T E R R A

TERRA

COOKING FROM THE HEART OF NAPA VALLEY

HIRO SONE and LISSA DOUMANI

Location Photography by Faith Echtermeyer

Food Photography by Hiroaki Ishii and Kaoru Sakuraba

Ten Speed Press

Box 7123

Berkeley, California 94707

www.tenspeed.com

Distributed in Australia by Simon & Schuster Australia, in Canada by Ten Speed Press Canada, in

New Zealand by Southern Publishers Group, in South Africa by Real Books, in Southeast Asia by

Berkeley Books, and in the United Kingdom and Europe by Airlift Book Company.

Cover and book design by Stefanie Hermsdorf

Copyediting by Carolyn Miller

Editorial development and headnote revision by Steve Siegelman

Photo on page xii by Barry Michlin

Line illustrations by Hiro Sone

Permissions acknowledgments:

Library of Congress Cataloging-in-Publication Data

Sone, Hiro.

   Terra : cooking from the heart of Napa Valley / Hiro Sone and Lissa Doumani.

     p. cm.

   ISBN 1-58008-149-5

   1. Cookery, American--California style. 2. Cookery--California--Napa Valley.

   3. Terra (Restaurant) I. Doumani, Lissa. II. Title

   TX715.2.C34 S66 2001

   641.59794'19--dc21   00-057758

Printed in Hong Kong

First printing, 2000

3 4 5 6 7 8 9 10 — 05 04 03 02 01

Contents

XI – The Story of Terra
XVII – A Day in Our Life at Terra
XXVI – Before You Start Cooking Our Recipes

1 – Appetizers

Grilled Miso-Marinated Beef Salad with Ginger-Mustard Vinaigrette
Fried Rock Shrimp with Chive-Mustard Sauce
Panzanella with Feta Cheese
Grilled Rare Tuna with Tomato-Cucumber Salad and Tahini Sauce
Miyagi Oysters in Ponzu
Wild Mushroom and Smoked Bacon Vol-au-Vent
Radicchio Salad with Parmesan-Balsamico Vinaigrette
Escabeche of Lake Smelt
Baked Mussels in Garlic-Parsley Butter
Petit Ragout of Sweetbreads, Mushrooms, Prosciutto, and White Truffle Oil
Fried Haricot Verts with Anchovy-Garlic Mayonnaise
Salmon and Tuna Tartare with Spicy Lemon-Ginger Vinaigrette and Sesame Tuiles
Goat Cheese and Artichoke Spring Rolls with Arugula and Tomato Salad
Warm Scallop Salad with Lemon-Coriander Vinaigrette
Dungeness Crab Salad with Avocado Mousse, Beets, and Ruby Grapefruit
Japanese Eggplant Salad
Lacquered Quail with Hong Kong Noodles
House-Cured Sardines with White Bean–Tomato Salad and Pesto
Tataki of Tuna with Whole-Grain Mustard and Soy Vinaigrette
Fricassee of Miyagi Oysters in Chardonnay Cream Sauce
Dungeness Crab Wontons with Spicy Sweet and Sour Sauce
Lobster Salad in Rice Paper
Gravlax on Potato Latkes with Dill Sour Cream
Sacramento Delta Crayfish with Thai Chili Mayonnaise
Foie Gras Terrine with Pear Chutney on Toast
More Passed Appetizers

45 – Soups

Tomato-Beet Gazpacho
Chanterelle Mushroom and Lentil Soup with Sautéed Foie Gras
Crème Vichyssoise with Caviar
Sopa de Ajo (Spicy Bread and Garlic Soup with Poached Eggs)
Soup Pistou with Goat Cheese Ravioli
Mussel Saffron Soup with Caramelized Onions and Garlic Croutons
Spring Garlic and Potato Soup with Morel Mushroom Croutons
Potage of Sweet Corn and Masa with Fried Soft-Shell Crab

61 – Pasta, Risotto, and Gnocchi

Bone Marrow Risotto with Braised Veal Shanks

Goat Cheese Ravioli with Fresh Tomato Sauce

Kabocha Pumpkin Ravioli with Pecorino Cheese

Foie Gras Tortelloni in Game Jus with Périgord Truffle and Fava Beans

Potato Gnocchi in Gorgonzola Cream Sauce

Chinese Egg Noodles with Gulf Shrimp, Shiitake Mushrooms, and Pea Tendrils

Spaghettini with Tripe Stew

Capellini with Smoked Salmon, Sevruga Caviar, and Lemon-Caper Vinaigrette

74 – Fish and Shellfish

Sautéed Maine Scallops on Garlic Mashed Potatoes with Chanterelle Mushrooms
    and Parsley Nage

Grilled Fillet of Pacific Salmon with Thai Red Curry Sauce and Basmati Rice

Croquettes of Copper River Salmon with a Ragout of Morel Mushrooms
    and Asparagus

Fricassee of Catfish with Tomato-Garlic-Caper Sauce

Pan-Roasted Local Halibut on Garlic Mashed Potatoes with Jus de Mer

Roasted Risotto-Stuffed Monterey Squid with Black Olive–Balsamico Vinaigrette

Acqua Pazza

Sautéed Pesto-Marinated Tai Snapper with Grilled Langoustines and
    Tomato–Black Olive Vinaigrette

Grilled Tournedos of Tuna and Fried Miyagi Oysters with Lemon-Caper Aioli

Poached Skate Wings on Napa Cabbage with Ponzu

Sautéed Alaskan Spot Prawns with Curry-Shrimp Sauce, Black Trumpet Mushrooms,
    and Snow Peas

Grilled Lingcod with English Peas and Peeky Toe Crab Risotto

Pan-Roasted California White Bass with Preserved-Lemon Beurre Blanc
    and Roasted Shad Roe

Broiled Sake-Marinated Chilean Sea Bass with Shrimp Dumplings in Shiso Broth

Pan-Roasted Medallions of Salmon on Brandade with Cabernet Sauvignon Sauce

Grilled Swordfish Steak on Caponata with Tuscan White Beans

109 – Meats

Grilled Spice-Rubbed Pork Chops with Yam Puree and Pickled Red Onions

Lamb Shanks Braised in Petite Syrah with Black Mission Figs

Grilled Duck Breast on Foie Gras and Sourdough Bread Stuffing with Sun-Dried Cherry Sauce

Paillards of Venison with French Fries

"Cassoulet" of Quail Confit with Pancetta and Lentils

Daube of Lamb Shoulder and Artichokes

Malfatti with Rabbit and Forest Mushrooms Cacciatore

Daube of Oxtail in Cabernet Sauvignon Sauce

Pan-Roasted Quail on Braised Endive with Sultanas and Napa Valley Verjus Sauce

Grilled Lamb Tenderloins on "Tagine" of Riblets with Minted Israeli Couscous

Grilled Dry-Aged New York Steak with Potatoes Aligot and Cabernet Sauvignon Sauce

Ossobuco with Risotto Milanese

Merlot-Braised Duck Legs with Wild Mushroom and Bacon Vol-au-Vent

Roasted Rack of Lamb with Ratatouille, Hummus, Tabbouleh, and Raita

Pork Belly "Kakuni" on Steamed Tatsoi with Wasabi

Grilled Quail on Eggplant and Goat Cheese "Lasagna" with Herbed Game Jus

Slow-Cooked Veal Cheeks on Roasted Yukon Gold Potatoes with Salsa Verde

Roasted Squab with Wild Mushroom Risotto and Pinot Noir Essence

Grilled Natural-Fed Veal Chops with Stir-Fried Japanese Eggplant in Miso Sauce

Medallions of Lamb with Anchovy–Black Olive Sauce and Artichoke Fritters

155 – Desserts

Almond Pithiviers with Meyer Lemon Ice Cream and Huckleberry Sauce

Apple Tart with Vanilla Ice Cream and Caramel Sauce

Fig Fritters with Ginger Ice Cream

Chocolate Truffle Cake with Espresso Ice Cream

Stone-Fruit Crostata

Lemon Crème Brûlée

Macadamia Nut Tart with Banana-Rum Ice Cream

Tart of Fromage Blanc with Caramelized Pears

Chocolate Bread Pudding with Sun-Dried Cherries and Crème Fraîche

Mixed Berry Shortcake with Caramel Sauce

Orange Risotto in Brandy Snaps with Passion Fruit Sauce

Pavlova with Frozen Yogurt and Tropical Fruit Salad

Baked Apple Crème Brûleé with Maple Cookies

Sunshine Cake with Cashew Brittle and Peach Compote

Sautéed Strawberries in Cabernet Sauvignon and Black Pepper Sauce with Vanilla Bean Ice Cream

Chocolate Mousseline on Pecan Sablé with Coffee Granité

Tiramisù

Apricot Tarte Tatin with Noyau Ice Cream

Feuilletée of Carmelized Bananas with Chocolate Fudge Sauce

195 – Basic Techniques and Recipes

Preparing Artichoke Hearts and Baby Artichokes
Deveining Foie Gras
Preparing Beets
Roasting and Peeling Bell Peppers
Blanching and Shocking Vegetables
Peeling and Seeding Tomatoes
Oven-Dried Tomatoes
Tomato Sauce
Clarified Butter
Garlic-Parsley Compound Butter
Mayonnaise
Aïoli
Terra House Vinaigrette
Lemon-Mustard Vinaigrette
Ponzu
Sake Marinade
Momiji Oroshi
Preserved Lemons
Pesto
Cutting Vegetables
Fontina Cheese Polenta
Mashed Potatoes, Garlic Mashed Potatoes
Veal Stock
Chicken Stock
Brown Chicken Stock
Lobster Stock
Fish Stock
Cooking and Shelling Lobster
Making Ravioli, Wontons, and Tortelloni
Almond Cream
Caramel Sauce
Crème Anglaise (Vanilla Custard Sauce and Vanilla Bean Ice Cream Base)
    Variations: Espresso Ice Cream, Banana-Rum Ice Cream,
    Ginger Ice Cream, Myers's Rum—Currant Ice Cream,
    Noyau Ice Cream, Meyer Lemon Ice Cream)
Pâte Sucrée
Vanilla Sugar

Acknowledgments
Versatile Recipes Index
General Index

The Story of Terra

by Lissa Doumani

We are always amazed that no matter what we say or serve, the first thing most people want to know is our story—how we met, how our relationship evolved, how we ended up building our dream restaurant in an agricultural hamlet that hadn't yet blossomed into one of the world's top destinations. In the decade since we opened Terra, we've told our story over and over, but until now, we've never really stopped to think about it…then again, it shouldn't come as a surprise that as chef-owners of a fine dining restaurant in the heart of Napa Valley we don't have much time to stop at all! Writing this book, however, has given us plenty of opportunities to reflect on the crazy mix of serendipity, beginner's luck, and downright foolishness that has made our story quite a tale and our restaurant one of a kind.

Like most partners, our relationship is a division of labor. Unlike many partners, we keep each other honest by candidly critiquing each other's work, constantly pushing one another to stay fresh and refine what we do. I am responsible for the front of the house, the desserts (I've been dubbed the pastry princess), the accounting, the PR, and most of the talking. Hiro creates all the menus, manages and trains the kitchen staff, and wields the sauté pan night in and night out while leading his team of chefs through the rigors and artistry of dinner service. In writing this book, the lines have blurred and we've both done a lot of everything. But in the interest of doing what comes naturally, we decided I would tell you our story, which begins at the now world-famous Spago in West Hollywood.

Late one night the week after Spago opened in 1983, I marched in, walked right up to owner Wolfgang Puck and asked how I could get a job in a restaurant like his. Wolf, as he's affectionately

known, suggested I sit at the bar for 15 minutes and told me he would come and talk to me when service was over. Well, a young woman sitting alone at a bar gets bought a lot of drinks, so when he came over about an hour later, the only thing I retained from our talk was that I should call him the next day. We began a series of stop-and-start conversations—the only type the professional kitchen allows—until Wolf finally asked me when I wanted to start working. I boldly named a date just a few days from then, and he said fine.

When I showed up for work, the only problem was that Wolf hadn't told anyone in the prep kitchen I was coming. So the kitchen manager, Kazuto Matsusaka, just looked at me in my street clothes and long, long red nails, and told me I wasn't to do anything until Wolfgang arrived. Eventually, I got to peel a case of asparagus. The next day, I was asked if I wanted to work with Nancy Silverton in pastry; she needed someone and anyone would do. Working alongside Nancy became one of the most formative experiences of my professional life. In addition to the technical pastry training I received, I also learned two rules that we still follow at Terra: Chocolate can diffuse almost any flare-up. And people like what they like—whether it's ketchup omelets, Tab, or iceberg lettuce, so give them what they want within reason.

After the first year of Spago in West Hollywood, Wolf and his business partner (and wife), Barbara, accepted an offer to build a Spago in Tokyo. It was agreed that the Tokyo chefs would have to come train in L.A. Enter Hiro Sone, a star culinary student from the finest cooking school in Japan, Ecole Technique Hoteliere Tsuji, where he had trained under the tutelage of such formidable French chefs as Paul Bocuse,

Pierre Troisgros, and Joel Robuchon. A country boy from a family of premium rice farmers for eighteen generations, Hiro was accustomed to the type of hard work and resourcefulness that reigned in Wolf's kitchen.

When Kazuto returned from the airport with Hiro, I kissed Kazuto hello and saw Hiro back away. He didn't know what to think of this affectionate "cleaning lady" in street clothes covered with chocolate. Hiro quickly realized his mistake, but the memory cemented an important difference in our styles. Even to this day, he remains immaculate while he works and I end up looking like a Jackson Pollock painting.

Soon after Hiro came to work, we had dinner together, talking and eating (probably flirting, too), as we prepared for the evening's work. I overheard Kazuto ask a friend how we were managing to talk, since Hiro didn't speak English and I didn't speak Japanese. Somehow, despite all the cultural differences and obstacles, we were able to communicate from the start, relying on the universal language of laughter to carry us through.

After two months of intensive training, it was

time for Hiro to go back to Tokyo. Despite the grueling pace and physical toll of the work—or maybe because of it—we had become close friends, which Wolf and Barbara had noticed. So Hiro went back to Tokyo and I immersed myself in the workings of Spago sans Hiro. Then Barbara and Wolf started to play Cupid. Sometimes late at night, Wolf would call Tokyo, get Hiro on the line, and then just hand the phone to me. I didn't know who would be on the other end but humored Wolf and was delighted to hear Hiro's voice, each of us accompanied by a kitchen concert in stereo. Later, when Barbara and Wolf were in Tokyo, Barbara had Hiro hold up a sign that read, "Lissa, I miss you madly, love Hiro." She took a picture, and casually gave it to me as she sorted the snapshots from their trip. Another time, when Wolf was doing a cooking demo in Tokyo, he told the class that Hiro trained in Los Angeles and that he had returned to Japan with a passion for American girls, or one specifically.

Ready for a new adventure after two years at the flagship Spago, I decided to cook and taste my way through a few more countries and kitchens. I headed for Sydney, planning to travel through Southeast Asia and end up in Japan. Hiro and I had continued to write each other, hoping our paths would cross again. And about a year later, they did.

Hiro and the Tokyo Spago manager, Johnny Romoglia, had been lobbying the management to hire me when I arrived in Japan. Only catch was, no one knew when I was coming. So Hiro only found out that I had arrived when we ran into each other in the elevator. We reconnected instantly. Hiro was proud to show me his town, and I was hungry to experience so many new things. He would take me to Tsukiji fish market to buy fish, a shopping experience unlike anything in America. Just looking at the rows and rows of fish stalls made us want to head right back into the kitchen. In what little free time we had, we sampled the cuisine of Tokyo's finest chefs and embarked on

expeditions all over the city to find the best neighborhood spots. That was a great time, working together in Tokyo, but the best part was that we discovered our relationship translated no matter the locale.

When it was time for me to go home, Hiro told me he wanted to move back with me. We felt our paths merging permanently, except for the small matter of finding work. Chefs spend so much time in the kitchen that if they don't work together, they never see each other. I called Wolfgang and asked him if he would hire Hiro if he moved to L.A. and Wolf said, "Of course." When Hiro asked his parents for their blessing, they agreed but only for a year. I used to wonder when the call would come for Hiro to pack up and move back home, and if I would be moving to Japan.

About the time that Hiro took over as chef at Spago, I left to become the pastry chef at Roy Yamaguchi's 385 North, also in Los Angeles. Hiro and I then spent much of our time together talking about what we thought made the ideal restaurant work, laying the foundation for what would become our business plan someday. Surprisingly, we agreed about almost everything, except the size of the dining room. Hiro wanted a restaurant of about 50 seats, where he could personally construct customized menus for a small circle of guests. I thought we'd work ourselves to death and still be in the red. I wanted a restaurant with 75 to 90 seats, where we could be ambitious and personal, but still balance the books. Little did we know that the perfect place would present itself—and become ours—almost overnight.

We had been looking for a space in Los Angeles to no avail. Everything we saw was too ugly, too expensive, or the wrong size. On September 11, 1988, at an ungodly hour, my dad called and asked us if we would be interested in the restaurant in the Hatchery building in the Napa Valley town of St. Helena. I sleepily said, "Sure," and hung up. When we woke up, we couldn't remember what Dad had called about. After tracking

him down and hearing more about the place, we decided it was a long shot that we simply had to try for. On September 19, Hiro and I flew up to see the space.

We still remember when we first walked up to the century-old fieldstone building with its arching French windows and graceful iron lanterns. It literally beckoned us in, bewitching us with its rustic warmth, European sophistication, and genuine antique feel. It was love at first sight— we were sold. So on September 26, 1988, we took over as the owners of the operational yet unnamed restaurant. It went so fast we didn't have time to overthink what we were doing.

In a stroke of good luck, no doubt aided by the speed with which the deal was done, we acquired the corporation that owned the restaurant. This meant that the restaurant could continue to run without us having to do the usual paperwork required by governmental agencies and suppliers for a start-up. How we were going to run a restaurant from Los Angeles while we got organized and Hiro worked for Wolf for at least another month was a mystery. Has someone ever done something so wonderful for you that you didn't know what to say? That was how we felt when Barbara Neyers offered to take care of things for us in the interim. She kept the restaurant running with the old menu still in place, and I flew up on weekends to work and learn how she did things. After a raucous Halloween party (a tradition we brought with us), we led the moving van to our new life in Napa Valley.

We like to joke that the day we walked into the kitchen, Hiro took the sauté pan out of the cook's hand in mid-toss and finished the dish. It certainly felt like that. We slowly changed the menu over the next couple of days and changed the name two weeks after that. I think if we had ever had kids, they still wouldn't be named—it's such an overwhelming responsibility. Finally, after considering a spate of names, we took a cue from our surroundings and settled on Terra. It evoked the Italian influence of the valley and, quite simply, the earth that we owe our inspiration to.

Probably the most daunting task was writing that first menu. We wanted to put everything we had talked about, tasted, and learned into it. The project became bigger than anything we had done before. Hiro had the good sense not to overextend himself and to let me do so either. As a result, the first menus we wrote were smaller than the one we offer now. It's usually the other way around.

Hiro and I had never run the front of a restaurant, done bookkeeeping, or used a computer (Hiro still can't). Yet here we were with a restaurant that kept all its accounts in a computer we inherited with the business and a reservation book filled with the names of local customers.

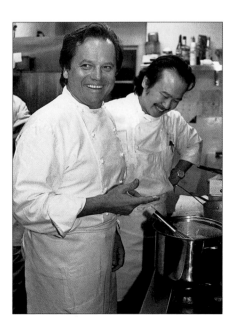

We did have one thing going for us: the generous support of family and friends. I grew up in Napa Valley (my family owned Stags' Leap Winery), so we had plenty of people coming by to wish us well, to eat, and to hope along with us. One night, business was ridiculously quiet when two local vintners, Bob Long and Bob Pecota, came in for dinner. They saw that there were only two other tables seated and told us to keep our spirits high, not to worry, and that everything would be okay. I think one of them had a crystal ball in his hip pocket.

For the first couple of years, we did everything ourselves, from fixing the plumbing to painting the sign hanging out front. (Some things we did better than others—after two disastrous attempts to paint our sign, we resigned ourselves to having no sign at all.) Hiro asked Jim Neal, a co-worker from Los Angeles, if he wanted to move up to Napa and be our sous chef. What we lacked in business experience we made up for with opinions. After dining all over Europe and Japan and eating our way through California and the U.S., we had learned what we wanted in service. We wanted a warm, comfortable environment where our customers could feel like our invited dinner guests without sacrificing the experience of a fine dining restaurant.

One of the changes we made early on was the size of the tables and the number of seats. We didn't want to lose seats, but the tables we inherited were really small for serious diners. We wanted our guests to leave Terra basking in the afterglow of an evening filled with great food and delicious wine shared with the good company they came with—not with the folks sitting nearby. Our ultimate goal was to have guests tell us that dinner at Terra was everything they had hoped it would be. That's a tall order when you consider that the local clientele and the visitors who come from all over the world have high expectations!

Being in Napa has given us the opportunity to work closely with the growers and producers of some of the best quality, hand-picked foods that are the cornerstone of our cooking. Over the years, these business relationships have grown into friendships that make our work all the more enjoyable. Because our community is small and relatively centralized, we have the luxury of going to many suppliers for foods, even if they only produce one or two items.

Our suppliers are often the first to show us exciting new offerings, whether newly available heirloom tomatoes or delicate greens. When this happens, we're careful to get to know the ingredient before we put it on the plate. Flavor evolution does not occur just because a new ingredient is available, but because you know how to use it. Hiro's food is characterized by its layers of flavors and textures. He believes this multidimensional quality lends each dish a depth that astounds with every bite, each forkful revealing yet another facet. This is easier to achieve with appetizers, which tend to be small yet can pack a powerful punch. Main courses present more of a challenge, since an intense flavor wouldn't be as successful in a larger portion, but at the same time you don't want the dish to be conservative or boring. The balance of these two courses, finished by dessert, is what Hiro strives to create each night.

Once Terra was established, the critics and food writers all wanted a two-word description for our cuisine. Breaking one of the basic restaurant marketing rules, we told them it was southern French and northern Italian in style with a Japanese sensibility. The usual response was silence, then, "But what kind of food is it?" Then we'd give the longer answer. We're classically trained in French and Italian cooking and apply those culinary techniques to what we create at Terra. Napa Valley shares much of the climate and vegetation of France and Italy, as well as an

appreciation for many of the same foods, so the French and Italian influence makes sense. Put more simply, every dish we make is a reflection of our experiences, both personal and professional. We don't put dishes on the menu just because we think they would be popular. Because of that guideline you won't find chicken served at Terra. We think chicken is mostly unremarkable and believe that people eat it throughout the week and want something they don't eat at home when they go out for a nice meal. We especially like to prepare offal and other less common rustic foods. We worry that as Americans cook less at home and have more money to spend on expensive cuts of meat, such staples from the past will be eradicated from the country's cuisine. That's why you'll find tripe and sweetbreads on our menu alongside goat cheese ravioli and fried rock shrimp, as we continue our mission to reconnect diners with foods that have unfairly fallen out of favor over the years.

In many restaurants you can't make substitutions or special requests. Chalk it up to our Spago roots, but we find this ridiculous. Just because a dish isn't on our menu doesn't mean it's not worth cooking. We know great cooks can cook anything and it will be memorable. So at Terra, the guests never get that no-substitutes treatment. And we don't have hard-and-fast rules about what is appropriate for each course either. If you want to order three appetizers instead of a main entrée, bon appétit!

When it comes to wine, we tell everyone to drink what they like and don't be afraid to try something different. We spend a lot of time trying to find less common varietals. There are countless bottles of Sauvignon Blanc, Chardonnay, Merlot, and Cabernet to choose from. What about trying a Pinot Blanc, Pinot Gris, Aligote, Pinor Noir, Syrah, Zinfandel, Mouvedre, or Sangiovese, among others? There are some unforgettable wine combinations, like Foie Gras and Sauterne, Lamb and Petite Syrah, Mussel Saffron Soup and Chardonnay. But what if you can't drink two bottles or you just feel like one wine? Or you've ordered a variety of dishes and one wine won't match all the different ingredients and flavors? To encourage diners to make the most of their time with us, we offer an array of by-the-glass selections and love to help our guests negotiate the list. We love to dine this way, and know it makes for a more enjoyable evening. At the other end of the spectrum are the special wine dinners we do for customers when they have an extraordinary wine to drink. We have done such dinners for groups as small as four and as large as 500. One of our favorite guests, the Duckhorns, regularly ask us to do a special duck dinner to go with their vineyard's remarkable Merlots and Cabernets. These dinners are fun and challenging,

and we usually get to try the wine before the dinner—an invitation we never refuse.

We hope that what sets us apart is that we take what we do very seriously, but we don't take ourselves too seriously. The wait staff and the kitchen staff like each other and approach their work with the same ethic and sense of humor we do. Then there are the customers who have been dining with us for so long that they feel like part of the operation. Sure, we have the usual surprises and upsets that come with running a fine dining restaurant in a destination locale, but we feel very lucky to be living this life. We cook from our hearts. We consider Terra an extension of our home, and each patron a friend coming over for dinner. Our cooking is a reflection of who we are—our heritages, our travels, our memories, and our own tastes. Each dish contains traces of Hiro's Japanese ancestry and his classical French and Italian training, plus the flavors of my Lebanese and European background and Napa Valley roots. Each of these components is fundamental to the food we prepare, and we hope that as you make our recipes you'll taste our history in them. ♪♪♪

A Day in Our Life at Terra

After people hear how Hiro and I ended up together in Napa Valley, they then want to know what it's like running Terra day in and day out. We thought a fresh set of eyes would probably do a better job of seeing all the things that go on here, so we asked Carol Doumani, who is a writer and also my aunt, to visit as an observer. To give you a glimpse of our lives, of how the day (and night) unfolds six days a week, 300 days a year, at our restaurant, here is Carol's account:

4:30 A.M. (yes, it really begins this early!)

I arrived at Terra bleary-eyed, knowing that one person is already inside and has started her busy day. The pastry chef, Susan, likes to work when she can be the only person in the kitchen, when the fragrance of sizzling garlic and the cacophony of pots and pans that comes from a kitchen full of cooks are absent, and all of the ovens and counters are hers alone.

As the front door swings open, I am enveloped by the intoxicating fragrance of sweet pastry crust, earthy yeast, and the heady aromas of fruit, almond, vanilla, and chocolate baking in the oven. Though the lights are out in Terra's dining room, with the help of the warm glow emanating from the kitchen, I can see that all the tables are set, ready and waiting for the first seating, still some twelve hours away. Through the arched windows of the fieldstone façade, dawn breaks in pinks and purples across the Valley, and I pause to think: This feast of sights and smells just might be worth getting up for.

Susan welcomes me into the kitchen with a smile, but no handshake, which, under the circumstances, is a good thing because she's up to her elbows in a huge bowl of dough. On the counter are peaches, nectarines, and plums, bowls of

finely chopped nuts, and more butter than I've ever seen assembled in one place. Watching her make the dozens of elements that will be assembled into six different desserts for the evening menu is like getting a crash course in the art and science of pastry from a choreographer. She rolls out dough, mixes batters, peels, slices, and sautés fruit, juggling baking sheets between refrigerator and oven, all in what appears to be a carefully rehearsed sequence of dance steps.

Lined up on the trays are the results of her work: twenty apple tarts, fourteen peach crostata, a battery of chocolate mousselines, a few dozen deftly shaped brandy snap tubes to hold the orange risotto (which she has also whipped up), and too many other sauces, cookies, shells, and candies to count. Four hours later, I congratulate myself for exercising remarkable restraint, having sampled only a few of that day's offerings when the temptation was to indulge in a dozen desserts, one taste at a time.

9:00 A.M.

Manny, the head prep cook, arrives through the back door, backlit by the morning sun, which has now climbed its way up the sky. It's a spectacularly clear Napa Valley day, and the small-town streets of St. Helena are still quiet—except, that is, for the delivery truck that's pulling up.

Manny checks in case after case of water, wine, and beer (rest assured, the Budweiser is strictly for the staff—everyone gets a glass of wine or a beer after their shift, and the King of Beers has its devotees).

An old Ford truck pulls up in front of the restaurant, and Terra's gardener, Christy Thollander, steps out. She's wearing overalls and a straw hat and carrying a flat of brilliant blue verbena to augment what is already blooming in the flowerbeds outside the entrance. Christy's father, Earl, is a well-known California artist, who coincidentally painted the first piece of art Lissa ever bought when she was sixteen years old—a picture of a moon over a rustic cabin. It's amazing how almost every person involved with the restaurant is connected to Hiro and Lissa in some other way. This kind of history is what gives the place so much of its soul and makes Terra a fixture in the community rather than just a good restaurant. It's one of those rare enterprises that embodies a way of life for everyone involved.

The sun is beating down now, and Christy liberally waters the flowerbeds as she talks about the four beds in the restaurant's garden, two of flowers and two of herbs. Right now, the stunning flowerbeds are awash with sunflowers that are easily six feet tall, and, at their base, with blue verbena, gerbera daisies, and sweet William. The herb beds are lush with rosemary, Thai basil, chives, rose geranium, and pineapple sage. Christy picks off a pale green leaf, rubs it between her hands, and holds it out for me to smell. It really does smell like pineapple.

11:00 A.M.

By the time Hiro and Lissa arrive, there are cases and cartons stacked in an organized jumble everywhere they will possibly fit. They come from vendors all over the Valley, and as far away as San Francisco, and they keep pouring in. Manny has checked in some of them—beverages, paper goods, and dry goods—but the produce is awaiting Hiro's discriminating eye before it's unpacked, examined, and approved.

Hiro says a quick hello and heads into the kitchen. He's in his white chef's jacket and baggy chef's pants, with his hair pulled into a tight knot at the back of his head. His warm,

relaxed manner and obvious eagerness to begin the day sets the tone. After twelve years of the same routine, you'd think that he would have grown weary from twelve to fourteen hours a day, six days a week, in the kitchen. But Hiro is in his element at Terra. This is where he wants to be. This is where his heart is. He sets out his knives on the stainless steel counter, ready to work.

Lissa heads for the dining room, ready to get on with the business of the day. Her arms are full of notebooks and mail, and a large bag is slung over her shoulder. She drops everything on the nearest table and heads for the espresso machine. I peek inside the bag and see that it's filled with handmade pottery sugar bowls. Moments later, double latte in hand, Lissa sets up shop at a table near the front door, where she will work well into the afternoon. I ask her about the sugar bowls, and she tells me that throwing pots is one of her hobbies, and that every so often she makes new sugar bowls and plates for the restaurant. "We wanted handmade plates but couldn't find any we liked, so I thought, well, maybe I can make them," she explains, as she picks up the phone to answer her first call of the day.

It's a travel agent inquiring about their next guest-chef engagement (Hiro and Lissa are invited all over the world to cook), and Lissa makes the arrangements. The next call is from Lissa's mentor and friend Nancy Silverton at Campanile and La Brea Bakery in Los Angeles. She wants to reserve a table for one of her chefs who will be in the Valley next Saturday. The restaurant is completely booked, but of course Lissa says yes. She can always figure something out.

11:30 A.M.

Watching Hiro at work is truly impressive. Many chef-owners in his position spend their days orchestrating the work, but not Hiro. There he is chopping carrots for the stock, a task the least-trained prep cook could be doing. With a

shrug, he explains that there aren't more important things he ought to be attending to—that everything is important.

Meanwhile, Manny whirls into action. He dumps a case of baby artichokes on the counter, and deftly starts cleaning them with a paring knife. I can't help staring at the pile, knowing that it would take a novice all morning and then some to work their way through that stack. Ten minutes later, Manny's on to the tomatoes, peeling, seeding, and dicing them into perfect *concassée*. He then turns his attention to several cases of local wild mushrooms, which he cleans and slices.

The pace in the kitchen begins to pick up. John, the sous chef, arrives, and he and Hiro run through the menu and the quantities of each dish they'll be preparing tonight. Sea bass sold well the night before—forty portions out of 162 dinners served—and today is Friday, so they're betting on selling even more fish.

Barney from Forni Brown Produce calls to tell Hiro that he'll be replacing the Lollo Rossa lettuce with red oak, since the Lollo Rossa is looking a little peaked. As he hands Lissa the phone, Hiro laughs and says, "Barney says the red oak is so fresh it doesn't even know it was picked yet." Now it's Lissa's turn to talk with Barney, whom she affectionately calls Captain Gossip. They catch up on all the news, following their golden rule: no bad news, just the good stuff.

12:00 NOON

The kitchen is humming. And so is Hiro. Stocks are simmering on the ten-burner stove, along with beets, sweetbreads, and white beans. John slices smoked salmon and covers each carefully prepared plate with plastic wrap. Manny asks Hiro how he wants the corn prepped, and keeps checking in deliveries as they arrive.

And the deliveries do just keep coming. A huge tower of boxes has made its way in through the back door. Peeking out from behind is Genna, Barney's daughter, and everyone greets her by calling out, "The lechuga girl is here!" Hiro starts poring over each box of lettuce, checking what seems like every last leaf. The quality is always perfect, but Hiro always checks. Genna secretly hands Lissa an egg carton, and Lissa gives a big smile as she asks, "Already?" Sure enough, Genna has delivered the most beautiful and fragrant *fraise de bois* (wild strawberries). I sneak a sample as Genna slips out and Matthew from Omega arrives with the fish order. On any given day, the large deliveries are interspersed with smaller offerings of figs, walnuts, Meyer lemons, corn, tomatoes, goat cheeese, and stone fruit all brought by local purveyors.

When the meat order arrives, Hiro drops everything to check the contents and weights, then immediately begins cutting everything up. He's particularly interested in a slab of pork belly which, he explains, will appear as a special tonight in a Japanese-inspired dish called "Kakuni." It's amazing that this huge hunk of what appears to be mostly fat can be transformed into something delectable.

1:00 P.M.

Now the kitchen is getting really crowded, with several more chefs settling in. Lissa is still working away, encircled by paperwork and answering the phones. It's time to stretch my legs and get a look at what's happening in the neighborhood. The building is a great starting point to do just that, tucked behind the main street of the town with vineyards in the distance on all sides. The building is as old as anything in town. Built in 1884, it first housed a foundry that forged small farming tools. After the turn of the last century, parts of the building were destroyed in two fires, and the foundry was closed. Later a glove factory moved in. For disbelievers, there's a fading sign proclaiming such wares stenciled on the front of the building. In the '40s, the glove factory gave way to a chicken hatchery. Later, the building was split in two,

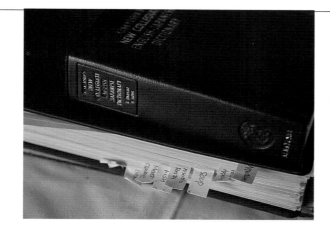

with offices on one side and a museum dedicated to writer and local Jack London on the other. Finally, in the '50s, the building was home to a restaurant, a humble little joint called the Hatchery Café, which changed hands and names throughout the following decades.

A loud pop from the kitchen followed by an ominous electrical fizzling sound draws me back into the kitchen. Hiro is sitting on the floor by the mixer. The massive machine had stopped working and he was trying to repair it when he got the wires crossed and gave himself a pretty good shock. He laughs it off, saying he needed an energy boost anyway. Lissa picks up the phone and calls a professional.

2:30 P.M.

Vanessa, the reservationist, has arrived, and she's making return calls to confirm or change reservations. She's also fielding incoming calls, juggling four lines at once without getting flustered, and doing her best to calmly address every caller's special request. In the summertime,

the 92-seat dining room books up a month ahead of time for weekday dinners and two months out for weekends. Part of Vanessa's job is pacing reservations so that there are only seven tables seated every thirty minutes to keep the kitchen and the floor staff from getting overwhelmed.

3:00 P.M.

Waving goodbye to Vanessa, with a reminder that she's only a phone call away, Lissa goes out to do the banking and a few other errands. Then she'll head home to have a bite to eat and put up her feet before dressing and returning to the restaurant to help brief the staff and greet the first guests. Thinking about how exhausting it is to host a dinner party for six in my own home, I'm awed by the fact that Lissa is host to more than 140 people every night.

3:30 P.M.

Hiro is sitting at a table in the dining room, writing out a list of tonight's specials. He makes the pork belly sound much more interesting than when he described it in the kitchen. The phones are still ringing off the hook.

Tim, the manager and sommelier, sits at another table, talking to John Buehler and Misha Chelini of Buehler Vineyards. Misha is a familiar face here, since she worked at Terra for seven years

both on the floor and making the pastries. Tim holds a glass of deep red Cabernet up to the light, then tastes it, remarking on the wine's characteristics.

The back door crashes open and a large green bush walks in. "Hi Kathy," shouts Hiro. "Hi everybody!" says the bush. Out from behind the greenery steps Kathy Hoffman, the brilliant florist who creates the massive arrangements that grace the restaurant's two dining rooms. Kathy, another Napa native, is the daughter of Don and Sally Schmitt. Don is the former mayor of nearby Yountville, and with Sally, their other daughter Karen, and Karen's husband, Tim, owns the Apple Farm, which produces over sixty varieties of organic apples, as well as cider and other apple products. Sally was the first person Lissa ever cooked with professionally, at the Vintage 1870 in Yountville.

4:30 P.M.

The servers begin to show up. As they come in, they seem more like old friends getting together for an evening of fun rather than co-workers clocking in. One of them, Gwen, comes in with a huge container. Hiro's eyes light up. "Chuck went fishing?" he asks, and Gwen just nods. Her husband likes to fish for salmon and sometimes catches females full of eggs. Hiro is always happy to take the eggs off Chuck's hands. Opening up the egg sacs, Hiro painstakingly separates and cleans the eggs, marinating them to make salmon caviar, which will be served with the salmon tartare later.

Each of the servers starts in on their work. One tackles the mountain of wine that was delivered, putting some of it in the wine racks for immediate use and setting some aside to go into the restaurant's aging cellar. Other servers polish glasses and silverware, stocking the items they will need for service throughout the evening. The bussers have also arrived and are cutting up limes, lemons, and butter and setting up coffee

No doubt, Kathy is inspired by the seasons and the restaurant's name. Her floral sculptures capture the essence of the land and the natural beauty of the Valley with branches, brambles, leaves, and flowers, all artfully amassed to create an illusion of spontaneity. Kathy takes a few surviving flowers from last week's arrangements and puts them in two tiny vases for the restaurant's restrooms.

service and filling ice bins. Tim fields questions regarding table set-up for the night's reservations.

5:00 P.M.

Staff dinner is served. Tonight it's roast pork, pasta with tomato sauce, salad, and desserts left over from the night before. The food is set out buffet-style on the pick-up counter and bussers' station. Everyone helps themselves to platefuls of food. They know it will be torture to serve Hiro's food all night on empty stomachs.

5:40 P.M.

Lissa returns in time for the staff meeting, where Hiro is briefing the staff on the specials, describing each dish in detail so that the servers can confidently answer any question a guest might have. One dish is especially complicated (the pork belly "kakuni"), so Hiro makes a sample for them to try. After Hiro is finished, it's Lissa and Tim's turn to go over service, noting the evening's special events: a sixtieth birthday at table forty-two and a marriage proposal at table nineteen. The restaurant often gets requests to present engagement rings. Tonight, there will be a ring tucked into a specially folded napkin. It's already waiting in the kitchen, carefully identified. "Make sure it goes to table twenty-four," says Hiro. There's a murmur of confusion amongst the staff before he smiles and says, "Just kidding. Make that table nineteen." Tim goes over the new wine additions, refreshing memories of

wines sampled at staff tastings. He also adds a couple of observations from the previous evening's service.

6:00 P.M.

The front door opens and the first guests, an elderly couple, walk in; Lissa greets them warmly and is clearly delighted to see them. They are the Gordons, and as Lissa introduces them to me, she explains that they have been coming to Terra almost twice a month since the restaurant opened.

Lissa and Hiro take a quick spin through the restaurant. As always, everything is tidy and the last-minute preparations are completed. Hiro is dressed in the same immaculate chef's jacket he put on seven hours ago. The mingling aromas emanating from the kitchen are absolutely mouth-watering.

6:30 P.M.

As I step back into the dining room, I see everyone in motion. More people have arrived and been seated and the specials are already being described at several tables. I watch as Lissa stops by a table where a guest is talking to a server about particular ingredients. She hands Lissa a card listing her allergies, and Lissa heads to the kitchen to confer with Hiro. It is important to them to be careful but still make the meal interesting. Lissa returns to the table to describe what they will prepare

for the guest, who is visibly pleased and relieved to escape another night of steamed vegetables!

7:00 P.M.

Back in the kitchen, Hiro is calling out the orders and each cook responds as they hear a dish from their station called. Three people are working in the pantry station, making all the cold appetizers and some parts of other dishes, plus later they will plate the desserts. A food runner zooms by with appetizers for table twenty-one. Sarah, who works the grill, appears cool and calm despite the constant waves of heat rolling over her. From another corner, a busser rushes in with a tray full of plates and deposits them with the dishwasher, hustling out as fast as he came in.

8:30 P.M.

The dining room is in full swing. Every table is full and Tim is talking with a customer about

the ideal wine for the meal ordered. Serious wine talk is to be expected in this part of the country, but sometimes it gets out of hand. A few weeks ago, a customer ordered a bottle of Chardonnay. The server, Patrick, presented the guest with a taste of the wine. The customer told Patrick to go ahead and serve the wine, but asked him to throw out the sample and get a fresh glass. As Patrick was pouring the guest's "fresh" glass of wine, the diner explained that all the sulfites in wine are only present in the top ounce, so once that is poured, the rest of the wine is clear, which is something most winemakers don't know. With all his training, Patrick smiled and said, "How interesting." Of course he knew the guest was repeating a myth, but thought it was a harmless mistake; correcting him would have tainted an otherwise wonderful memory of a great evening.

During service Lissa seems to be everywhere and to watch everything. She tries to be by the door to greet arriving guests, and once they are seated, she walks the "track" around the dining rooms. The way the restaurant is laid out, the staff can follow a circular path through the front, both dining rooms, and the back. I'm surprised to see her appearing in one room and then in the other from the opposite direction. While walking through the restaurant, Lissa is available as an extra set of hands, to help take care of anything that is needed: clearing a table, pouring more wine, being always on the lookout for a table that needs more water or bread. The servers know that they can ask Lissa for help with anything (except opening Champagne). Everyone works as skilled, graceful members of a team.

11:00 P.M.

The evening continues to go smoothly, but I start to wane. Tim has promised a wine tasting at the end of the night, so I hold on. As the night winds down, the high energy is replaced with the

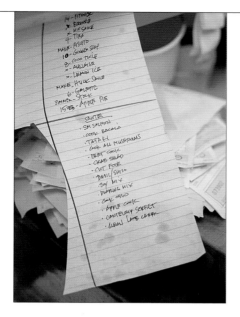

sense of calm that comes with surviving another successful evening. Each person has his or her job to do. I go looking for Hiro and finds him standing in the refrigerator. It's not because he needs to cool down (which is a reasonable assumption when you feel the heat emanating from the kitchen), but because he is taking the nightly inventory so orders can be placed for tomorrow.

11:30 P.M.

In the kitchen, the sous chef is writing down a prep list for Manny and the pastry chef. Hiro will augment it with his ideas for specials. This is just a game plan; the menu can change depending on the surprises the morning deliveries may bring. Each person is cleaning and organizing his or her station to minimize tomorrow's work. I wander back into the dining room and see that tables are reset and everything is put away.

12:00 MIDNIGHT

The last guests have just left, and Tim sets up the monthly staff wine tasting, loading down a large table with enough wine bottles sheathed in paper bags and glasses for a large army—or, in our case, just a small, thirsty one. The wine is bagged so that no one will judge a wine by the winery. Each staff member has a sheet for their tasting notes. At first, I wonder how any of them will make it home after trying so much wine. However, this is a tasting, not a drinking, session; everyone slurps and holds a taste of wine in their mouths, then spits it unceremoniously into a tableside bucket. They discuss and rate the wines, saying the first thing that comes to mind, not some fancy adjective from the wine lexicon. The top wines from each tasting are added to future wine lists, providing a few more flavors to profile for the inquisitive guests who want to know more.

1:00 A.M.

Tim counts the money, and Hiro and Lissa sit and replay the evening's events. Once they've decompressed, they turn their thoughts to tomorrow, feeling tonight as they do each night—that it's a privilege to walk into this glorious building the next day and start the whole routine in motion again. ♪♪♪

Before You Start Cooking
Our Recipes

We're not going to pretend that the recipes in this book are simple. What we've tried to present here is the food we serve at Terra— the food we love to cook and eat—adapting it, when necessary, for home cooks and home kitchens.

Many of these dishes have several components and require a fair amount of organization and planning. But what we can also tell you is that, for the most part, these recipes don't require special skills or a degree from a culinary academy. Follow these simple guidelines and follow your nose. You'll be rewarded with dishes you can really be proud of.

1. Read the recipe from start to finish before you do anything—shopping, meal planning, thinking about wine, and, most of all, cooking. Do you have a clear sense of what the finished dish will look and taste like and how to fit it into the meal? Do you have the right equipment for preparing and serving it? Is there enough time in your life to make the dish, or hands to help you?

2. As you read, visualize the cooking process step by step.

3. Measure, weigh, and prep as much as you can before you begin. Group together the prepared ingredients for each dish to avoid confusion in the heat of the moment. Set out the equipment and serving items you'll need, and give your oven and/or grill at least 15 minutes to preheat.

4. Relax and have fun! If you've approached things in an organized way, everything will go smoothly, and you'll actually enjoy yourself!

Sharing good food with people you care about—whether it's foie gras or a fried egg—is one of the great pleasures of life. These recipes don't just come from our kitchen. They come from our hearts. And we hope they'll find a place in yours.

Essential Ingredients

Following are fundamental ingredients you will come across again and again in our recipes. Please be sure to make the effort to find and use these particular items, most of which are available in your neighborhood markets (a few items may be found in ethnic or specialty markets). You'll find that a specific ingredient really makes a difference in the outcome of the dish!

BUTTER: We always use unsalted or sweet butter. We feel that there is never a reason to add salt to a recipe through butter. Salt acts as a preservative in the butter, which means that salted butter may not be as fresh as unsalted.

CHOCOLATE: Always use bittersweet chocolate, of which there are many excellent products. We use a bittersweet couverture chocolate, which has a very high cocoa butter content. Different brands of chocolate will have different proportions of cocoa butter, so their performance in a recipe may vary. If you are having trouble with a recipe, look for Callibaut bittersweet, which is the brand we use. It is available through gourmet stores and mail order.

CREAM: Restaurant cream is 40 percent fat and is very difficult to find in retail stores. Choose the richest cream you can find, usually called heavy cream or manufacturer's cream.

EGGS: We use extra large and prefer hormone-free and cage-free eggs.

FLOUR: All-purpose flour and pastry flour are not interchangeable. All-purpose flour has a higher protein (more than double) than pastry flour, so it develops more gluten, which gives the flour strength so it can hold up to the heat or bind and thicken a dish. When baking cakes, pastry dough, or cookies, however, you want a soft flour that will crumb easily. If you don't have pastry flour, you can use all-purpose flour, but delete 1 tablespoon for each cup of flour called for in the recipe. Another technique is to use all-purpose flour to cake flour in a 2 to 1 ratio (for example, if the recipe calls for 1½ cups flour, use 1 cup all-purpose flour and ½ cup cake flour).

MISO: Miso is the fermented paste of soybeans and rice, primarily. The lighter misos have less fermentation and a milder flavor, and the darker misos have longer fermentation and a stronger flavor. For our recipes, use darker miso, aka (red) miso and Hatcho miso, which is very dark brown. Aka miso can also be used for miso soup. All misos will keep for up to a year in the refrigerator.

OLIVE OIL AND EXTRA VIRGIN OLIVE OIL: Most of our recipes call for pure olive oil, but not extra virgin. Pure olive oil is very versatile, it has a mild flavor, and it is good when sautéing or marinating meat, fish, or vegetables before cooking. Cooking will mask the nuances of extra virgin olive oil, which tends to have more olive flavor and more fruitiness and spiciness (olive oils from different producers will vary in flavor). Save extra virgin olive oil for when its bright taste can shine in a dish, on a salad, or with fresh vegetables. Some people prefer to eat bread with extra virgin olive oil instead of butter. We get our olive oil from the Napa Valley Olive Oil Mfg. Co. (707-963-4173).

PUFF PASTRY: We don't make our own puff pastry dough for many reasons, primarily having to do with space, time, heat, and patience. Very good quality commercial products are available, but be sure to always use one made with unsalted butter. These can be found in the freezer sections of markets. Some bakeries also sell puff pastry dough. If you want to make your own, you can follow one of any number of good recipes; we recommend the one in Nancy Silverton's *Desserts*.

RICE VINEGAR: There are two kinds. We use unseasoned rice vinegar for all our dishes. The seasoned vinegar has sugar in it and is used primarily for flavoring sushi rice.

SAKE AND MIRIN: These may seem similar, but they are very different. Sake is a Japanese rice wine that is primarily for drinking but can also be used for cooking. As with wine, the sake you use should be of a quality that you would drink; it will keep, refrigerated, for about one to two months once opened. Mirin is sweet sake that is for cooking purposes only. It keeps much longer and does not need refrigeration.

SALT: All our recipes use kosher salt unless otherwise written. Kosher salt has a different crystal formation than table salt and has no additives. It also adheres more and dissolves quicker. If you are using table salt instead, remember: 1 tablespoon of table salt is equal to 2 tablespoons of kosher salt.

SOY SAUCE: We use Japanese soy sauce that is made of fermented soybeans and wheat. Do not substitute Chinese soy sauce or light soy sauce (Japanese light soy sauce actually has more salt than regular does). Low-sodium soy sauce would be fine. We don't recommend using tamari unless you have a wheat allergy; tamari has a different flavor.

VEGETABLE OIL FOR FRYING: We use primarily canola oil but would also recommend peanut oil. Only use oils that have a high smoke point.

RED AND WHITE WINE: Always use a dry wine of a quality you would drink. Never use wines made for cooking, which have salt added. ♪♪♪

APPETIZERS

Grilled Miso-Marinated Beef Salad
with Ginger-Mustard Vinaigrette

*Hiro says that what makes this salad so special is the way the tender slices of warm grilled steak help release the flavor of all the other ingredients. Lissa would tell you it's the beautiful combination of colors. We're both right. Have all the ingredients ready before you grill the steaks, so you can put everything together quickly while the meat is still hot. Be sure to use red miso (also called **aka miso**) in the marinade; other kinds will impart a very different flavor. Because miso does not break down the fibers in meat quickly, you can marinate the steaks for up to 24 hours.*

Miso Marinade

1 tablespoon red miso
2 tablespoons plus 1½ teaspoons sugar
¼ teaspoon grated peeled fresh ginger
¼ teaspoon grated garlic
1 tablespoon Asian (toasted) sesame oil
½ teaspoon soy sauce
1 tablespoon mirin

1 (12-ounce) New York steak, trimmed of all fat
    and silver skin and cut into 4 thin steaks

Ginger-Mustard Vinaigrette

1½ teaspoons peeled and chopped ginger
¼ teaspoon chopped garlic
¼ cup rice vinegar
1 tablespoon soy sauce
1 tablespoon packed brown sugar
1½ teaspoons Asian (toasted) sesame oil
Pinch of crushed red pepper flakes
1 tablespoon corn oil
2¼ teaspoons Dijon mustard

Rice Noodles (optional)

Vegetable oil for deep-frying
8 dried flat, ½-inch wide rice noodles

Vegetable Salad

1 Japanese cucumber, or ½ hothouse cucumber,
    halved lengthwise and cut on the diagonal
    into ⅛-inch-thick slices about 2 inches long
¼ carrot, peeled, halved lengthwise, and cut
on the diagonal into ⅛-inch-thick slices
    about 2 inches long
2 tablespoons thinly sliced red onion
1½ ounces haricots verts, stemmed and
    blanched (page 198)
2 Roma (plum) tomatoes, each cut into 6 wedges
1 tablespoon crushed roasted peanuts

8 large radicchio leaves
2 cups mesclun or your favorite small-leaf lettuce mix

Garnish

2 teaspoons chopped fresh chives
8 fresh cilantro sprigs

To make the marinade, whisk together all the ingredients in a medium bowl. Add the steak, cover, and marinate for 1 hour in the refrigerator, turning twice.

Prepare a fire in a charcoal grill or preheat a gas grill.

To make the vinaigrette, purée all the ingredients in a blender for 1 minute. Strain and set aside.

To deep-fry the rice noodles, heat 3 inches of oil in a large saucepan to 350°. Add a few rice noodles, taking care not to crowd the pan. Cook until the noodles are puffed but still white, about

30 seconds. Using tongs, transfer the rice noodles to paper towels to drain. Repeat with the remaining noodles. Set aside.

TO MAKE THE SALAD, combine the cucumber, carrot, red onion, haricots verts, tomatoes, and peanuts in a large bowl, and set aside.

TO COOK THE STEAK, remove the steak slices from the marinade. Grill the steak for about 1 minute per side for medium rare. Or, heat a large grill pan or nonstick skillet over high heat and sauté the steak for 1 minute per side for medium rare. Cut the steak into strips about ¼ inch wide and 3 inches long. Add the steak to the salad and toss with the vinaigrette.

TO SERVE, take 2 radicchio leaves and fit them together to make a bowl. Repeat to make 4 bowls. Place each bowl in the center of a plate, then divide the mesclun among the radicchio bowls and top with the tossed salad. Sprinkle with the chives. Top each with 2 fried rice noodles and 2 cilantro sprigs. 🌶️🌶️🌶️

Fried Rock Shrimp with Chive-Mustard Sauce

When people ask us what our specialties are, we're always somewhat hesitant to mention this one. After all, fried shrimp is something you can get in any chain restaurant in America. But the truth is, this is one of our best-loved and most requested dishes. What makes our version so good is the rock shrimp. They're like no other shrimp—fat little balls of flavor that are totally addictive. Rock shrimp have a very hard shell, which until fairly recently made them difficult to process commercially and thus hard to find. In the early '90s, new technology for removing the shell became widely available and rock shrimp are now sold everywhere. Whoever developed that machinery deserves a prize—or at least a plate of these fried shrimp.

If you can't find fresh rock shrimp, frozen are fine; be sure to defrost them in the refrigerator. Fresh or frozen, rock shrimp always need to be deveined.

Chive-Mustard Sauce
1½ teaspoons egg yolk (½ yolk)
1 tablespoon plus 1 teaspoon Dijon mustard
⅛ teaspoon salt
2 teaspoons rice vinegar
2 tablespoons freshly squeezed lemon juice
6 tablespoons corn oil
Pinch of cayenne pepper
⅛ teaspoon paprika
3 tablespoons heavy cream
1 tablespoon plus 1½ teaspoons
　chopped fresh chives

Vegetable oil for deep-frying
1½ cups pastry flour
Pinch of cayenne pepper
½ teaspoon paprika
20 ounces shelled large rock shrimp, deveined (page 69)
1 tablespoon water
Salt to taste

4 cups mesclun or your favorite small-leaf lettuce mix
1 teaspoon Terra house vinaigrette (page 201)
1 tablespoon chopped fresh chives
1 lemon, cut into 4 wedges and seeded

To start the chive mustard sauce, combine the egg yolk, mustard, salt, vinegar, and lemon juice in a food processor. With the machine running, gradually add the corn oil in a thin stream. Add the cayenne, paprika, and cream, and process for 5 seconds. Transfer to a medium bowl. Cover and refrigerate until the shrimp are ready. Just before serving, fold in the chives.

Preheat the oven to 250°.

To deep-fry the shrimp, heat 3 inches of oil in a deep, heavy pot to 375°. Combine the flour, cayenne, and paprika in a medium bowl. Moisten the shrimp with the water, then toss one-quarter of the shrimp in the flour mixture, making sure each one is individually coated. Transfer them from the flour to a wire-mesh strainer in a single layer and wait 10 seconds for the coating to set. Gently shake the strainer to remove any excess flour, then carefully drop the shrimp into the oil. Cook for 1 to 1½ minutes, or until crisp but not browned. Using a wire-mesh skimmer or slotted metal spoon, transfer the shrimp to paper towels to drain, then place on a baking sheet pan and keep warm in the oven. Repeat with the remaining 3 batches of shrimp. Sprinkle all the shrimp with salt.

TO SERVE, finish the sauce by folding in the chives, then divide the sauce among 4 warmed 10-inch plates. In a large bowl, toss the mesclun with the vinaigrette and mound 1 cup in the center of each plate. Arrange the shrimp around the salads. Sprinkle with the chives and place a lemon wedge on the side of each plate. ♪♪♪

Photo: Barney (and Lucy) in the lettuce fields at Forni Brown

Panzanella with Feta Cheese

Our Italian customers sometimes raise an eyebrow at the thought of a Japanese chef making panzanella, the classic bread salad of central Italy. But Hiro just smiles and tells them his grandmother was Italian. Panzanella is usually prepared by soaking torn pieces of day-old bread in water, then tossing them with oil, vinegar, and tomatoes. In our version, we skip the water and let the bread absorb the vinaigrette and some of the juice from the tomatoes, making the salad more intensely flavored. Instead of the traditional torn bread, Hiro starts with crunchy garlic-rubbed croutons and tosses them with a rainbow of local vine-ripened tomatoes, basil, cucumber, and red onion in a lively anchovy vinaigrette. He tops the salad with a local goat's milk feta cheese, Italian Taleggio or Gorgonzola, or California Teleme. Panzanella shows up on our menu the moment tomatoes are at their peak, and it stays there all summer long. No one ever leaves any on their plate. Not even the Italians.

Balsamico and Caper Vinaigrette

½ cup extra virgin olive oil

2 tablespoons balsamic vinegar

1 tablespoon sherry wine vinegar

1 tablespoon capers

1½ teaspoons chopped anchovy fillets

½ teaspoon chopped garlic

½ teaspoon caper juice

Salt and freshly ground black pepper to taste

½ baguette, or enough for 1½ cups croutons

1 clove garlic, peeled

6 vine-ripened tomatoes, cut into 1-inch chunks

1 Japanese cucumber or ½ hothouse cucumber, quartered lengthwise, then cut crosswise into ½-inch-thick pieces

¼ cup thinly sliced red onion

2 teaspoons chopped fresh basil

Salt and freshly ground black pepper to taste

12 kalamata olives

12 yellow pear tomatoes or Sweet 100 cherry tomatoes

½ cup crumbled feta cheese

2 tablespoons extra virgin olive oil

4 fresh basil sprigs

TO MAKE THE VINAIGRETTE, combine all the ingredients in a blender and purée for 1 minute. Set aside.

TO MAKE THE CROUTONS, preheat the oven to 500°. Slice the baguette in half lengthwise. Rub all over with the garlic, then cut in half again lengthwise. Cut these strips into ¾-inch cubes. Spread the bread cubes on a baking sheet pan, crust side down, and bake just until golden brown and crisp on the outside but still soft inside, about 3 minutes. Watch carefully. Let cool.

TO MAKE THE PANZANELLA, combine the tomatoes, cucumber, onion, basil, croutons, and the vinaigrette in a large bowl. Toss well. Season with salt and pepper.

TO SERVE, divide the panzanella among 4 bowls or plates. Arrange 3 olives and 3 pear tomatoes on each salad. Top with the feta cheese, drizzle with extra virgin olive oil, and garnish with a basil sprig. ♪♪♪

Grilled Rare Tuna
with Tomato-Cucumber Salad and Tahini Sauce

Serves 4

This Middle Eastern–style tuna appetizer is a nod to Lissa's Lebanese background. Hiro has loved the flavors of Lebanese home-cooking ever since he married into the family, and Lissa's always delighted to see how those flavors turn up in his cooking at Terra. In Lebanon, this dish would be made with swordfish or shark and served with caramelized onions. We think the use of tuna and the addition of the fresh, crunchy salad make the dish lighter and more intriguing.

Look for tahini made from roasted sesame seeds, which is much more flavorful than the kinds made from unroasted seeds. Sumac is a remarkable Middle Eastern seasoning made from the dried berries of a Mediterranean bush. It has a distinctly sour flavor and beautiful reddish-purple color that can add a little extra touch of sparkle to a dish.

Tahini Sauce
½ cup Middle Eastern–style tahini paste
¼ cup hot water
¼ teaspoon grated garlic
⅓ cup freshly squeezed lemon juice
Salt and freshly ground white pepper to taste

Salad
2 large tomatoes, cut into ½-inch dice
2 Japanese cucumbers or 1 hothouse cucumber,
 cut into ½-inch dice
2 teaspoons finely chopped red onion
2 tablespoons fresh flat-leaf parsley leaves
1 teaspoon freshly squeezed lemon juice
1 tablespoon extra virgin olive oil
Salt and freshly ground black pepper to taste

1 globe eggplant
2 tablespoons olive oil
Salt and freshly ground black pepper to taste
4 (3- to 3½-ounce) sashimi-grade tuna steaks,
 ¾ inch thick

Garnish
2 teaspoons pine nuts, toasted (page 68)
12 kalamata olives
½ teaspoon sumac (optional)

PREPARE A FIRE in a charcoal grill or preheat a gas grill.

TO MAKE THE TAHINI SAUCE, combine the tahini paste, water, and garlic in a food processor and process until smooth. Add the lemon juice and process again; if the tahini is still too thick, add more water, up to ½ cup (it should be thick, but not like peanut butter). Season with salt and pepper. Set aside.

TO MAKE THE SALAD, toss together all the ingredients in a medium bowl. Cover and refrigerate until needed.

TO COOK THE EGGPLANT, cut four ¾-inch-thick disks from the thickest part of the eggplant. Brush each slice with ¼ tablespoon of the olive oil, season with salt and pepper, and grill 3 to 4 minutes per side, or until golden brown and soft. Or, preheat the broiler and broil 4 inches from the heat source, 3 to 4 minutes per side.

TO COOK THE TUNA, brush the steaks with the remaining 1 tablespoon olive oil and season with salt and pepper. Grill for 1 to 2 minutes per side, or until lightly browned on the outside and rare inside. Or, heat a grill pan or skillet over high heat until very hot, and sauté the steaks for 1 to 2 minutes per side, or until lightly browned on the outside and rare inside.

TO SERVE, spread 3 tablespoons of the tahini sauce on each of 4 plates. Place 1 slice of eggplant in the center of each plate. Mound the salad evenly over the eggplant and top with a tuna steak. Sprinkle with the pine nuts, olives, and sumac.

Miyagi Oysters in Ponzu

Serves 4

This is a traditional Japanese way to serve oysters that's relatively unknown in the West. The tartness of the lemon and the saltiness of the soy sauce in the ponzu bring out the altogether different saltiness of the oysters, and the combination is unforgettable. We serve these oysters in Chinese porcelain soup spoons. If you don't have 24 of them on hand, you can use the oyster shells instead. Or, simply put a half-dozen shucked oysters in a beautiful bowl, add the ponzu and top with a large ball of momiji oroshi (omitting the radicchio).

24 small Miyagi oysters or other small
  Pacific oysters, scrubbed and rinsed
1 cup ponzu (page 202)

2 tablespoons chopped fresh chives
⅔ cup momiji oroshi (page 202)
2 cups loosely packed radicchio chiffonade

CAREFULLY SHUCK THE OYSTERS, reserving the oyster liquor. Strain the liquor through cheesecloth into another bowl. Gently rinse the oysters in a bowl of cold water, drain well, and transfer to the bowl of the oyster liquor. Cover and refrigerate until ready to use.

TO SERVE, chill 24 Chinese soup spoons, or rinse and drain the bottom, rounded shell of each oyster. Drain the oysters and put 1 oyster in each spoon or shell. Spoon in the ponzu to fill the spoon or shell, and sprinkle with chives. Top with a ¼-inch ball of momiji oroshi. Divide the radicchio among 4 plates, making a mound in the center. Surround each mound of radicchio with 6 of the spoons with the handles facing out, or with the filled shells.

Wild Mushroom and Smoked Bacon Vol-au-Vent

Serves 4

Mushrooms and bacon are such a natural combination—a marriage of flavors that bring out the best in each other. We serve this in flaky pastry shells, which soak up some of the rich sauce and become meltingly tender. Try to buy bacon produced by a small company. You'll find that it's usually less salty and has a truer smoked flavor than commercial brands. We use a locally made apple wood-smoked bacon that has a clean, fruity sweetness. You can make a vegetarian version of this dish by omitting the bacon and the stock and adding a little Parmesan cheese to the cream sauce.

Vol-au-Vent

14 ounces all-butter puff pastry

1 egg yolk

¼ teaspoon water

Mushroom Sauce

2 teaspoons unsalted butter

1 slice bacon, cut into ¼-inch-wide strips
  (about 1 tablespoon)

1 tablespoon minced shallot

6 ounces wild mushrooms, cleaned and cut
  into bite-size pieces

⅛ teaspoon minced garlic

Pinch of chopped fresh thyme

¼ cup veal stock (page 207)

2 cups heavy cream

Salt and freshly ground black pepper to taste

Garnish

4 fresh thyme sprigs

2 teaspoons chopped fresh chives

TO MAKE THE VOL-AU-VENTS, preheat the oven to 400°. On a lightly floured board, roll the puff pastry out into a 7 by 14-inch rectangle 3/16 inch thick. Using a 3½-inch round cookie cutter, cut out 8 rounds from the sheet of puff pastry. Using a 2½-inch round cookie cutter, cut out 4 rounds from the center of 4 of the large rounds to form rings. In a small bowl, combine the egg yolk with the water to make an egg wash. Brush the rings and the smaller rounds with the egg wash. Place the rings, brushed side down, on top of the larger rounds so that the 3½-inch rounds are a double thickness on the outside. Match the ring up carefully and don't press hard; the puff pastry will puff better if it is not pressed down. Brush the tops of the rings only with the egg wash, being careful not to let any of it drip down the sides of the puff pastry. Place the vol-au-vents and the 2½-inch rounds on a baking sheet pan lined with parchment paper, and refrigerate for at least 15 minutes. Bake for about 15 minutes, or until golden brown on top and cooked through on the bottom. Keep warm in a 200° oven, or reheat them in a 350° oven for 2 minutes just before serving.

TO MAKE THE SAUCE, melt the butter in a large sauté pan or skillet over high heat. Add the bacon and shallots, lower the heat to medium, and sauté until the shallots are soft, about 3 minutes. Add the mushrooms and garlic, increase the heat to high, and sauté for 2 minutes longer. Add the thyme, stock, and cream, and bring to a boil. Lower the heat to a simmer and cook until the sauce thickens slightly, about 3 minutes. Season with salt and pepper.

TO SERVE, place 1 vol-au-vent in the center of each of 4 warmed plates. If the centers of each vol-au-vent are puffed up, tap them down gently with your finger to make a well; be careful not to break through the bottom. Divide the sauce and mushrooms among the wells of the vol-au-vents, putting most of the sauce inside and the extra around the outside. Garnish each well of mushrooms with a sprig of thyme, then set a 2½-inch round on top. Sprinkle with chives.

Radicchio Salad
with Parmesan-Balsamico Vinaigrette

Serves 4

Hiro came up with this salad when he was the chef at Spago in Los Angeles. It was so good, we decided to save it for when we opened our own place. That turned out to be a wise decision. It was one of the first dishes on our menu when we opened, and it's remained there to this day, a favorite with our regular customers. Depending on the variety and where it's grown, radicchio can have a bitter flavor. Before you use it, taste a leaf. If you want to reduce the bitterness you can soak it for up to 30 minutes in cold water. Any leftover salad can be sautéed (in its dressing) and served as a side dish with meat or game.

¼ baguette, or enough for ¾ cup croutons

Parmesan-Balsamico Vinaigrette
¼ teaspoon grated garlic
1 tablespoon Dijon mustard
1 tablespoon balsamic vinegar
1 tablespoon sherry wine vinegar
2 tablespoons corn oil
¼ cup extra virgin olive oil
Salt and freshly ground white pepper to taste

2 heads radicchio, about 4½ inches in diameter, halved and cored
⅔ cup freshly grated Parmesan cheese

To MAKE THE CROUTONS, preheat the oven to 350°. Cut the baguette into ½-inch cubes. Spread the bread cubes on a rimmed baking sheet pan and bake until golden brown, 4 to 5 minutes. Set aside.

TO MAKE THE VINAIGRETTE, whisk together the garlic, Dijon mustard, balsamic vinegar, and sherry vinegar in a small bowl. Mix together the corn oil and extra virgin olive oil, then slowly whisk it into the vinegar mixture. Season with salt and pepper. Set aside.

Separate the radicchio leaves and soak them in cold water for 10 minutes, or longer if necessary. Drain and dry (with a lettuce spinner, if you have one). Cover with a damp towel and refrigerate until ready to use.

To SERVE, combine the radicchio, croutons, vinaigrette, and ⅓ cup of the Parmesan cheese in a large bowl, tossing well so each leaf is coated with vinaigrette. Divide the salad among 4 chilled plates and sprinkle with the remaining Parmesan cheese.

Need a Hand?

WHISKING OR STIRRING INGREDIENTS IN A LARGE BOWL CAN BE TRICKY WHEN YOU'RE ALONE IN THE KITCHEN, AND THE BOWL WANTS TO ROCK AND ROLL TO THE BEAT OF A DIFFERENT DRUMMER. TRY THE TRICK WE USE AT THE RESTAURANT: HOLDING A DISH TOWEL BY OPPOSITE CORNERS, ROLL IT INTO A ROPE. LAY THE TOWEL IN A CIRCLE ABOUT THE SIZE OF THE BOTTOM OF THE BOWL AND PLACE THE BOWL IN THE CENTER OF THE CIRCLE TO HOLD IT IN PLACE.

Escabeche of Lake Smelt

*Before there was refrigeration, people all over the world discovered that preparing fresh fish in an acidic marinade could help preserve it for a few extra days. In Spain, fish was first crisp-fried, then steeped in a vinegar marinade, a style of cooking that has come to be known as **en escabeche**. The vinegar penetrates the fish to the bones and softens them enough to make the smaller ones edible. We love the flavor that this two-step technique gives to fish and to the delicate pickled vegetables that steep along with it. If lake smelt are not available surf smelt or white bait are a fine substitute.*

Marinade

1 cup rice vinegar

1 cup dry white wine

2/3 cup sugar

1 tablespoon plus 1 teaspoon salt

Pinch of crushed red pepper flakes

4 bay leaves

1½ teaspoons coriander seeds

1 teaspoon black peppercorns

1 carrot, peeled and sliced into
   1/16-inch-thick rounds

1 small onion, peeled, halved, and sliced
   1/8 inch thick

1 cup water

Vegetable oil for deep-frying

1 pound small lake smelt (about 3½ inches long)

Salt and freshly ground black pepper

1 cup all-purpose flour

Garnish

1 tablespoon chopped fresh chives

12 chive flowers (optional)

To MAKE THE MARINADE, combine all the ingredients in a large nonreactive saucepan. Bring to a boil, decrease the heat, and simmer for 1 minute. Set aside and keep hot.

TO DEEP-FRY THE SMELT, heat 3 inches of oil in a deep, heavy pot to 360°. Season the smelt with salt and pepper, then dredge in the flour and pat between your hands to shake off the excess. Deep-fry the smelt in batches for 2 to 3 minutes, or until golden brown. Don't overcrowd the pot or the smelt won't get crisp and will overcook. Using a wire-mesh skimmer or slotted metal spoon, transfer the smelt to paper towels to drain. When all the smelt are done, put them in a nonreactive container, then pour the hot marinade over them. Let cool to room temperature, then refrigerate for at least 3 hours, or until cold, up to 2 days.

TO SERVE, arrange the smelt with some of the vegetables from the marinade on each plate, spoon some of the marinade over the smelt, sprinkle with the chives, and decorate with the chive flowers.

Baked Mussels in Garlic-Parsley Butter

Serves 4

These mussels prepared in the style of escargot are heaven for anyone who loves snails, and perfect for people with "escargophobia" as well. You'll need 4 escargot dishes—the ceramic ones with 6 holes and a little handle, not the shallow plates used to serve escargot in the shell. You can fill the dishes ahead of time, wrap them in plastic, and refrigerate them until you're ready to finish them in the oven. The smell of the bubbling butter and garlic as these come to the table does just what an appetizer should do: It makes people hungry. Make sure you've got plenty of crusty bread on hand to sop up the sauce.

28 black mussels, scrubbed and debearded;
   this includes a few extras, in case some don't open
½ teaspoon minced garlic
⅓ cup dry white wine
⅔ cup garlic-parsley compound butter (page 200),
   at room temperature
2 tablespoons tomato sauce (page 200)
1 tablespoon chopped fresh flat-leaf parsley

IN A SMALL SAUCEPAN, combine the mussels, garlic, and wine. Cover and place over high heat. Steam the mussels until they open, 3 to 4 minutes. Discard any mussels that do not open. Drain over a bowl to catch the cooking liquid, then strain the cooking liquid through cheese-cloth. Let cool. Gently remove the mussels from the shells, then put them in the cooling liquid. Cover and refrigerate until using; this will keep the mussels moist and flavorful.

Preheat the oven to 500°. Drain the mussels (the cooking liquid can be frozen for another use), then place a mussel in each of the 6 holes of each escargot dish. Cover each hole with compound butter to the top, then put ¼ teaspoon tomato sauce on top of each hole. Place the 4 dishes on a baking sheet pan and bake until the butter starts to bubble, 6 to 8 minutes. Sprinkle with parsley and place each dish on a separate plate. Be careful, as the butter is hot. ♪♪♪

How to Clean Mussels

AS SOON AS YOU GET THE MUSSELS HOME, PUT THEM IN A LARGE BOWL, TOSS ON A HANDFUL OF SALT, AND SHAKE THE BOWL TO BEGIN CLEANING THE SHELLS. IF THERE ARE ANY FIBERS ON THE SURFACE OF THE SHELLS, USE A WIRE SCRUBBER TO REMOVE THEM. RINSE THE MUSSELS IN COLD WATER, PUT THEM BACK IN THE BOWL, COVER THEM WITH A DAMP CLOTH, AND REFRIGERATE THEM UNTIL YOU'RE READY TO USE THEM. THE BEARD—THE FIBROUS STRAND THAT COMES OUT FROM BETWEEN THE TWO HALVES OF THE SHELL AND IS USED BY THE MUSSEL TO ATTACH ITSELF TO A ROCK OR OTHER SURFACE—MUST BE TAKEN OFF RIGHT BEFORE COOKING, SINCE REMOVING IT KILLS THE MUSSEL. TAKE THE MUSSEL IN ONE HAND AND, WITH YOUR OTHER HAND, GRAB THE BEARD BETWEEN YOUR THUMB AND THE TIP OF A SPOON AND PULL HARD (OR, IT MAY BE EASIER TO JUST USE YOUR FINGERS). IF YOU'RE SERVING THE MUSSELS WITHOUT THEIR SHELLS, DON'T BOTHER BEARDING THEM BEFORE YOU COOK THEM. ONCE THE SHELLS ARE OPEN AND THE MUSSELS ARE COOKED, IT'S MUCH EASIER TO REMOVE THE BEARD. ANY COOKED MUSSELS THAT DON'T OPEN ARE DEAD AND SHOULD BE DISCARDED.

Petit Ragout of Sweetbreads, Mushrooms, Prosciutto, and White Truffle Oil

Serves 4

When people ask us about the best dishes at Terra, we always start by recommending sweetbreads, especially this warm ragout enriched with veal stock and wild mushrooms. Then we usually explain that they're not brains. Sometimes, people are a bit reluctant to give them a try, but so far, we've had no complaints—and lots of converts. Once, though, when Lissa asked a customer how she was enjoying her meal, she replied that the sweetbreads were delicious, but not very sweet. Lissa explained that this is a savory dish and left it at that. She didn't have the heart to tell her what she was eating; better to just let her enjoy it.

Hiro says he can always tell when Lissa's been recommending the sweetbreads, because the order will come in with a request for mashed potatoes to be added to the plate—her favorite way to eat them. If you're serving them as a main course, mashed potatoes do make a wonderful addition, but for an appetizer, it can be a lot of food.

20 ounces veal sweetbreads
3 tablespoons rice vinegar
2 tablespoons salt
1 teaspoon freshly ground black pepper

Sauce
1 tablespoon unsalted butter
1 teaspoon minced garlic
2 teaspoons sherry wine vinegar
3 tablespoons dry white wine
3 cups veal stock (page 207) or brown
   chicken stock (page 208)
1 tablespoon tomato puree
Salt and freshly ground black pepper to taste

1 tablespoon unsalted butter
3 ounces wild mushrooms, cleaned and cut
   into bite-size pieces
Salt and freshly ground black pepper to taste
¼ cup rice flour
¼ cup all-purpose flour
3 tablespoons clarified butter (page 200)
1 tablespoon julienned prosciutto
¼ cup fava beans, blanched for 1 minute (page 198)
   and peeled
2 teaspoons chopped fresh flat-leaf parsley

Garnish
½ teaspoon white truffle oil (optional)
⅓ cup loosely packed chervil sprigs

To prepare the sweetbreads, put them in 1 gallon of ice water to soak overnight; this will remove any blood left in them. The next day, bring 8 cups water to a boil in a large saucepan. Add the rice vinegar, salt, and pepper, lower the heat to a low simmer, add the sweetbreads, and gently poach them for 4 to 5 minutes, or until firm but medium rare. Transfer to a bowl of ice water and let cool for 10 minutes. Drain and pat dry with a towel. Clean off any visible membrane or veins. Cut into ½-inch-thick medallions.

TO MAKE THE SAUCE, melt the butter in a large saucepan over medium heat. Add the garlic and sauté just until it starts to caramelize. Add the vinegar and wine, and bring to a boil. Add the stock and tomato purée, and return to a boil. Lightly season with salt and pepper. Set aside and keep warm.

TO MAKE THE RAGOUT, melt the butter in a sauté pan or skillet over high heat. Add the mushrooms and sauté for 1 to 2 minutes. Lightly season with salt and pepper and set aside.

In a medium bowl, mix together the rice flour and all-purpose flour. Season the sweetbreads with salt and pepper, then dredge them in the flour mixture. In a large sauté pan or skillet, heat the clarified butter over high heat until hot. Add the sweetbreads and sauté until crisp and golden brown, about 1½ minutes per side. Transfer them to the sauce and add the mushrooms, prosciutto, fava beans, and parsley. Bring to a boil, lower the heat, and simmer for 1 minute. Season with salt and pepper.

TO SERVE, spoon the ragout into 4 warmed shallow bowls. Drizzle with the white truffle oil and top with chervil sprigs.

Fried Haricots Verts
with Anchovy-Garlic Mayonnaise

Serves 4

This delicate appetizer is inspired by the light frying technique of tempura and the flavors of fritto misto. We make it with haricots verts, the very small, thin French-style green beans. If you can't find them, blue lake or yellow wax beans will also work well. The secret to golden color and crispy texture: Fry just a few beans at a time. This takes a little more time and patience, but it keeps the oil temperature constant and ensures that the beans stay separate and fry evenly. This recipe comes with a little bonus: The Anchovy-Garlic Mayonnaise makes a wonderful Caesar salad dressing.

1½ pounds small haricots verts or
   baby Blue Lake beans, stemmed

Anchovy-Garlic Mayonnaise
1½ teaspoons egg yolk (½ yolk)
1 tablespoon Dijon mustard
2 tablespoons plus 1 teaspoon rice vinegar
⅔ cup olive oil
½ teaspoon minced garlic
1½ teaspoons chopped anchovy fillets
1 teaspoon freshly squeezed lemon juice,
   plus more if needed
Salt and freshly ground black pepper to taste

Batter
2 eggs
½ cup pastry flour
⅛ teaspoon minced garlic
1 tablespoon freshly grated Parmesan cheese
1 teaspoon olive oil
1 tablespoon water
Pinch each of salt and freshly ground
   black pepper
Vegetable oil for deep-frying
Salt to taste

4 large radicchio leaves (optional)
12 yellow cherry tomatoes
12 red cherry tomatoes
1 teaspoon chopped fresh flat-leaf parsley
3 tablespoons freshly grated Parmesan cheese
1 lemon, cut into 4 wedges and seeded

To make the haricots verts, bring a pot of salted water to boil. Add the haricots verts and blanch them for 1 to 2 minutes, then drain and plunge them into a bowl of ice water. Drain and pat dry. If the haricots verts are tiny, blanch them for just 30 to 45 seconds. It's best to test them every 30 seconds; they will cook again and should still have some crispness after the first cooking.

TO MAKE THE MAYONNAISE, combine the egg yolk, mustard, and rice vinegar in a food processor. With the machine running, gradually add the olive oil in a thin stream, then add the garlic, anchovy, and lemon juice. Adjust the acidity with more lemon juice, if necessary. Season with salt and pepper.

TO MAKE THE BATTER, whisk together all the ingredients in a bowl. Cover and refrigerate until you are ready to fry the haricots verts.

Preheat the oven to 250°.

Heat 3 inches of oil in a deep, heavy pot to 360°.

Put the haricots verts in the batter and coat well. Drop the haricots verts one by one into the oil in batches so the oil temperature doesn't drop and the haricots verts don't stick together. Fry until golden brown and crisp, 2 to 3 minutes. Using a wire-mesh skimmer or slotted metal spoon, transfer the beans to paper towels to drain. Place the beans on a baking sheet pan, season with salt, and keep warm in the oven while frying the remaining beans.

TO SERVE, spread 4 plates with the mayonnaise and place 1 large radicchio leaf in the center of each plate. Divide the haricots verts among the radicchio leaves, then arrange the cherry tomatoes around each plate. Sprinkle with the parsley and Parmesan and place a lemon wedge on the side of each plate. 🔥🔥🔥

Salmon and Tuna Tartare with Spicy Lemon-Ginger Vinaigrette and Sesame Tuiles

Serves 4

Use only absolutely fresh sashimi-grade fish, since it is served raw, and don't add the vinaigrette until the last minute because the acid in the vinaigrette will "cook" the fish, turning it opaque and milky-colored. Tobiko caviar—especially the wasabi-flavored kind—can be hard to find, but it's worth looking for. Its crunchy texture makes a perfect contrast to the soft, silky tartare. Sambal chili is an Indonesian or Malaysian hot chili paste available in Asian markets.

Sesame Tuile

2 tablespoons sesame seeds
¼ teaspoon sugar
Pinch of salt
Pinch of cayenne pepper
1 egg white
2 teaspoons cornstarch
4 wonton wrappers
Vegetable oil for deep-frying

Spicy Lemon-Ginger Vinaigrette

2 tablespoons freshly squeezed lemon juice
1½ teaspoons rice vinegar
1 tablespoon plus 1 teaspoon soy sauce
1 teaspoon sambal chili
⅛ teaspoon grated peeled fresh ginger
⅛ teaspoon grated garlic
1 tablespoon plus 1 teaspoon Asian (toasted)
   sesame oil

Ponzu Mayonnaise (optional)

½ teaspoon ponzu (page 202)
2 tablespoons mayonnaise (page 201)

Tobiko Oil

1 tablespoon wasabi tobiko
1 tablespoon extra virgin olive oil

Tartare

6 ounces sashimi grade tuna fillet,
   cut into ¼-inch dice
6 ounces sashimi grade salmon fillet,
   cut into ¼-inch dice

1 teaspoon finely chopped red onion
2 teaspoons minced fresh chives
3 tablespoons tomato concassée (page 199)
4 teaspoons wasabi tobiko (optional)

1 cup upland cress or daikon sprouts, rinsed
   and drained, for garnish

T O MAKE THE TUILES, combine the sesame seeds, sugar, salt, and cayenne in a shallow bowl. In a small bowl, whisk together the egg white and cornstarch. Thinly brush one side of each wrapper with the egg white mixture. Press the wrappers, brushed side down, on the sesame mixture. Heat 1 inch of oil in a deep, heavy pot to 310°. Deep-fry the wrappers for about 2 minutes per side, until golden brown. Using a wire-mesh skimmer or slotted metal spoon, transfer to paper towels to drain.

TO MAKE THE VINAIGRETTE, whisk together all the ingredients in a small bowl. Set aside.

TO MAKE THE MAYONNAISE, whisk together the ponzu and mayonnaise in a small bowl, and set aside.

TO MAKE THE TOBIKO OIL, whisk together the wasabi tobiko and extra virgin olive oil in a small bowl, and set aside.

TO MAKE THE TARTARE, just before serving, combine all the ingredients in a medium bowl. Add the vinaigrette and mix well.

TO SERVE, place a 3-inch-diameter, 1¼-inch-high ring mold in the center of a chilled plate and fill with the tartare. Press down lightly. Carefully remove the ring and repeat with the remaining tartare. Divide the upland cress into 6 tumbleweed-shaped balls and put one on top of each circle of tartare. Drizzle the mayonnaise around the tartare. Drizzle the tobiko oil around the mayonnaise. Place a tuile next to each tartare.

Goat Cheese and Artichoke Spring Rolls
with Arugula and Tomato Salad

Serves 4

Although these delicate spring rolls are fried, their texture and flavor are surprisingly light. We sometimes make them a little smaller and serve them as passed cocktail appetizers (page 43). Lumpia wrappers can usually be found in the refrigerator section of Filipino or Asian markets.

Spring Rolls

¾ cup fresh goat cheese without a rind

⅓ cup cold mashed potatoes (page 206)

¼ cup freshly grated Parmesan cheese

½ cup coarsely chopped cooked baby artichokes
  (page 196), lightly squeezed to remove water

½ teaspoon chopped fresh basil

Pinch of freshly ground white pepper

2 teaspoons cornstarch

1 egg white

8 lumpia wrappers (6 inches square)

Whole-Grain Mustard Vinaigrette

4 teaspoons sherry wine vinegar

4 teaspoons extra virgin olive oil

2 teaspoons whole-grain mustard

Salt and freshly ground black pepper to taste

Vegetable oil for deep-frying

Arugula and Tomato Salad

8 cups loosely packed baby arugula

1 cup ½-inch-diced peeled tomato

1 tablespoon thinly sliced red onion

Garnish

12 kalamata olives

2 tablespoons freshly grated Parmesan cheese

To make the filling, in a mixer using a paddle attachment, combine the goat cheese, potatoes, Parmesan, artichokes, basil, and pepper, and beat until well incorporated, 2 to 3 minutes.

To assemble the spring rolls, in a small bowl whisk together the cornstarch and egg white to make an egg wash. Divide the filling into 8 cylinders, each 1 inch thick and 3 inches long. Lay out a wrapper in a diamond shape on a work surface. Place a goat cheese cylinder horizontally on the bottom third of the wrapper. Bring the bottom point up over the goat cheese and tuck the point underneath it. Begin rolling tightly until you reach the side points, then fold the sides in at a neat angle. Continue rolling until there is a triangle about 2 inches from the top. Brush the edges of the wrapper with the egg wash and complete rolling. Transfer to a baking sheet pan, seam side down. Cover with a towel and refrigerate. Repeat with the remaining wrappers.

To make the vinaigrette, whisk together the ingredients in a small bowl. Preheat the oven to 250°.

To deep-fry the spring rolls, heat 3 inches of oil in a deep, heavy pot to 360°. Deep-fry the spring rolls 2 at a time until golden brown, 3 to 4 minutes. Using tongs, transfer the spring rolls to paper towels to drain, then place them on a baking sheet pan and keep warm in the oven.

While the spring rolls are cooking, toss the salad ingredients with the vinaigrette in a medium bowl. Divide the salad among 4 plates and top each with 2 spring rolls. Arrange the olives around the spring rolls and sprinkle the rolls with Parmesan cheese.

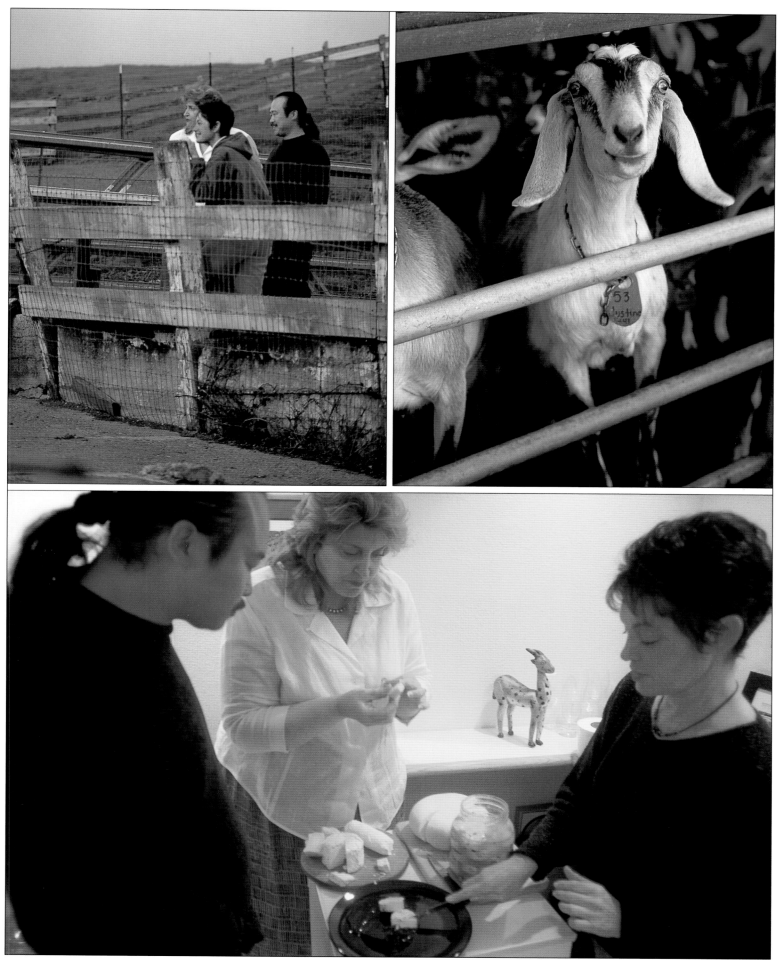

At Laura Chenel's Goat Farm

Warm Scallop Salad
with Lemon-Coriander Vinaigrette

Serves 4

"Warm" is the key to this delightful dish. The scallops are just barely cooked, then dressed with a warm vinaigrette that brings out their sweetness. Because they're served almost raw, it's important that the scallops be sashimi grade and very fresh. Be careful to avoid overcooking them; they're ready when their tops have just turned white. Even if they look a little too raw, remember that the warm plate and the dressing will continue to cook them.

1 pound large sashimi grade sea scallops,
   hinge muscle removed

Lemon-Coriander Vinaigrette

1 teaspoon coriander seeds
½ cup extra virgin olive oil
¼ cup freshly squeezed lemon juice
Salt and freshly ground white pepper to taste
¼ cup tomato concassée (page 199)
2 tablespoons minced fresh chives

⅓ cup chervil sprigs, for garnish

Choosing Good Scallops

SCALLOPS ARE OFTEN TREATED WITH A PRESERVATIVE TO INCREASE THEIR SHELF LIFE AND WATER CONTENT; IF YOU FIND SCALLOPS SITTING IN A POOL OF MILKY LIQUID, AND THEY'RE VERY WHITE AND FIRM, CHANCES ARE THEY'VE BEEN PROCESSED IN THIS WAY. A GOOD SCALLOP, WHETHER FRESH OR PREVIOUSLY FROZEN, WILL BE TRANSLUCENT AND HAVE A SLIGHT PINKISH-ORANGE COLOR; IT WILL ALSO BE SOFT, AND NOT PERFECTLY SHAPED.

RINSE THE SCALLOPS in cold water and pat dry with paper towels. Slice the scallops into ¼-inch-thick discs. Divide the scallops among 4 chilled 8 to 10-inch rimmed plates, arranging them in a single layer starting from the center of the plate. Try to cover the entire inside surface of each plate with scallops; they should be touching slightly. Cover each plate with plastic wrap and refrigerate.

TO START THE VINAIGRETTE, toast the coriander seeds in a small sauté pan or skillet over high heat for about 1 minute, or until fragrant. Transfer immediately to a bowl to stop the cooking. Let the pan cool slightly, then add the olive oil, lemon juice, coriander seeds, salt, and pepper, and whisk well. Whisk in the tomato concassée.

TO SERVE, preheat the oven to 450°. Remove the plastic wrap from the plates. Set the plates in the oven and heat until the surface of the scallops just start to turn opaque but the inside is still raw; this can take as little as 30 seconds, depending on your oven. Meanwhile, finish the vinaigrette by warming it in the sauté pan over medium heat, but don't let it boil. Remove from the heat and stir in the chives. Spoon the vinaigrette over the warmed scallops, scatter the chervil sprigs on top, and serve immediately.

Dungeness Crab Salad
with Avocado Mousse, Beets, and Ruby Grapefruit

Serves 4

Crab and avocado is one of those classic combinations that always seems to work. It looks dressed up, but it's actually quite easy to put together. Like so many restaurant dishes, what makes it seem a little more sophisticated is the presentation. If you don't have access to Dungeness crab, you can also use blue crab.

Crab Salad

1 pound fresh lump Dungeness crabmeat,
  picked over for shell

2 teaspoons minced red onion

1/3 cup finely diced celery

1/4 teaspoon chopped fresh basil

1/2 cup mayonnaise (page 201), or store bought

3 tablespoons tomato concassée (page 199)

Avocado Mousse

1 ripe avocado, peeled, pitted,
  and coarsely chopped

Juice from 1/2 lime

1/4 teaspoon coarsely chopped fresh cilantro

Pinch of grated garlic

2 tablespoons sour cream

Salt and freshly ground white pepper to taste

2 golf ball–sized red beets, steamed, peeled,
  and cut into 6 wedges

12 Ruby Red grapefruit segments

24 Sun Gold, Sweet 100, or other
  cherry tomatoes, stemmed

2 tablespoons Whole-Grain Mustard Vinaigrette
  (page 22)

1 teaspoon chopped fresh chives

8 fresh cilantro sprigs

To make the crab salad, combine all the ingredients in a medium bowl. Refrigerate for no more than 30 minutes.

To make the avocado mousse, put the avocado, lime juice, cilantro, and garlic in a food processor and puree until smooth. Add the sour cream and process until smooth. Season with salt and pepper.

To assemble the salads, place a 3-inch-diameter, 1½-inch-high ring mold in the center of each of 4 chilled plates and fill three-quarters full with the crab salad; smooth the top. Fill the rest of the ring with the avocado mousse, smooth the top with the back of a knife, then carefully remove the ring. Repeat with the remaining salads.

To serve, alternate 3 beet wedges with 3 grapefruit segments and 6 tomatoes around each salad. Drizzle each with 1½ teaspoons of the vinaigrette, sprinkle with chives, and top each with 2 sprigs of cilantro.

 To Segment Citrus

With a very sharp serrated knife, cut the top off the fruit. Cut down the sides from the top, slicing just deep enough to remove the peel and white pith. Finally, cut off the bottom. You should now have a whole fruit, completely cleaned of all pith and peel. Working over a bowl to catch the juices, cut along either side of the membranes between each segment, releasing the segments as you go and working your way all around the fruit. Keep the segments in their juice until you need them.

Japanese Eggplant Salad

Serves 4

We love eggplant in every way imaginable. This salad of tender fried eggplant and wax beans in a sake marinade is a traditional Japanese dish that you might find in a bento box or as part of a kaiseki meal. We present it in a more Western fashion, but the flavors are as haunting as the original version. We like it best in its simplest form, but on occasion, if we get very fresh squid or Hokki Gai clams, we grill them and toss them into the mix. Momiji oroshi is grated daikon seasoned with cayenne and paprika; you can adjust its spiciness to taste. It's important in this recipe because it helps the ponzu adhere to the eggplant, making its flavor more intense.

8 Japanese eggplants (1½ inches thick and
   4 inches long)
Vegetable oil for deep-frying
2 tablespoons sake marinade (page 202)
5½ ounces yellow wax beans, stemmed and
   blanched (page 198)
⅓ cup momiji oroshi (page 202)
1 tablespoon chopped fresh chives
½ cup ponzu (page 202)
½ cup upland cress or daikon sprouts,
   rinsed well and drained
½ teaspoon sesame seeds, toasted (page 68)

PEEL THE EGGPLANTS LENGTHWISE, leaving strips of skin unpeeled to make a striped pattern. Cut the eggplants lengthwise into 5 wedges, then cut those in half crosswise. In a large bowl, whisk 2 quarts water with 1 tablespoon salt and soak the eggplants in the salted water for 15 minutes to remove the bitterness. Drain the eggplant and carefully pat dry with paper towels to remove all the moisture (you don't want any water on the eggplant when you deep-fry them).

Heat 2 inches of oil in a deep, heavy pot to 300°. Add as many eggplant pieces as will fit without overcrowding and deep-fry for about 1 minute, or until they are cooked through but not browned. Using a wire-mesh skimmer or slotted metal spoon, transfer the eggplant to a metal colander in a single layer. Pour hot water over the eggplant for 15 seconds to remove the residual oil, then transfer to a bowl of ice water to cool. Remove and pat dry. Repeat the process for the remaining eggplant.

Place the eggplant in a large bowl, add the sake marinade, and toss gently. Marinate in the refrigerator for 15 minutes. Add the yellow wax beans, momiji oroshi, chives, and ponzu and gently combine.

TO SERVE, divide the salad among 4 chilled shallow bowls. Top with the upland cress and sprinkle with toasted sesame seeds.

Lacquered Quail with Hong Kong Noodles

Serves 4

The first time Hiro saw a man deep-frying a whole turkey on TV, he thought, "This guy is crazy." But for days afterward, he couldn't stop thinking about how he might use this technique—perhaps on a slightly smaller scale, so as not to scare anyone. What he settled on was quail, which first steep overnight in a soy-ginger marinade. When they're deep-fried, the sugar in the marinade caramelizes and they take on a deep mahogany color reminiscent of Peking duck. Served over a simple cold noodle salad, they're a great way to start a meal. Frying the quail requires careful attention and a gentle touch, as their skin is quite fragile. But the results are truly worth the effort. If Hong Kong noodles or Chinese egg noodles are not available, use capellini.

Soy-Ginger Marinade

⅓ cup soy sauce
1 (1-inch) piece of fresh ginger, sliced
1 clove garlic, smashed
⅓ cup sugar
1 cup water
Pinch of crushed red pepper flakes
1 tablespoon cornstarch mixed with
   1 tablespoon water

4 bone-in quail (about 6 ounces each)
Vegetable oil for deep-frying
10 ounces Hong Kong noodles or
   Chinese fine egg noodles
¼ cup loosely packed julienned carrot
¼ cup loosely packed julienned Japanese cucumber
   or hothouse cucumber
¼ cup loosely packed julienned red bell pepper
½ cup Ginger-Mustard Vinaigrette (page 2)

Garnish

1 tablespoon chopped fresh chives
1 tablespoon sesame seeds, toasted (page 68)
12 garlic chive flowers (optional)
8 fresh cilantro sprigs

THE DAY BEFORE SERVING, make the marinade and marinate the quail: In a small saucepan, combine the soy sauce, ginger, garlic, sugar, water, and pepper flakes. Bring to a boil and gradually whisk in the cornstarch mixture. Bring back to a boil. Remove from the heat and let cool. Pour the marinade into a medium bowl, add the quail, and turn well to coat. Cover and marinate in the refrigerator overnight.

Preheat the oven to 250°.

TO DEEP-FRY THE QUAIL, heat 3 inches of oil to 360°. Drain the quail and pat dry with paper towels. Add 2 quail and deep-fry for 3 to 4 minutes, or until dark brown, turning with tongs to get an even color (be careful not to break the skin of the quail while turning). Transfer the quail to paper towels to drain, then place them on a baking sheet pan and keep warm in the oven. Repeat with the remaining quail.

WHILE THE QUAIL ARE COOKING, prepare the noodles: Bring a large pot of salted water to boil. Add the noodles and cook for about 2 minutes, or until tender. Drain in a colander, then rinse with cold water until the noodles are completely cool. Drain well. In a medium bowl, combine the noodles, carrot, cucumber, bell pepper, and all but ¼ cup of the vinaigrette, and toss well.

TO SERVE, divide the noodles among 4 plates, creating a nest in the center of each plate. Cut each quail in half and put 2 halves on each plate, on either side of the noodles. Drizzle the remaining vinaigrette around the noodles. Sprinkle with chives and sesame seeds. Arrange 3 flowers and 2 cilantro sprigs on each plate. ♪♪♪

House-Cured Sardines
with White Bean–Tomato Salad and Pesto

Serves 4

If you've never experienced fresh sardines, you're in for a tasty surprise. The difference between fresh sardines and the canned ones we're all familiar with is as pronounced as the difference between fresh and canned tuna. Fresh sardines are usually relatively inexpensive, and curing them in salt, olive oil, and basil is quite easy to do, especially if you ask the fishmonger to clean and bone them for you. Cure them as soon as you get them home; once they're in the olive oil, they will keep for up to two days. We think their mild, earthy flavor goes perfectly with a light salad of white beans. They also make a fine addition to an antipasto platter.

Cured Sardines

1 teaspoon salt

4 (5- to 6-ounce) fresh sardines, filleted,
   boned, and skinned

2 tablespoons extra virgin olive oil

1 teaspoon fresh basil chiffonade

White Bean Salad

⅔ cup cooked white beans

12 oven-dried tomatoes (page 199)

2 tablespoons lemon-mustard vinaigrette (page 201)

2 teaspoons fresh basil chiffonade

Salt and freshly ground black pepper to taste

½ cup thinly sliced onion, soaked in ice water
   for 1 hour (to make onion crispy and remove
   bitterness), then drained

4 teaspoons lemon-mustard vinaigrette (page 201)

4 teaspoons pesto (page 203)

12 dry-cured olives

1 tablespoon chopped fresh chives

To cure the sardines, sprinkle ½ teaspoon of the salt evenly over the surface of a baking sheet pan. Lay the sardine fillets in a single layer on the salt, then sprinkle the remaining ½ teaspoon salt over the top. Cover with plastic wrap and refrigerate for 1 hour. Pat the fillets dry with paper towels. Gently toss with the olive oil and basil. Cover and refrigerate again.

To make the salad, combine all the ingredients in a medium bowl.

To serve, lay 2 sardine fillets on the center of each of 4 chilled plates, former skin side up, then spoon the white bean salad in a line across the sardines. Put a tomato in the center and on either side of the fillets. Mound the onion slices on top of the salad, then drizzle the vinaigrette over the onions. Drizzle the pesto around the sardines. Arrange the olives on the pesto. Sprinkle with chives.

Tataki of Tuna
with Whole-Grain Mustard and Soy Vinaigrette

These days, the term "tataki" has come to mean fish or meat that is seared on the outside and raw on the inside. In classical Japanese cuisine the technique is more complicated, but modern chefs have adapted it to highlight the excellent quality of local fresh ingredients. Use only impeccably fresh sashimi grade tuna and plan to eat it the day you buy it. If you don't like raw tuna, this is probably not the dish for you, since the tuna is seared for only a few seconds. Cooking it through would result in dry fish that won't work with the other ingredients and flavors.

Tataki

½ teaspoon coarsely ground black pepper

1 pound sashimi grade tuna loin, cut into
   triangle strips 2 inches on all sides

1 tablespoon olive oil

Whole-Grain Mustard and Soy Vinaigrette

3 tablespoons whole-grain mustard

1 tablespoon soy sauce

1 tablespoon rice vinegar

2 tablespoons tomato concassée (page 199)

1 tablespoon minced fresh chives

2 tablespoons extra virgin olive oil

4 cups mesclun or your favorite small-leaf
   lettuce mix

1 tablespoon minced fresh chives

TO MAKE THE TATAKI, sprinkle pepper over all sides of the tuna strips. Heat the olive oil in a large non-stick sauté pan or skillet over high heat until it starts to smoke. Carefully place the tuna in the pan and sear for 5 seconds per side. Transfer the tuna to a baking sheet pan and refrigerate.

TO MAKE THE VINAIGRETTE, whisk together all the ingredients in a small bowl.

TO SERVE, using a very sharp knife, cut the tuna into ¼-inch-thick triangles. Arrange the tuna on 4 chilled plates like flower petals, leaving the center open. Divide the mesclun into 4 mounds and place in the center of each plate. Drizzle the vinaigrette over the tataki and a little on the mesclun. Sprinkle with chives. 🌿🌿🌿

Fricassee of Miyagi Oysters
in Chardonnay Cream Sauce

Serves 4

Not far from us, in West Marin County, is Tomales Bay, famous for its beautiful oysters. The first time Hiro called one of the local oystermen to ask what was fresh, he got a huge surprise. They told him they had Miyagi oysters. Hiro is from Miyagi, Japan, and he couldn't believe he had found oysters from his hometown halfway across the world. In fact, what we buy here are actually oysters grown from oyster seeds from Miyagi, but the connection is still a very special one for us. If you buy already shucked oysters, make sure you ask for the oyster liquor, too. You'll need a bit of it to enrich the sauce.

20 small Miyagi oysters or other small fresh
   Pacific oysters, scrubbed and rinsed

Chardonnay Cream Sauce
2 teaspoons unsalted butter
2 teaspoons minced shallot
1/4 teaspoon minced garlic
1 cup Chardonnay
1/4 teaspoon Champagne vinegar
1 1/2 cups heavy cream
2 pinches of saffron threads
Salt and freshly ground white pepper to taste

2 tablespoons unsalted butter
2 tablespoons julienned carrot
2 tablespoons julienned leek
Salt and freshly ground pepper to taste
1 1/2 ounces small chanterelles or any other
   wild mushroom, cleaned
1/4 teaspoon minced garlic
Freshly squeezed lemon juice (optional)

Garnish
2 teaspoons chopped fresh chives
1 tablespoon salmon caviar
20 fresh chervil sprigs

Preheat the oven to 350°.

CAREFULLY SHUCK THE OYSTERS, reserving the oyster liquor. Strain the liquor through a fine-mesh sieve and reserve 2 tablespoons. Scrub and reserve 8 of the nicest rounded (bottom) oyster shells.

TO MAKE THE CREAM SAUCE, melt the butter in a medium saucepan over medium heat. Add the shallot and garlic and sweat over low heat until soft, about 2 minutes. Add the wine and vinegar and reduce over high heat until 1 tablespoon remains. Add the cream, saffron, and reserved oyster liquor, and bring to a boil. Lightly season with salt and pepper (be careful not to oversalt, as the oysters are already salty). Set aside and keep warm.

In a small sauté pan or skillet, melt 1 tablespoon of the butter over medium heat and sweat the carrot and leek over low heat for about 2 minutes, or until crisp-tender. Season with salt and pepper and transfer to the sauce.

In the same pan, sauté the chanterelles and garlic in the remaining butter over high heat for 2 to 3 minutes; season with salt and pepper Add to the sauce and bring to a boil. Add the oysters, decrease the heat, and simmer for 2 to 3 minutes, just until the edges curl and the oysters are firm,

but not cooked through. Taste and adjust the seasoning, adding lemon juice if the sauce is not acidic enough. Set aside and keep warm.

TO SERVE, put the oyster shells on a baking sheet pan and heat them in the oven for 3 minutes, or until warm. Place 2 oyster shells in the center of each of 4 warmed plates. Evenly and quickly divide the fricassee among and around the oyster shells and sprinkle with chives. Scatter the salmon caviar and chervil over the fricassee.

Dungeness Crab Wontons
with Spicy Sweet and Sour Sauce

Makes 36 wontons; serves 6 as a first course

In the classic tradition of Chinese dumpling-making, the filling for these wontons is made by first puréeing uncooked scallops and shrimp, which become a binder for the whole crabmeat. If you can't find rock shrimp, uncooked medium-size shrimp will work. Once you get the hang of it, wontons are quite easy to make, and you can stuff and fold them up to 3 hours ahead of time. One important cautionary note: Avoid overfilling. The extra moisture from too much filling can cause the wontons to explode or develop large bubbles on their surfaces.

Filling

8 ounces shelled rock shrimp,
  deveined (page 69)

4 ounces scallops

½ beaten egg (about 1 tablespoon)

½ teaspoon grated peeled fresh ginger

¼ teaspoon grated garlic

1 tablespoon soy sauce

1½ teaspoons mirin

1 tablespoon sugar

Pinch of freshly ground white pepper

1 tablespoon Asian (toasted) sesame oil

7½ ounces fresh lump Dungeness, blue,
  or king crabmeat, picked over for shell

1 egg yolk

½ teaspoon water

36 wonton wrappers

Spicy Sweet and Sour Sauce

¼ cup sugar

⅓ cup plus 1 tablespoon rice vinegar

⅔ cup water

1½ teaspoons soy sauce

¼ cup hoisin sauce

½ teaspoon paprika

½ teaspoon crushed red pepper flakes

Pinch of salt

1½ teaspoons cornstarch mixed with
  1½ teaspoons water

Vegetable oil for deep-frying

Garnish

1 tablespoon chopped fresh chives

1 teaspoon sesame seeds, toasted (page 68)

12 fresh cilantro sprigs

To MAKE THE FILLING, combine the shrimp, scallops, egg, ginger, garlic, soy sauce, mirin, sugar, and white pepper in a food processor and process until smooth. With the machine running, gradually add the sesame oil through the feed tube and process to mix. Transfer the mixture to a medium bowl and fold in the crabmeat.

In a small bowl, combine the egg yolk and water to make an egg wash for the wonton wrappers. To assemble the wontons, follow the directions on page 212. Use about 1 tablespoon of the filling for each wonton.

TO MAKE THE SAUCE, combine all the ingredients except the cornstarch in a small saucepan. Bring to a boil, then lower the heat to a simmer. Stir the cornstarch mixture and gradually whisk it into the sauce. Bring the sauce back to a boil, whisking constantly, then remove it from heat. Set aside and keep warm.

Preheat the oven to 250°.

TO DEEP-FRY THE WONTONS, heat 2 inches of oil in a deep, heavy pot to 360°. Add as many wontons

Dungeness Crab Wontons with
Spicy Sweet and Sour Sauce

Lobster Salad in Rice Paper (p. 36)

as will fit without overcrowding and cook until crisp and golden brown, 2 to 3 minutes. Using a wire-mesh skimmer or slotted metal spoon, transfer the wontons to paper towels to drain, then place them on a baking sheet pan and keep warm in the oven. Repeat with the remaining wontons.

TO SERVE AS A PASSED APPETIZER, fill a bowl with the warm sauce and put it in the center of a large serving platter. Arrange the wontons around the bowl, then sprinkle with the chives and toasted sesame seeds and garnish with the cilantro sprigs.

TO SERVE AS A FIRST COURSE, spoon the sauce onto the center of 6 dinner plates, then stack 6 wontons on each plate. Sprinkle with the chives and toasted sesame seeds and garnish each plate with 2 cilantro sprigs.

Gravlax on Potato Latkes
with Dill Sour Cream (p. 38)

Sacramento Delta Crayfish
with Thai Chili Mayonnaise (p. 39)

Having a Party?

WE'VE DESIGNED THE APPETIZERS IN THIS SECTION TO BE SERVED AS PASSED APPETIZERS RATHER THAN INDIVIDUAL SERVINGS. EACH RECIPE YIELD IS FOR 12 PEOPLE, 2 TO 4 PIECES PER PERSON. MAKE A VARIETY OF APPETIZERS IN A QUANTITY SUITABLE TO YOUR OCCASION. FOR EXAMPLE, TO PRECEDE A SIT-DOWN DINNER, HAVE ENOUGH APPETIZERS FOR 3 OR 4 PIECES PER PERSON. FOR A COCKTAIL PARTY, FIGURE 8 TO 9 PIECES PER PERSON, OR 6 TO 7 IF YOU'RE SUPPLEMENTING THE PASSED APPETIZERS WITH DISPLAYS OF CRUDITÉS AND DIP, CHEESE TRAYS, ETC. ALWAYS MAKE A LITTLE EXTRA. YOU'LL BE AMAZED AT HOW MANY BITES YOUR FRIENDS CAN EAT.

Foie Gras Terrine
with Pear Chutney on Toast (p. 40)

Lobster Salad in Rice Paper

Makes 12 rolls; serves 4 as a first course

We love to serve these delicate rolls as passed appetizers or as a plated first course (figure three per person). Rice paper wrappers are sold in many markets that carry Asian products. They're thin and brittle and can be a little tricky to work with until you get a feel for the process of softening them in water and handling them with a light touch. You can replace the lobster in this recipe with crabmeat, shredded chicken, thin slices of Chinese-style barbecued pork, grilled beef (the steak strips from the Grilled Miso-Marinated Beef Salad, page 2, work well) or just use the vegetables without meat or seafood.

Dipping Sauce

1 teaspoon Thai fish sauce

2 tablespoons soy sauce

1 cup rice vinegar

⅓ cup freshly squeezed lime juice

¼ cup sugar

Lobster Salad

2 Maine lobsters (1¼ pounds each),
   cooked and shelled (page 211)

⅓ cup julienned peeled carrot

⅓ cup julienned Japanese or hothouse cucumber

1 cup loosely packed chiffonade of butter lettuce

⅓ cup tomato concassée (page 199)

⅓ cup finely diced fresh papaya

⅛ teaspoon minced peeled fresh ginger

3 tablespoons coarsely chopped toasted peanuts

1 tablespoon fresh cilantro leaves

1 teaspoon chiffonade of fresh mint leaves

12 round rice paper wrappers (8 inches in diameter)

Garnish

3 tablespoons chopped toasted peanuts

8 fresh cilantro sprigs

To MAKE THE DIPPING SAUCE, whisk together all the ingredients in a small bowl. Cover and refrigerate.

TO MAKE THE LOBSTER SALAD, coarsely dice the lobster meat. In a medium bowl, combine the lobster with all the remaining salad ingredients.

TO ASSEMBLE, fill a large bowl with room-temperature water and put the rice paper wrappers in one at a time to soften for about 20 seconds. Carefully remove the wrappers from the water and store between damp kitchen towels in a single layer; don't let them touch, or they will glue together.

Lay 1 wrapper on a work surface. Spoon about ¼ cup of the lobster salad in a line across the lower third of the rice paper. Fold the smaller end up over the lobster salad and lightly pull it tight. Fold the sides in about ½ inch, then continue rolling the rice paper up to the top. Place the rolls seam side down between layers of damp towels (don't let them touch). Repeat with the remaining wrappers and lobster salad.

TO SERVE, pour the dipping sauce in a ramekin and place it in the middle of a large chilled platter. Cut the rolls in half and arrange them cut side up around the ramekin. Sprinkle with the toasted peanuts and place the cilantro sprigs over the top.

An additional decorative touch is to tie each roll with 2 pieces of chive. To do this, blanch 24 long pieces of chive for 2 seconds then shock in ice water. The chive should be pliable but not so soft that it doesn't stay in one piece. Take 2 chives for each roll and tie them around the roll, each one about ¼ inch from the ends. Do this gently so the chive doesn't break. Trim the ends from each chive and cut the rolls in half. ♪♪

Gravlax on Potato Latkes
with Dill Sour Cream

Makes about 20 latkes

Home-cured salmon, or gravlax, is actually very easy to prepare. Serve it on miniature potato pancakes, and your friends will suddenly appreciate you for the amazing cook you are. This recipe can be scaled up to cure a whole side of salmon. Gravlax is great to have around for snacking or tossing into scrambled eggs or omelets. To serve this dish as a first course, make larger pancakes and serve one per person with the gravlax draped over part of the latke and the dill sour cream drizzled in a zigzag over the plate.

Gravlax

¼ cup salt

1 tablespoon sugar

1½ teaspoons freshly ground black pepper

½ cup chopped fresh dill

1 (2-pound) salmon fillet with skin,
   at least 1 inch thick

Dill Sour Cream

1 cup sour cream

2 teaspoons minced shallot

1 teaspoon chopped fresh dill

1 teaspoon freshly squeezed lemon juice

Salt and freshly ground white pepper to taste

Potato Latkes

2 tablespoons minced onion

3 cups peeled and shredded potato (do these
   at the last minute, so they don't brown)

½ cup pastry flour

1 egg

1 teaspoon baking powder

⅛ teaspoon salt

Pinch of freshly ground pepper

4 tablespoons clarified butter (page 200)

Dill sprigs, for garnish

TO MAKE THE GRAVLAX, in a medium bowl combine the salt, sugar, pepper, and dill. On a non-reactive baking sheet pan long enough to hold the salmon, spread half of the salt mixture and lay the salmon skin side down. Cover the salmon with the rest of the salt mixture, then place another baking sheet pan of the same size on top of the salmon. Place 4 pounds of weight on the top pan (large cans or bricks work well). Refrigerate overnight.

The next day, wash the salmon in cold running water and pat dry with a kitchen towel. Remove the pin bones (page 105) and cut thinly on the diagonal. Place the slices in a single layer on a plate covered with plastic wrap. Refrigerate until ready to use.

TO MAKE THE DILL SOUR CREAM, whisk together the sour cream, shallot, dill, and lemon juice in a small bowl. Season with salt and pepper, cover, and refrigerate.

Preheat the oven to 250°.

TO MAKE THE LATKES, combine the onion, potato, pastry flour, egg, baking powder, salt, and pepper in a medium bowl. In a large sauté pan or skillet, heat 2 tablespoons of the clarified butter over medium heat until hot. Spoon 1 tablespoon of the potato mixture for each latke into the pan and cook until golden brown, about 1 minute per side. Using a slotted metal spatula, transfer the latkes to paper towels to drain, then place them on a baking sheet pan and keep warm in the oven. Repeat with the remaining potato mixture, adding more clarified butter as needed.

TO SERVE, spoon a scant teaspoon of the dill sour cream onto each latke and cover with a piece of gravlax. Garnish with a very small dill sprig.

Sacramento Delta Crayfish
with Thai Chili Mayonnaise

Makes about 60 crayfish; serves 4 as a first course

One Christmas, we threw an "all the heads you can suck" party. Don't be shocked—we are talking about crayfish. True crayfish lovers know that sucking on the heads to get all the juices and the tomalley is every bit as important a part of the experience as eating the meat. Many areas have local crayfish, and we love to use our own variety, but Louisiana crayfish are another excellent option. Make sure they're all alive when you buy them.

These make a really unusual passed appetizer, but they're also great at an outdoor party, heaped in a huge pile with corn on the cob and small red potatoes on the side.

Court Bouillon

1½ gallons water

1 onion, sliced

1 carrot, peeled and sliced

1 stalk celery, sliced

1 stalk lemongrass, sliced (optional)

1 tablespoon coriander seeds

1 lemon, halved

1 head garlic, halved crosswise

¼ cup salt

Thai Chili Mayonnaise

½ to 1 teaspoon Thai red curry paste
   (depending on how hot you like it)

1 teaspoon sugar

1 teaspoon soy sauce

1 cup mayonnaise (page 201)

4 pounds live crayfish

Garnish

1 tablespoon sesame seeds, toasted (page 68)

1 tablespoon chopped fresh chives

4 fresh cilantro sprigs

To MAKE THE COURT BOUILLON, combine all the ingredients in a large stockpot. Bring to a boil, lower the heat to a simmer, and cook for 45 minutes. Strain and return to the pot. Bring to a simmer.

MEANWHILE, TO MAKE THE MAYONNAISE, whisk together the curry paste, sugar, and soy sauce in a small bowl until smooth. Whisk in the mayonnaise. Refrigerate until ready to serve.

TO CLEAN THE CRAYFISH, carefully pick each one up by grabbing it between the tail and body. If it's alive, it will raise its claws. Discard any that don't move. Scrub each with a kitchen brush under running water, especially the legs and under the tail. Grab the middle tail fin, twist it 180 degrees, and gently pull. This will remove the sandy intestinal tract. Throw that part away and place the cleaned crayfish in another bowl. Repeat to clean the remaining crayfish.

TO COOK THE CRAYFISH, boil them in the simmering court bouillon for 2 to 3 minutes. Drain and immerse in a bowl of ice water until cool; drain again. Split each crayfish in half lengthwise.

TO SERVE AS A PASSED APPETIZER, arrange the crayfish in a single layer, claws facing out, on a large platter. Drizzle the mayonnaise over the crayfish, sprinkle with the sesame seeds and chives, and garnish with cilantro sprigs.

TO SERVE AS A FIRST COURSE, divide among 4 plates in a single layer, claws facing out. Drizzle the mayonnaise over the crayfish, then sprinkle with the sesame seeds and chives. Garnish each plate with a cilantro sprig.

Foie Gras Terrine
with Pear Chutney on Toast

Makes 48 appetizers

This is about the most decadent dish you can make—expensive, but worth every penny. Spread it on small toast points to pass, or serve half-inch slices as a first course with a few thin baguette croutons or toast points on each plate. This recipe uses a whole foie gras, but you could halve the recipe if you don't need as many appetizers.

1 whole grade A foie gras (about 1½ pounds)
1½ teaspoons salt
½ teaspoon freshly ground white pepper
1 teaspoon sugar
Pinch of freshly ground nutmeg
1½ teaspoons Cognac
1½ teaspoons bourbon

Pear Chutney
2 Bosc pears, peeled, cored, and
   cut into ⅓-inch dice
2 tablespoons dry black currants
½ cup verjus
4 teaspoons sugar
Pinch of freshly ground black pepper

12 (¼-inch-thick) slices of brioche or egg bread,
   4 inches by 4 inches

To make the terrine, devein the foie gras (page 197). Spread the foie gras out on a nonreactive baking sheet pan. Mix together the salt, pepper, sugar, and nutmeg in a small bowl, then sprinkle evenly over the foie gras. Sprinkle with the Cognac and bourbon, then gently mix together with your hands. Cover with plastic wrap and refrigerate overnight.

The next day, let the foie gras come to room temperature for about 2 hours, or until soft.

Preheat the oven to 250°.

Tightly pack the foie gras into a 6 by 3 by 2-inch terrine mold. Cover with the mold's lid. Place the terrine in a 110° water bath, then place it in the oven for 15 to 20 minutes, or until the

How to Use a Water Bath

Using a water bath, or bain-marie, means to place a sauce or ingredient in a container (pan, bowl, baking dish, etc.) in water. It is a way to cook or keep food hot without exposing it to direct heat, which might cause it to burn or separate. To make a water bath, fill a pan with a few inches of hot water and place the container inside the pan. Depending on the use, place it in the oven to cook or on the stove with a very low heat to keep warm.

terrine has released about 2 tablespoons of fat. Remove it from the oven and the water bath. Using a large spoon, transfer the melted fat from the top of the terrine to a bowl. Refrigerate the fat. Let the terrine cool to room temperature.

Cover the terrine loosely with plastic wrap. Cut a doubled cardboard piece to fit inside the terrine mold and place 2 pounds of weight evenly on top of the cardboard. Refrigerate the terrine overnight.

The next day, remove the weights, cardboard, and plastic wrap. Transfer any fat that is still on the top of the terrine to the bowl with the other fat. Smooth the top of the terrine and refrigerate for 15 minutes. Meanwhile, melt the foie gras fat in a small sauté pan over very low heat. Strain through a fine-mesh sieve. Let cool to 100° to 95°. Pour over the top of the foie gras terrine, making sure the whole surface is covered evenly with the fat to keep the terrine from oxidizing. Refrigerate until the fat is set, then cover with plastic wrap. The terrine can be kept refrigerated for up to 1 week; keep any cut edges covered with plastic wrap.

TO MAKE THE CHUTNEY, combine all the ingredients in a small sauté pan over medium heat and cook, stirring gently, until almost all the liquid has evaporated and the pear is cooked through, 3 to 4 minutes. Remove from the heat and let cool.

TO SERVE, preheat the oven to 350°. Cut the crusts off the bread and then cut each slice into 4 triangles. Place the triangles on a rimmed baking sheet pan and toast until golden brown, about 5 minutes. Let cool to room temperature.

Cut the terrine into 12 slices and cut each slice into 4 triangles (dip the knife in hot water before each slice so that it will cut easily and leave a clean edge). Place the foie gras triangles on each of the toast triangles and top with a ¼-teaspoon mound of pear chutney. ♪♪♪

Salmon and Tuna Tartare on Cucumber Discs with Wasabi Tobiko

Makes 24 appetizers

1 recipe of Salmon and Tuna Tartare with Spicy Lemon-Ginger Vinaigrette (page 20), without the garnish
24 (¼-inch-thick) slices hothouse cucumber
3 teaspoons wasabi tobiko

Make the tartare with the vinaigrette as instructed in the recipe. Mound bite-size portions (about 1½ tablespoons) of the tartare on top of the cucumber slices. Top with ⅛ teaspoon wasabi tobiko. Place the disks on a platter. 🍃🍃🍃

Miyagi Oysters in Ponzu

Makes 24 appetizers

Follow the recipe on page 202. To serve, place the oysters on one large platter rather than 4 individual plates. 🍃🍃🍃

Wild Mushroom and Smoked Bacon Vol-au-Vent

Makes 24 appetizers

1 recipe of Wild Mushroom and Smoked Bacon
    Vol-au-Vent (page 11)
2 teaspoons finely chopped chives

When cutting out the puff pastry for the vol-au-vents, roll out the pastry as directed on page 11, and instead use a 2-inch pastry cutter to make 24 discs. Next, use a ¼-inch cutter and lightly press into the center of each disc. Do not press through, just halfway. Brush the egg wash on the discs and bake as instructed. Remove from the oven and let cool. Using a sharp paring knife, carefully cut out the middle circle and set aside. Push down slightly on the inside of each pastry to make a little pocket. When making the sauce as directed on page 11, slice the mushrooms a little smaller so they will fit inside the pastry. Spoon the sauce into each vol-au-vent, sprinkle with chives, and top each with the pastry circle, like a hat.

Goat Cheese and Artichoke Spring Rolls

Makes 24 appetizers

1½ recipes Goat Cheese and Artichoke
    Spring Rolls (page 22)
24 pieces tomato concassée (page 199)
24 (1-inch-long) pieces chive (about 3 to 4 chives)

Make the spring rolls as instructed in the recipe. Cut each spring roll in half and stand on a platter with the cut sides facing up (you may need to trim a small amount off the bottom to get them to stand). Top each spring roll with a piece of the tomato concassée and garnish with a chive piece so it is sticking out from the top of each spring roll.

SOUPS

Tomato-Beet Gazpacho

Here's an easy chilled soup to make in the summer, when the weather is hot and tomatoes are at their best. The beets give it a shocking magenta color and a deep, sweet flavor. Make it early in the day or even a day ahead so the flavors blend and develop. Tomatoes vary widely in acidity, so adjust the vinegar according to your own taste. This soup is beautiful served in glass bowls.

½ cup torn white bread with no crust

1 cup water

3 cups coarsely chopped ripe tomatoes

½ cup coarsely chopped cooked and peeled red beets

Pinch of minced garlic

2 teaspoons extra virgin olive oil

Sherry wine vinegar to taste (adjust the amount depending on the acidity of the tomatoes)

Pinch of cayenne pepper

Salt and freshly ground black pepper to taste

1 tablespoon ¼-inch-diced cucumber

1 tablespoon ¼-inch-diced sweet onion

1 tablespoon ¼-inch-diced yellow pepper

4 fresh cilantro sprigs

½ teaspoon extra virgin olive oil

TO MAKE THE GAZPACHO, soak the bread in the water to soften. In a blender, puree the tomato, beets, garlic, and the bread and water until smooth. Strain through a medium-mesh sieve to remove the seeds and skins from the tomatoes. Transfer to a medium bowl and whisk in the olive oil and vinegar. Season with the cayenne, salt, and pepper. Refrigerate until well chilled.

TO SERVE, combine the cucumber, onion, and bell pepper in a small bowl. Divide the soup among 4 chilled shallow bowls and top each serving with a mound of the vegetable mixture. Garnish with a cilantro sprig and drizzle with the olive oil.

Chanterelle Mushroom and Lentil Soup
with Sautéed Foie Gras

The earthy fall flavors of lentils, mushrooms, and truffle oil make this soup hearty and soothing. The foie gras adds a really special touch, but if you don't want to use it, don't let that stop you from serving the soup on its own with warm crusty bread.

Soup

2 tablespoons unsalted butter
½ teaspoon minced garlic
½ cup finely chopped onion
6 ounces chanterelle mushrooms, cleaned
  and thinly sliced
½ cup green French lentils (lentilles de Puy)
4 cups chicken stock (page 208)
Salt and freshly ground black pepper to taste

Sautéed Foie Gras

8 ounces grade A foie gras, cut into
  4 (½-inch-thick) slices
Salt and freshly ground black pepper
Flour for dusting
½ teaspoon clarified butter (page 200)

Garnish

1 teaspoon chopped fresh chives
½ teaspoon white truffle oil
Pinch of sea salt

To make the soup, preheat the oven to 350°. In an ovenproof casserole over medium heat, melt the butter, add the garlic and onion, and sauté for 2 to 3 minutes, or until light brown. Add the mushrooms and sauté 2 to 3 minutes longer. Add the lentils and stock. Bring to a boil, skim off any foam that develops, and season with salt and pepper. Lower the heat to a simmer, cover, and place the casserole in the oven. Cook for about 30 minutes, or until the lentils are very soft. Puree the soup in a blender. Return the soup to the casserole. Taste and adjust the seasonings. Set aside and keep hot, or reheat before serving.

When the soup is ready to serve, sauté the foie gras: Season it with salt and pepper, then dust with flour. Heat a heavy, medium skillet over high heat until it starts to smoke, then decrease the heat to low and add the clarified butter. Swirl the butter around in the skillet to evenly distribute it, and immediately add the foie gras. Sauté for about 20 seconds per side, or until golden brown (the foie gras will smoke a lot while cooking). Using a slotted metal spatula, transfer the foie gras to paper towels to drain. Serve immediately.

TO SERVE, ladle the hot soup into 4 warmed bowls. Place a slice of foie gras in the center of each bowl of soup. Sprinkle with chives and a drizzle of white truffle oil. Sprinkle a tiny amount of sea salt directly on the foie gras.

Crème Vichyssoise
with Caviar

Vichyssoise didn't originate in Vichy, or even in France. It was actually invented in New York in 1917 by a French chef at the Ritz-Carlton hotel. We just thought you'd like to know. We garnish our version with caviar, but it's great "straight up" as well. You can make a lighter version by substituting milk or half-and-half for some or all of the heavy cream.

The consistency of this soup will vary depending on the chicken stock you use. Canned broth is less gelatinous than homemade stock when chilled and will produce a thinner soup, so if you use canned broth, increase the amount of potato. Crème Vichyssoise is always served chilled, but this soup is incredible served hot. Just adjust the thickness with chicken stock and omit the caviar.

1 tablespoon unsalted butter

⅔ cup sliced leek (white part only),
   rinsed and drained well

11 ounces peeled and thinly sliced Yukon Gold
   or russet potatoes (about 2 cups)

2 cups chicken stock (page 208)

2 cups heavy cream

Salt and freshly ground white pepper to taste

1 tablespoon chopped fresh chives

Caviar, as much as you can afford
   (hopefully 4 teaspoons or more)

TO MAKE THE SOUP, in a large saucepan over medium heat, melt the butter, add the leek, and sauté the leek for 2 to 3 minutes, or until tender but not browned. Add the potatoes and sauté 2 to 3 minutes longer, until tender but not browned. Add the stock and bring to a boil. Skim off any foam that develops, then lower the heat and simmer until the potatoes are very tender, about 20 minutes. Add the cream and return to a boil. Transfer the soup to a food processor and puree until smooth, then strain through a fine-mesh sieve. Season with salt and pepper. Let cool, then refrigerate until chilled. Adjust the consistency of the soup before serving: If it is too thick, whisk in a little milk (but not too much, as you want the caviar to sit on top of the soup).

TO SERVE, ladle the soup into 4 chilled bowls. Sprinkle with chopped chives and garnish with as large a dollop of caviar as you like placed in the center of the soup. 🌶🌶🌶

Sopa de Ajo
(Spicy Bread and Garlic Soup with Poached Eggs)

Serves 4

Late one night when we came home tired and hungry from the restaurant, Hiro disappeared into the kitchen, and ten minutes later, he emerged with this most amazing soup. It was as if he had whipped it up out of nothing. It's rich and garlicky and you probably have everything to make it in your kitchen right now. If you don't love garlic as much as we do, just use a little less. We finish the soup with the egg in small sauté pans, but you can use any ovenproof bowl, soup crock, or small soufflé dish. At the table, tell everybody to stir the egg right into the soup to enrich it.

Croutons

1 tablespoon olive oil

½ teaspoon minced garlic

½ baguette, cut into ¾-inch dice (about 2 cups)

½ teaspoon paprika

Soup

1 tablespoon olive oil

1 tablespoon minced garlic

1 teaspoon paprika

⅛ teaspoon cayenne pepper

5 cups chicken stock (page 208)

Salt and freshly ground black pepper

4 large eggs

1 teaspoon chopped fresh chives

To MAKE THE CROUTONS, preheat the oven to 350°. Combine the olive oil and garlic in a bowl, add the diced bread, and toss until well coated. Transfer to a baking sheet pan and bake until golden brown, about 5 minutes. Return the croutons to the bowl, sprinkle with the paprika, and toss well.

TO MAKE THE SOUP, heat the olive oil and garlic in a large saucepan over medium heat until the garlic is lightly browned. Remove from the heat and quickly stir in the paprika and cayenne so they do not burn and taste bitter. Immediately add the stock and bring to a boil. Season to taste with salt and pepper. Set aside and keep warm.

TO SERVE, preheat the oven to 500°. Add the croutons to the soup and bring to a boil, shaking the pan gently so that all the croutons are moistened. Carefully place 4 hot ovenproof serving bowls on a baking sheet pan. Divide the soup among the 4 bowls. Break an egg into the center of each dish. Gently spoon a tablespoon of the soup over each egg. Bake for 4 to 5 minutes, or until the white of the egg turns opaque but the yolk is still runny. Remove from the oven, place on a plate, and sprinkle with the chives. ♪♪

Soup au Pistou
with Goat Cheese Ravioli

We think this is the perfect spring soup. The pistou, France's answer to pesto (but don't substitute pesto here), is added at the last minute for intense fresh-herb flavor. Keep the pistou recipe handy. You'll find it's a great condiment in its own right, drizzled over grilled vegetables or served alongside chicken, fish, or steak. The ravioli couldn't be easier to make, thanks to a secret shortcut: They're made with wonton wrappers.

Goat Cheese Ravioli

1 cup fresh goat cheese without a rind
¼ cup freshly grated Parmesan cheese
2 egg yolks
Freshly ground white pepper to taste
½ teaspoon water
18 wonton wrappers

Pistou

1 teaspoon coarsely chopped garlic
2 tablespoons coarsely chopped fresh basil
1 tablespoon coarsely chopped fresh flat-leaf parsley
2 tablespoons extra virgin olive oil
2 teaspoons coarsely chopped tomato
Pinch each of salt and freshly ground black pepper

Soup

2 tablespoons olive oil
2 teaspoons chopped garlic
Pinch of crushed red pepper flakes
½ cup ¼-inch-diced onion
¼ cup ¼-inch-diced celery
¼ cup ¼-inch-diced carrot
¼ cup ¼-inch-diced peeled turnip
⅓ cup ¼-inch-diced zucchini

½ cup ¼-inch-diced eggplant
⅓ cup ¼-inch-diced leek (white part only)
½ teaspoon dried basil
7 cups chicken stock (page 208)
½ cup tomato concassée (page 199)
½ cup tomato puree
⅔ cup cooked white beans
Salt and freshly ground black pepper to taste
2 tablespoons freshly grated Parmesan cheese,
   for garnish

To make the filling, combine the goat cheese, Parmesan cheese, 1 of the egg yolks, and the pepper in a heavy-duty mixer with the paddle attachment. Beat until smooth, about 1 minute.

In a small bowl, combine the remaining egg yolk and water to make an egg wash for the wonton wrappers. To assemble the ravioli, follow the directions on page 212. Use a scant table-spoon of the filling for each ravioli.

To make the pistou, grind all the ingredients together in a mortar with a pestle until smooth. If you don't have a mortar and pestle, use a small food processor.

To make the soup base, heat the olive oil, garlic, and chili flakes in a large saucepan over medium heat and sauté until the garlic is lightly browned. Add the onion, celery, and carrot. Increase the heat to high and sauté, stirring often with a wooden spatula, until the vegetables are soft, about 3 minutes. Add the turnip, zucchini, eggplant, leek, and basil, and sauté 5 minutes longer. Add the stock, concassée, and tomato purée. Bring to a boil, skim off any foam that develops, and lower the heat to a very low simmer. Cook for about 10 minutes, then add the white beans and cook 10 minutes longer. Season with salt and pepper. Set aside and keep warm.

TO COOK THE RAVIOLI, bring a large pot of salted water to boil. Add the ravioli and cook until translucent, about 3 minutes. Drain the ravioli and divide them among 6 warmed serving bowls. Add the pistou to the soup and simmer for 5 seconds. Ladle the soup over the ravioli and sprinkle with the Parmesan cheese. ♪♪♪

Browning Garlic

MANY OF OUR RECIPES BEGIN WITH BROWNING GARLIC. THIS IMPARTS A NUTTY, TOASTY FLAVOR TO A DISH AND MELLOWS THE FLAVOR OF THE GARLIC. IN MOST CASES, WE START WITH EVERYTHING AT ROOM TEMPERATURE—GARLIC, FAT, AND PAN. MANY COOKBOOKS RECOMMEND ADDING THE GARLIC TO A HOT PAN, BUT WE FEEL THAT STARTING THE PROCESS AT ROOM TEMPERATURE AND STIRRING CONSTANTLY ALLOWS THE GARLIC TO COOK MORE GRADUALLY, RELEASING MORE OF ITS FLAVOR. IT ALSO HELPS YOU AVOID BURNING THE GARLIC. WHEN A RECIPE DOES CALL FOR ADDING GARLIC TO A HOT PAN, IT'S IMPORTANT TO STIR CONTINUOUSLY AND TO ADD THE LIQUID (WINE, WATER, OR STOCK) OR VEGETABLE THE MOMENT THE GARLIC TURNS LIGHT BROWN, TO STOP IT FROM CARAMELIZING TOO MUCH. IF GARLIC GETS TOO BROWN OR BURNS, THROW IT AND THE OIL OR BUTTER AWAY, AND START OVER. THERE'S NO WAY TO SAVE BURNT GARLIC AND IT WILL GIVE THE DISH A STRONG BITTER FLAVOR.

Mussel Saffron Soup
with Caramelized Onions and Garlic Croutons

When Hiro created this soup, he was melding two culinary ideas: traditional French onion soup, with its slow-cooked onions and slab of toast, and Provençal shellfish cooked with saffron and cream. The result is a very sexy soup with the soulful flavors of saffron, onions, and the sea, which brings to mind the great fish soups of France.

Garlic Croutons

12 baguette slices, about ¼ inch thick
  and 3 inches long
½ teaspoon herbes de Provence
1 clove garlic

Caramelized Onions

2 tablespoons unsalted butter
2 onions, halved and thinly sliced

Mussel Saffron Soup

40 black mussels (about 3 pounds),
  scrubbed and debearded (page 15)
½ cup dry white wine
1 tablespoon olive oil
2 teaspoons minced garlic
Pinch of crushed red pepper flakes
½ cup chopped onion
½ cup tomato puree
2½ cups heavy whipping cream
2 cups chicken stock (page 208)
1 teaspoon saffron threads
Salt and freshly ground black pepper to taste
1 tablespoon chopped fresh chives

TO MAKE THE GARLIC CROUTONS, preheat the oven to 350°. Arrange the baguette slices in a single layer on a baking sheet pan and sprinkle with the herbes de Provence. Bake until golden brown, 3 to 4 minutes. Rub each crouton with the garlic clove. Set aside.

TO CARAMELIZE THE ONIONS, melt the butter in a medium sauté pan or skillet over low heat. Add the onions and sauté until caramel brown, about 30 minutes, stirring occasionally.

TO MAKE THE SOUP, combine the mussels and wine in a large, heavy nonreactive pot over high heat. Cover and cook, shaking the pot occasionally, until the mussels open, 4 to 5 minutes. Discard any mussels that do not open. Drain, reserving the mussel liquor. Shell the mussels. Strain the reserved mussel liquor through a fine-mesh sieve.

In a large, nonreactive saucepan over medium heat, add the olive oil, garlic, and pepper flakes, and sauté until the garlic is light brown. Add the onion and sauté until tender, about 5 minutes. Add the reserved mussel liquor, the tomato puree, cream, and stock. Bring to a boil and skim off any foam that develops. Lower the heat, add the saffron, and simmer for about 5 minutes. Season with salt and pepper.

TO SERVE, add the shelled mussels and caramelized onions to the soup and bring just to a boil. Remove from heat. Place 2 garlic croutons in each of 6 warmed soup bowls. Divide the hot soup and mussels among the bowls and sprinkle with chives. ♪♪♪

Spring Garlic and Potato Soup
with Morel Mushroom Croutons

Serves 4

There are certain foods that awaken us to the arrival of a new season. Morels and spring garlic are two of them, and this spring soup brings out the best in both. If it's not spring try the version with leek and garlic, and experiment with other kinds of wild mushrooms. You'll have an entirely different soup—one that tastes more like a hot Vichyssoise—but that's the beauty of seasonal cooking.

Soup

2 tablespoons unsalted butter

1 cup coarsely sliced spring garlic,
   including the green stem,
   or 1 cup sliced leek and 1 clove garlic

1 russet potato (about 1 pound), peeled
   and sliced ¼ inch thick

Salt and freshly ground white pepper to taste

3 cups chicken stock (page 208)

1 cup heavy cream

Morel Croutons

4 baguette slices, ¼ inch thick and 3 inches long

2 tablespoons unsalted butter

1 tablespoon minced shallot

1 ounce morels, cleaned and halved
   if larger than ½ inch in diameter

2 tablespoons brown chicken stock (page 209)
   or chicken stock (page 208)

1 teaspoon chopped fresh flat-leaf parsley

Salt and freshly ground black pepper to taste

TO MAKE THE SOUP, melt the butter in a large saucepan over medium heat, add the spring garlic, and sauté until soft. Add the potato and sauté until the outside of the potato is translucent, 2 to 3 minutes. Lightly season with salt and pepper, then add the chicken stock and bring to a boil. Lower the heat to a simmer and cook until the potato is very soft, about 20 minutes. Add the cream and bring to a boil. Puree in a blender until smooth. Strain through a medium-fine-mesh sieve. Rinse the pan and return the soup to the pan. Taste and adjust the seasoning. Cover to keep warm. Set aside.

TO MAKE THE CROUTONS, preheat the oven to 350°. Spread the baguette slices on a rimmed baking sheet pan and bake until golden brown, 3 to 4 minutes. Keep warm. Heat the butter and shallot in a medium sauté pan over high heat, and sauté the shallot until it starts to caramelize. Add the morels and sauté until soft, about 2 minutes. Add the stock and bring to a boil, then add the parsley and remove from heat. Season with salt and pepper.

TO SERVE, divide the soup among 4 warmed bowls, mound the morels on the croutons, and place 1 crouton in the center of each bowl of soup. Drizzle the morel pan juices over the soup and croutons.

Potage of Sweet Corn and Masa
with Fried Soft-Shell Crab

Serves 4

This velvety soup gets its mysterious flavor from the addition of a corn tortilla. Corn, masa, and soft-shell crabs share a natural, earthy sweetness that makes them wonderfully complementary. If you can't find fresh soft-shell crabs, ask your fishmonger for frozen ones. Or, you can omit the crab entirely and simply garnish the soup with a little homemade salsa.

Potage

3 ears sweet corn
2 tablespoons unsalted butter
½ onion, sliced
2 teaspoons chopped garlic
½ carrot, peeled and sliced
1 (6-inch) corn tortilla, coarsely chopped
3 cups chicken stock (page 208)
1 cup heavy cream
Salt and freshly ground white pepper to taste

Red Bell Pepper Coulis

1 red bell pepper, seeded and coarsely chopped
½ cup chicken stock (page 208)
⅛ teaspoon chopped jalapeño
Salt and freshly ground white pepper to taste

Crab Batter

1 egg
⅓ cup milk
¼ cup all-purpose flour
2 tablespoons freshly grated Parmesan cheese
Salt and freshly ground black pepper

Vegetable oil for deep-frying
4 soft-shell crabs, cleaned (page 59)
½ cup fine cornmeal
8 fresh cilantro sprigs, for garnish

TO MAKE THE POTAGE, cut the kernels from the corn and reserve 2 tablespoons. With the back of the knife, scrape down the length of the ears, catching the milk from the corn in a bowl. Set this aside with the corn kernels.

In a large, heavy saucepan over high heat, melt the butter, add the onion, garlic, and carrot, and sauté until soft, 3 to 5 minutes. Add the corn (except for the reserved 2 tablespoons), corn milk, tortilla, stock, and cream. Bring to a boil, lower the heat to a simmer, and cook for 3 minutes. Puree in a blender until smooth. Strain the soup through a medium-fine-mesh sieve. Season with salt and pepper. Rinse the pan and return the soup to the pan. Set aside and keep warm.

TO MAKE THE COULIS, combine all the ingredients except the salt and pepper in a small saucepan. Cover, bring to boil, lower the heat to a simmer, and cook until the pepper is very soft, 5 to 7 minutes. Puree in a blender until smooth. Strain through a fine-mesh sieve. Season with salt and pepper, and set aside.

Preheat the oven to 250°.

TO MAKE THE BATTER, whisk together the egg, milk, flour, and Parmesan in a medium bowl. Lightly season with salt and pepper.

TO DEEP-FRY THE CRAB, heat 2 inches of oil to 350°. Working with 1 crab at a time, dip a crab in the batter, dredge it in the cornmeal, and drop it in the oil. Cover and deep-fry for about 3 minutes, or

until golden brown and crisp. (Be sure to cover the pot, as the crabs have a lot of liquid in them and can explode, scattering the hot oil.) Using tongs, transfer the crab to paper towels to drain, then place on a baking sheet pan and keep warm in the oven. Repeat with the remaining crabs.

To SERVE, divide the potage among 4 warmed shallow bowls and place a crab in the center of each bowl. Drizzle the red bell pepper coulis around the crab, and sprinkle the coulis with the reserved corn kernels. Top each crab with 2 cilantro sprigs. ♪♪♪

Cleaning Soft-Shell Crabs

BE SURE TO BUY CRABS THAT ARE ALIVE AND KICKING; THEY CAN'T REALLY MOVE TOO MUCH, BUT IF YOU PICK ONE UP, THE LEGS SHOULD MOVE. USE SCISSORS TO CUT OFF THE HEAD JUST BELOW THE FEELERS. LIFT THE SHELL ON THE TOP AND TO THE SIDE OF THE CRAB, AND YOU WILL SEE THE GILLS, LONG TAPERED PLASTIC-LOOKING TUBES. USING THE SCISSORS, CAREFULLY CUT THESE OUT FROM BOTH SIDES OF THE CRAB. PULL UP THE TAIL FLAPS—A LONG PIECE OF SHELL THAT FITS AGAINST THE UNDERSIDE—AND CUT IT OFF AT THE BASE.

PASTA, RISOTTO AND GNOCCHI

Bone Marrow Risotto with Braised Veal Shanks

Serves 4

With a little planning, you can make ossobuco one night and then use the leftovers to make this very special risotto the next. If you don't want to have both in such quick succession, just freeze some of the ossobuco meat and sauce. At Terra, we serve this dish with a tall roasted marrow bone in the center. It makes for quite an impressive presentation. If you'd like to try this, ask your butcher to cut 4 veal marrow bones, each 3 inches long, with large openings so you can get the marrow out. Season the bones with salt and freshly ground pepper, then roast them in a preheated 400° oven for 15 to 20 minutes. Serve them piping hot. Marrow can be quite unappealing when it's cold.

2 cups Ossobuco sauce (page 134)

2½ to 3 cups chicken stock (page 208)

2 tablespoon unsalted butter

1 teaspoon chopped garlic

¼ cup chopped onion

2 cups arborio rice

⅓ cup dry white wine

¾ cup diced meat from about
   1 piece of cooked Ossobuco (page 134)

2 tablespoons marrow from about
   1 piece of cooked Ossobuco (page 134)

½ cup freshly grated Parmesan cheese

Salt and freshly ground black pepper to taste

2 teaspoons Gremolata (page 134), for garnish

IN A SMALL SAUCEPAN, heat the ossobuco sauce to a simmer. In another small saucepan, heat the chicken stock to a simmer. In a large saucepan over medium heat, melt the butter, add the garlic and onion, and sauté until translucent, about 4 minutes. Add the rice and sauté for about 3 minutes, stirring with a wooden spoon until the outside of the rice becomes opaque. Add the wine and bring to a boil. Stir constantly, scraping the entire bottom of the pan until almost all the wine is absorbed by the rice. Add the simmering ossobuco sauce, meat, and bone marrow. Return to a boil, then lower the heat to a simmer. Stir constantly until almost all the liquid is absorbed. Add ½ cup of the simmering chicken stock. The rice should be kept at a fast simmer and not a boil as you stir and add stock. Stir the rice constantly until almost all the stock has been absorbed. Repeat the process until the rice is tender but firm. (Total cooking time for the rice is 12 to 14 minutes after the ossobuco sauce is added.) Add the Parmesan cheese and mix well. Season with salt and pepper.

TO SERVE, divide the risotto among 4 warmed shallow bowls. Sprinkle with the gremolata.

Goat Cheese Ravioli
with Fresh Tomato Sauce

It's no surprise that the secret of the barely cooked tomato sauce in this recipe is the tomatoes. If you can find them, use either heirloom or homegrown tomatoes. The combination of brilliant red and yellow tomatoes against the white ravioli looks like a Jackson Pollock painting.

Fresh Tomato Sauce

1 cup peeled, seeded, and diced red heirloom tomato (page 199); reserve juice and seeds

1 cup peeled, seeded, and diced yellow heirloom tomato (page 199); reserve juice and seeds

2 teaspoons minced red onion

2 tablespoons extra virgin olive oil

1 teaspoon rice vinegar

¼ teaspoon paprika

Pinch of cayenne pepper

Salt and freshly ground black pepper to taste

16 Goat Cheese Ravioli (page 52)

Garnish

1 tablespoon chiffonade of fresh basil, plus 4 fresh basil sprigs

1 tablespoon extra virgin olive oil

2 tablespoons freshly grated Parmesan cheese

To make the sauce, strain the reserved tomato juice and seeds and combine with the tomatoes, onion, olive oil, vinegar, paprika, and cayenne pepper in a medium bowl. Season with salt and pepper. Cover and refrigerate for at least 1 hour or up to 3 hours.

To finish the dish, bring a large pot of salted water to boil. Add the ravioli and cook until they become translucent, about 3 minutes; drain. Heat the sauce in a large saucepan over high heat just until hot, and add the ravioli. Simmer for just 10 seconds; you don't want to overcook the sauce, which should keep its fresh flavor and color.

To serve, spoon the ravioli and sauce into 4 warmed shallow bowls, sprinkle with the basil chiffonade, drizzle with the extra virgin olive oil, sprinkle with Parmesan cheese, and garnish with a sprig of fresh basil.

Kabocha Pumpkin Ravioli
with Pecorino Cheese

Serves 4

*This dish is our adaptation of Tortelli di Zucca, a specialty of northern Italy that Hiro learned to make while doing a **stage** at Dal Pescatore restaurant in Canneto sull'Oglio. The classic Italian filling is made with butternut squash. Hiro thought he'd try it with kabocha, the most popular pumpkin in Japan, where it's prized for its sweetness and density. We think it lends just the right balance to the saltiness of the pecorino. Serve these ravioli as a first course, a main dish for lunch, or as a side dish with grilled chicken or quail.*

Kabocha Pumpkin Filling

2½- to 3-pound kabocha pumpkin or butternut squash

½ cup freshly ground pecorino cheese

1 to 1½ tablespoons firmly packed brown sugar

Pinch of freshly ground nutmeg

Salt and freshly ground black pepper to taste

1 egg yolk

¼ teaspoon water

36 wonton wrappers

3 tablespoons unsalted butter

3 cups chicken stock (page 208)

Salt and freshly ground pepper to taste

2 cups spinach leaves, cleaned and stemmed

3 tablespoons freshly ground pecorino cheese,
   for garnish

To make the filling, preheat the oven to 350°. Cut the pumpkin in half and remove the seeds. Place the pumpkin, cut sides down, on a baking sheet pan lined with aluminum foil and roast in the oven for 30 to 40 minutes, or until soft. Scrape off and discard the brown part of the pumpkin that was against the baking sheet pan. Scoop out the flesh and press it through a food mill or a ricer. Let cool. Combine the pumpkin, cheese, brown sugar, and nutmeg in a medium bowl. Taste for sweetness; you may need to add a little more brown sugar. Lightly season with salt and pepper.

Combine the egg yolk with the water to make an egg wash. To assemble the ravioli, see the directions on page 212. Use 1 scant tablespoon of the filling for each ravioli.

To finish the dish, bring a large pot of salted water to a boil. In a large saucepan over high heat, brown the butter. Carefully add the chicken stock, bring to a boil, and season lightly with salt and pepper. Lower the heat to a simmer. Add the ravioli to the boiling water and cook until they become translucent, about 3 minutes; drain. While the ravioli drains, add the spinach to the chicken stock and stir to wilt, then add the ravioli and simmer for 10 seconds.

To serve, divide the ravioli, spinach, and sauce among 4 warmed shallow bowls and sprinkle with pecorino cheese.

Foie Gras Tortelloni in Game Jus
with Périgord Truffle and Fava Beans

Serves 6

This dish is absolutely simple in its presentation, but wonderfully complex in the eating. As you bite into the tortelloni, they explode with the rich flavor and silky texture of warm foie gras. And the added luxury of black truffles from Périgord puts the whole thing right over the top. If you don't have time to make your own terrine, buy a high-quality foie gras pâté made only with the livers and seasonings.

6 ounces Foie Gras Terrine (page 40)

2 egg yolks

2 ounces Périgord truffle, or ½ teaspoon
   black truffle oil

½ teaspoon water

24 wonton wrappers

3 cups game stock (page 209) or
   brown chicken stock (page 209)

6 fava bean pods, shucked, blanched
   for 1 minute, and peeled

1 tablespoon cold unsalted butter

Salt and freshly ground black pepper to taste

To make the filling, combine the foie gras terrine and 1 of the egg yolks in a small food processor and puree until smooth. Transfer to a small bowl. Chop ½ ounce of the Périgord truffle and fold it into the pureed foie gras. If using truffle oil, fold ¼ teaspoon into the pureed foie gras. Cover and refrigerate for 1 hour.

In a small bowl, combine the remaining egg yolk and water to make an egg wash for the wonton wrappers. To assemble the tortelloni, follow the directions on page 212. Use 2 teaspoons of the foie gras mixture for each tortelloni.

To finish the dish, bring a large pot of salted water to boil. Meanwhile, bring the game stock to a boil in a large saucepan. Slice the remaining truffle, $\frac{1}{16}$ inch thick. Add the tortelloni to the boiling water, and once it returns to a boil, lower the heat to a simmer. Gently cook the tortelloni for 2 to 3 minutes, then drain and transfer to the game stock. Add the fava beans, truffle slices, and butter. Gently shake the pan to incorporate the ingredients, and bring the mixture back to a boil. Season with salt and pepper.

To serve, ladle the tortelloni into warmed shallow bowls and divide the sauce, fava beans, and truffles evenly among them. If using truffle oil, drizzle a few drops over each serving.

Potato Gnocchi
in Gorgonzola Cream Sauce

Serves 4

Here's a really good basic gnocchi recipe that also works well with a tomato or mushroom sauce. For this version, look for a good-quality Italian Gorgonzola. Rice the potatoes while they're still hot; they'll be easier to handle, and their texture will be fluffier and less glutinous, resulting in lighter gnocchi. This is a great choice for a dinner party because you can make the gnocchi and the sauce earlier in the day and put them together just before serving. These gnocchi make a fine first course, and they're also a perfect side dish with grilled steak.

Gnocchi

2 pounds large russet potatoes

1 egg

1 to 1¼ cups all-purpose flour

⅔ cup freshly grated Parmesan cheese

¼ cup ricotta cheese

Pinch of ground nutmeg

Rice flour for dusting

Gorgonzola Cream Sauce

1½ cups heavy cream

¼ cup freshly grated Parmesan cheese

½ cup Italian Gorgonzola cheese

1 tablespoon unsalted butter

Salt and freshly ground white pepper to taste

1 cup 1-inch strips spinach or radicchio

1 tablespoon pine nuts, toasted

To MAKE THE GNOCCHI, preheat the oven to 400°. Place the potatoes on a baking sheet pan. Bake until soft, about 1 hour. Peel while hot, then press through a ricer or food mill into a medium bowl. Add the egg, 1 cup of the flour, Parmesan cheese, ricotta, and nutmeg, and mix well. Add more flour if the dough is still sticky. (Each potato has a different moisture content, so you have to adjust each time you make the gnocchi.) Knead in the bowl for about 1 minute, or until the dough comes together. Lightly flour a work surface with rice flour. Cut the dough into 4 pieces and roll each piece into a ¾-inch-thick rope. Cut each rope on the diagonal into 1½-inch-long pieces and transfer to a baking sheet pan lined with parchment paper and sprinkled with rice flour. Cover with a dry towel and refrigerate for up to 1 day.

TO MAKE THE SAUCE, combine the cream, cheeses, and butter in a large saucepan and bring just to a boil while whisking until smooth. Season with salt and pepper. Set aside and keep warm.

TO FINISH THE DISH, bring a large pot of salted water to boil. Add the gnocchi and cook for about 2 minutes, or until they are all floating on the surface. Meanwhile, add the spinach to the sauce and bring to a boil. Using a wire-mesh skimmer, transfer the gnocchi from the pot to the sauce. Swirl the pan to gently coat the gnocchi.

TO SERVE, divide the gnocchi and sauce among 4 warmed shallow bowls and sprinkle with pine nuts. ♩♩

How to Toast Nuts and Seeds

PREHEAT THE OVEN TO 325°. SPREAD THE NUTS OR SEEDS IN A SINGLE LAYER ON A BAKING SHEET PAN AND PUT IN THE OVEN. CHECK AFTER 2 MINUTES, AND EVERY MINUTE THEREAFTER, STIRRING OCCASIONALLY, UNTIL THE NUTS ARE A LIGHT GOLDEN BROWN.

Chinese Egg Noodles with Gulf Shrimp, Shiitake Mushrooms, and Pea Tendrils

*Pea tendrils, the shoots and leaves that appear on the top of new pea plants in the early days of spring, are tender little greens that taste like a cross between peas and spinach. They have a relatively short growing season and can be hard to find. Look for them in Asian produce markets, where they're sometimes sold under their Cantonese name, **dau miu.** If you can't find them, substitute spinach and a few sprigs of watercress. If fresh Chinese noodles are not available, use dried ones or fresh angel-hair pasta. And if you don't have time to make lobster or shrimp stock, you can use a rich chicken stock instead. Having said all that, we want to encourage you to try to round up all the ingredients we use for this recipe at least once. Once you do, the dish comes together very quickly, and it's an experience no one should miss.*

Lime-Soy Mixture

1 tablespoon freshly squeezed lime juice
1 teaspoon Thai yellow curry paste
¼ teaspoon grated peeled fresh ginger
¼ teaspoon grated garlic
1 tablespoon soy sauce
1 teaspoon Asian (toasted) sesame oil
½ teaspoon sugar

10 ounces Chinese egg noodles
3 tablespoons unsalted butter
20 medium shrimp, shelled and deveined
Salt and freshly ground white pepper
8 shiitake mushrooms, cleaned, stemmed,
  and sliced ¼ inch thick
1½ cups lobster stock (page 210)
  or shrimp stock (page 210)
3 cups pea tendrils, loosely packed

To MAKE THE LIME-SOY MIXTURE, whisk together all the ingredients in a small bowl. Set aside.

TO PREPARE THE NOODLES, bring a large pot of salted water to boil. Add the noodles and cook until al dente, about 2 minutes; drain.

TO ASSEMBLE, melt the butter in a large, preferably nonstick sauté pan or skillet over high heat until it starts to foam. Season the shrimp with salt and pepper. Add the shrimp and the shiitake mushrooms and sauté until the shrimp start to turn pink, about 2 minutes. Add the lobster stock and bring to a boil, then lower the heat to a simmer. Add 2 tablespoons of the lime-soy mixture to the shrimp and mushrooms, then add the noodles and pea tendrils and toss to combine. Simmer for 10 seconds.

TO SERVE, divide among 4 warmed shallow bowls.

 Deveining Shrimp ——————

THE INTESTINAL "VEIN" SHOULD BE REMOVED FROM A SHRIMP BEFORE COOKING, BOTH FOR COSMETIC REASONS AND BECAUSE, ESPECIALLY IN LARGER SHRIMP, IT CONTAINS GRIT, WHICH IS UNPLEASANT TO EAT. NOT EVERY SHRIMP WILL HAVE ONE, THOUGH. TO REMOVE, USING A BAMBOO SKEWER, INSERT THE POINTED END ABOUT 1/8 INCH DEEP INTO A SHRIMP ACROSS THE CENTER OF THE CURVE. GENTLY PULL UP ON THE SKEWER, AND A THIN DARK STRAND SHOULD COME OUT. KEEP PULLING UNTIL IT COMES FREE OF THE SHRIMP; DISCARD.

Spaghettini with Tripe Stew

When Hiro started cooking in Japan, one of his first jobs was cleaning tripe. And now, when he prepares it, he still thinks about those early days and the chef who inspired him to pursue a career in cooking. Tripe isn't for everyone, but we think that a lot more people would love it if they could just taste a well-prepared version. That's why we've had it on the menu at Terra since the day we opened, sometimes served as in this recipe and sometimes as an appetizer without the pasta. One of our servers had a ready answer for the often-asked question, "What kind of fish is tripe?" With a perfectly straight face, he would reply, "Oh, that would be a land fish."

Blanched Tripe

2 pounds honeycomb tripe, cleaned well
2 gallons water
¼ cup rice vinegar
½ carrot
1 stalk celery
½ onion
5 bay leaves
1 teaspoon black peppercorns
2 fresh thyme sprigs
1 tablespoon salt

Stew

2 tablespoons olive oil
1 tablespoon chopped garlic
1 cup chopped onion
½ cup chopped peeled carrot
½ cup chopped celery
¼ teaspoon crushed red pepper flakes
½ teaspoon dried basil
⅔ cup dry white wine
3 cups chicken stock (page 208)
1 cup tomato puree
1 cup tomato concassée (page 199)
Salt and freshly ground black pepper
⅔ cup cooked white beans

1 pound spaghettini
⅔ cup freshly grated Parmesan cheese
2 teaspoons chopped fresh basil
1 tablespoon chopped fresh flat-leaf parsley
2 tablespoons extra virgin olive oil
Salt and freshly ground black pepper to taste

To BLANCH THE TRIPE, put it in a large stockpot with the water and bring to a boil. Skim off any foam that develops. Add the vinegar, return to a boil, and skim again. Add the remaining ingredients, and place a lid smaller than the pot inside the pot to hold the tripe underwater. Simmer for 45 minutes, or until the tripe can be pierced with a bamboo skewer. Drain and transfer to a rimmed baking sheet pan to cool. Remove any fat from the tripe and cut the tripe into 2½ by ½-inch strips. Set aside.

TO MAKE THE STEW, preheat the oven to 350°. In a large ovenproof saucepan over high heat, heat the olive oil and garlic and sauté until the garlic is lightly browned. Add the onion, carrot, celery, pepper flakes, and dried basil. Sauté for 3 to 4 minutes, until the onion is translucent. Add the blanched tripe and wine. Bring to a boil, then add the chicken stock, tomato puree, and tomato concassée, and return to a boil. Skim and season with salt and pepper. Cut a circle of parchment paper that just fits inside the pan. Place the paper on the stew to cover. Cook in the oven for 1 to 1½

hours, or until the tripe is tender. Remove the paper and place the pan over medium heat on top of the stove. Add the white beans and simmer for 5 minutes.

TO FINISH THE DISH, bring a large pot of salted water to boil. Add the spaghettini and cook until al dente; drain. Stir ⅓ cup of the Parmesan cheese, the fresh basil, parsley, and 1 tablespoon of the extra virgin olive oil into the stew. Season with salt and pepper. Add the cooked spaghettini and mix well; return to a boil.

TO SERVE, divide the pasta and stew among 4 warmed shallow bowls. Sprinkle with the remaining extra virgin olive oil and the remaining ⅓ cup Parmesan cheese. 🍃🍃🍃

Capellini with Smoked Salmon, Sevruga Caviar, and Lemon-Caper Vinaigrette

Serves 4

We think this is the ultimate cold pasta dish. The richness of the smoked salmon, the saltiness of the caviar, and the tangy acidity of the vinaigrette create a different flavor balance with every bite. We like to use sevruga caviar, but if that's not in your budget, buy the best you can. Don't make this dish ahead of time. The pasta needs to be cooked and cooled just before tossing with the other ingredients. If it sits, the flavors will become muddy as the acid in the vinaigrette breaks down the caviar and the pasta. Tobiko, or flying fish roe, has a mild flavor and a delicately crunchy texture.

Lemon-Caper Vinaigrette

1 teaspoon minced capers
Pinch of grated garlic
2 tablespoons plus 2 teaspoons
  extra virgin olive oil
2 teaspoons rice vinegar
2 teaspoons freshly squeezed lemon juice
¼ teaspoon soy sauce
Pinch of freshly ground white pepper

4 ounces dried capellini pasta
4 ounces thinly sliced smoked salmon,
  cut into 3 by ½-inch strips
¼ cup tomato concassée (page 199)
1 teaspoon chopped shallot
1 tablespoon chopped fresh chives
1 tablespoon tobiko caviar

2 Japanese cucumbers, or 1 hothouse cucumber,
  cut into very thin circles on a mandoline or
  with a very sharp knife
4 teaspoons sevruga caviar
12 fresh chervil sprigs

To make the vinaigrette, whisk together all the ingredients in a small bowl. Set aside.

TO COOK THE CAPELLINI, bring a large pot of salted water to boil. Add the capellini and cook for about 3 minutes, or until the pasta is cooked a little more than al dente. Drain the pasta and immerse it in ice water to chill. Drain again and gently press to squeeze out any excess water. In a medium bowl, combine the capellini, smoked salmon, tomato concassée, shallot, chives, tobiko caviar, and vinaigrette. Mix well with your fingers to keep from breaking the pasta.

TO SERVE, place a 3-inch metal ring or a 3-inch-diameter glass or bowl as a guide in the center of a chilled large plate. Overlap the cucumber slices in a circular pattern around the ring; remove the ring or bowl and repeat with the remaining plates. Place an equal amount of the capellini mixture in the center of each plate. Spoon 1 teaspoon of the sevruga caviar on top of each mound, then top with 3 chervil sprigs. ♪♪♪

FISH AND SHELLFISH

Sautéed Maine Scallops on Garlic Mashed Potatoes with Chanterelle Mushrooms and Parsley Nage

Serves 4

The combination of scallops, chanterelles, and vibrant green parsley sauce is strikingly beautiful on the plate, and just as pleasing on the palate. Nage, by the way, is a French word that literally means "swimming" and refers to a dish served with a brothy sauce.

Parsley Nage

2 teaspoons minced shallots
⅓ cup dry white wine
½ cup heavy cream
Salt and freshly ground white pepper to taste
1 bunch flat-leaf parsley, stemmed
½ cup packed spinach leaves
⅔ cup chicken stock (page 208)
Pinch of minced garlic
1 tablespoon unsalted butter
4½ ounces chanterelle mushrooms,
 cleaned and cut or torn into bite-size pieces

3 tablespoons clarified butter (page 200)
20 ounces large scallops, cleaned (hinge removed)
Salt and freshly ground white pepper
2 tablespoons all-purpose flour
2 tablespoons unsalted butter
8 peeled baby carrots, blanched (page 198)
4 baby yellow squash, blanched (page 198)
12 sugar snap peas, blanched (page 198)
2 cups hot garlic mashed potatoes (page 206)
4 fresh flat-leaf parsley sprigs, for garnish

To START THE NAGE, combine the shallots and wine in a small, heavy nonreactive saucepan. Bring to a boil and cook until reduced to 2 tablespoons. Add the cream and return just to a boil. Season lightly with salt and pepper. Set aside and keep warm.

Bring a pot of salted water to boil. Add the parsley and spinach and blanch for 10 seconds (page 198). Drain and immerse in ice water until cold. Drain, squeeze out all the excess water, and coarsely chop. Combine in a blender with the cold stock and garlic and process until smooth. Season lightly with salt and pepper. Strain through a fine-mesh sieve, pressing the solids with the back of a large spoon to extract all the liquid. Reserve the liquid and discard the solids. Melt the butter in a medium sauté pan or skillet over high heat, add the chanterelle mushrooms, and sauté for 2 minutes. Set aside.

TO SAUTÉ THE SCALLOPS, heat the clarified butter in a large sauté pan or skillet over high heat until hot. Season the scallops with salt and pepper, dust with flour on both sides, and sauté until golden brown, about 1 minute per side. Remove the pan from the heat and let the scallops rest in the pan for 1 minute.

Meanwhile, finish preparing the nage: Reheat the cream mixture and add the parsley-spinach puree and the chanterelle mushrooms. Bring just to a boil, then remove from the heat. Taste and adjust the seasoning. Set aside and keep warm.

At the same time, melt the butter in a medium sauté pan or skillet over medium heat, add the carrots, squash, and sugar snap peas, and sauté until heated through, about 2 minutes. Season with salt and pepper.

TO SERVE, put ½ cup garlic mashed potatoes in the center of each of 4 warmed shallow bowls. Spoon the mushroom and parsley nage evenly around the potatoes, then place one fourth of the scallops on top of each serving of mashed potatoes. Arrange the carrots, squash, and sugar snap peas on and around the scallops. Garnish with the parsley sprigs.

Grilled Fillet of Pacific Salmon
with Thai Red Curry Sauce and Basmati Rice

Serves 4

This is another customer favorite we can never take off our menu. It has something for everyone: a spicy red curry sauce that cuts through the richness of the salmon, a cool crisp cabbage salad for contrast, and nutty basmati rice to sop it all up. We've taught this dish in many cooking classes, and at first we wondered if it might be a little too complicated for the home cook. But we have been pleasantly surprised time and again when people come into the restaurant and tell us they make it at home. Funny thing though: They still order it when they come to Terra.

Basmati Rice

1 cup basmati rice

½ teaspoon unsalted butter

1½ cups water

2 cups loosely packed thinly sliced cabbage

⅓ cup loosely packed julienned cucumber

2 tablespoons cilantro leaves

2 tablespoons mint leaves

Thai Red Curry Sauce

2 teaspoons peanut oil

1 teaspoon minced garlic

1 teaspoon minced peeled fresh ginger

1 teaspoon coriander seeds, cracked

1½ teaspoons curry powder

1½ teaspoons Thai red curry paste

1½ teaspoons paprika

½ teaspoon ground cumin

1¼ cups unsweetened coconut milk

2 tablespoons plus 2 teaspoons tomato puree

2 teaspoons soy sauce

1 tablespoon plus 1½ teaspoons firmly packed
  brown sugar

4 (6-ounce) king or Atlantic salmon fillets,
  each ¾ inch thick

1 tablespoon olive oil

Salt and freshly ground black pepper

½ teaspoon soy sauce

2 teaspoons rice vinegar

1 tablespoon coarsely chopped roasted peanuts

P REPARE A FIRE in a charcoal grill or preheat a gas grill.

T O MAKE THE RICE, preheat the oven to 350°. Wash the rice in a colander under cold running water for 1 minute, then drain well and set aside for 10 minutes. In a small ovenproof saucepan, combine the rice, butter, and water. Cover with a tight-fitting lid and cook over high heat until strong steam comes out from under the lid. Remove from the heat, put the pan in the oven, and bake for 12 to 14 minutes, or until the rice is tender and all the water is absorbed. Set aside and keep warm.

T O START THE SALAD, combine the cabbage, cucumber, cilantro, and mint in a medium bowl, and toss well. Cover and refrigerate.

T O MAKE THE SAUCE, in a medium saucepan over a medium heat, heat the peanut oil and sauté the garlic and ginger until the garlic is lightly browned. Remove the pan from the heat and add the coriander seeds, curry powder, curry paste, paprika, and cumin. Decrease the heat to low and sauté for about 2 minutes to release the oils and flavors; be careful not to burn the mixture. Stir in the coconut milk, tomato puree, soy sauce, and brown sugar. Increase the heat, bring the sauce almost to a boil, and remove from the heat. (Don't let the sauce boil, or the sauce will separate.) Keep warm or reheat gently before serving.

MEANWHILE, TO COOK THE SALMON, brush the fillets with the olive oil and season with salt and pepper. Grill the fillets for about 2½ minutes per side for medium rare, or until browned on the outside but still slightly translucent in the center. Or, heat a grill pan or skillet over high heat until very hot and cook the fillets for about 2½ minutes per side for medium rare, or until browned on the outside but still slightly translucent in the center.

TO FINISH THE SALAD, toss the cabbage mixture with the soy sauce and rice vinegar in a large bowl. To serve, place about ½ cup rice in the center of each of 4 warmed plates. Ladle ½ cup sauce around the rice, then place a fillet on top of the rice. Top each fillet with a tall mound of the cabbage salad. Sprinkle the sauce with the peanuts.

Croquettes of Copper River Salmon
with a Ragout of Morel Mushrooms and Asparagus

Serves 4

Make these golden breaded fillets in the spring, when morels, asparagus, and Copper River salmon (which has a fresh, clean flavor and deep red-orange color) are in season. We use Japanese-style panko bread crumbs to coat the fish. They're made from shredded fresh bread and are larger and more rough textured than ordinary breadcrumbs. The result is a lighter, crispier crust that keeps the salmon moist and sweet inside.

Salmon Croquettes

4 Copper River or king salmon fillets, cut into
   1¼-inch-wide by 1¼-inch-high by 4-inch-long strips

Salt and freshly ground black pepper

½ cup all-purpose flour

1 egg

2 tablespoons milk

½ cup panko (Japanese bread crumbs)
   or regular dried bread crumbs

Vegetable oil for deep-frying

Ragout

2 tablespoons unsalted butter

¼ cup julienned leek (white part only)

¼ cup julienned peeled carrot

¼ cup sliced onion

3 ounces morel mushrooms, cleaned

2 tablespoons veal stock (page 207) or
   brown chicken stock (page 209)

1 cup heavy cream

4 jumbo asparagus, trimmed, blanched for 2 minutes
   (page 198), and cut 1-inch-long pieces

Garnish

½ teaspoon medium-coarse sea salt

12 fresh chervil sprigs

⅓ cup Pinot Noir Essence (page 148)

1 tablespoon chopped fresh chives

TO MAKE THE CROQUETTES, season the salmon strips with salt and pepper, then dredge in the flour to coat evenly; pat off the excess. Whisk together the egg and milk until completely incorporated, then dip each strip in the mixture, making sure to coat evenly. Dredge in the panko to coat evenly. Set aside. Preheat 3 inches of oil in a deep, heavy pot to 370°.

TO MAKE THE RAGOUT, melt the butter in a medium saucepan over medium heat and sauté the leek, carrot, and onion until soft, about 2 minutes. Add the morels and sauté for 1 minute. Add the veal stock and cream and bring just to a boil. Set aside and keep warm. Just before serving, add the asparagus and heat for about 2 minutes.

TO DEEP-FRY THE CROQUETTES, add as many croquettes as will fit in the pot of preheated oil without overcrowding and cook until golden brown, about 3 minutes. Using a slotted metal spatula, transfer the croquettes to paper towels to drain.

TO SERVE, finish the ragout by adding the asparagus and heating. Divide the ragout among 4 warmed plates. Cut each croquette into 3 pieces and place them around the ragout, cut side up. Sprinkle a bit of sea salt on each piece of croquette and garnish each with a chervil sprig. Drizzle with the Pinot Noir essence around the outside of the ragout and croquettes and sprinkle with chives.

The Principles of Deep-Frying

1. **Always use plenty of oil.** Don't skimp here; deep-frying needs to be just that. When it's done correctly at the proper temperature, the oil forms a "skin" on the surface of the ingredient which keeps it from being absorbed into the food; as a result, the food gets crisp and won't be greasy. Shallow frying produces very different results.

2. **Start with fresh oil.** Used frying oil contains small particles of food that may burn when the oil is reheated, imparting a bitter flavor. Also, oil breaks down and oxidizes as it heats, affecting its performance. Commercial frying oils have stabilizers that help prevent this problem. If you do decide to reuse oil after frying, strain it through a coffee filter to remove food particles.

3. **Dry before you fry.** If ingredients are covered with surface moisture, this moisture will turn to steam and spatter on contact with the oil, which can be dangerous. The evaporation of excess moisture also lowers the oil temperature. Use paper towels to dry the ingredients as thoroughly as you can.

4. **Don't overfill the pot.** Crowding will cause the oil temperature to drop and may keep the ingredients from cooking evenly. It can also cause food to cook together in clumps instead of frying in individual pieces. A good rule of thumb: don't fill the pot more than half full with oil, and stop adding ingredients when the oil level reaches the three-quarter mark.

5. **Keep the temperature constant.** Use an oil thermometer, and adjust the heat to keep the oil consistently at the temperature recommended in the recipe. Wait, if necessary, until the oil returns the right temperature before adding more ingredients—deep frying is a process that can't be rushed.

Here's a guide to the basic frying temperatures you'll need for our recipes.

300°F – Oil blanching (precooking ingredients without letting them color). Examples: Japanese Eggplant (page 151), French Fries (page 117)

320°F – Ingredients that cook quickly, but have some moisture in them that needs to evaporate before they can begin to color. Example: Sesame Tuiles (page 20).

340°F – Ingredients that have a medium density and that you want to cook a bit before they start to color. Example: Haricots Verts (page 18).

360°F – Ingredients that need to be sealed quickly. Example: Lacquered Quail (page 28), Spring Rolls (page 22), finishing French Fries (page 117), Catfish (page 82)

Fricassee of Catfish
with Tomato-Garlic-Caper Sauce

Serves 4

We're glad to see catfish getting more popular as today's farmed varieties become more widely available. They're sweet and clean-tasting, and their firm flesh makes them easy to work with—especially when you're deep-frying. The secret to great frying is to use a thermometer to keep the temperature constant. We also like to use heavy old-fashioned iron skillets to keep the heat even. If you still feel that catfish has too muddy a flavor, try soaking the fillets in milk for about 3 hours before cooking.

Vegetable oil for deep-frying

Tomato-Garlic-Caper Sauce
2 tablespoons unsalted butter
1 tablespoon sliced garlic
1½ cups ½-inch-diced peeled tomatoes
2 teaspoons capers
2 teaspoons chopped fresh flat-leaf parsley
1 teaspoon chopped fresh basil
20 niçoise olives
1 teaspoon freshly squeezed lemon juice
1½ cups chicken stock (page 208)
Pinch of cayenne pepper
Salt and freshly ground black pepper to taste

20 ounces skinless catfish fillet, cut into 1 by 3-inch strips
Salt and freshly ground black pepper
1 cup all-purpose flour
4 cups hot fontina cheese polenta (page 206)

Preheat 2 inches of oil in a deep, heavy pot to 360°.

To make the sauce, in a large sauté pan or skillet, sauté the butter and garlic over medium heat until the garlic is lightly browned. Add the remaining ingredients except salt and pepper, and bring to a boil. Season with the salt and pepper. Set aside and keep warm.

To deep-fry the catfish, season the catfish with salt and pepper, then dredge in the flour to coat evenly; pat off the excess. Add as many pieces of catfish as will fit in the pot of preheated oil without overcrowding and cook until golden brown and crispy, 2 to 3 minutes, depending on the thickness of the fish. Using a slotted metal spatula, transfer the catfish to paper towels to drain.

To serve, bring the sauce back to a boil. Add the catfish all at once, return to a boil, then lower the heat to a simmer and cook for 10 seconds. Place 1 cup of polenta into each of 4 warmed shallow bowls. Divide the catfish and sauce equally among the bowls.

Pan-Roasted Local Halibut
on Garlic Mashed Potatoes with Jus de Mer

Serves 4

This dish is like two wonderful meals in a single bowl—a perfect, simple halibut fillet and a lusty shellfish "stew"—with creamy mashed potatoes to bring it all together. Every forkful is a revelation. Here in California, we're lucky to have very high-quality local halibut that weigh in at ten to fifteen pounds— small by halibut standards. We love their delicate fresh flavor. If you can't get the California variety, use the freshest Alaskan or East Coast halibut you can find.

Croutons

4 baguette slices, ½ inch thick and 6 inches long
2 teaspoons olive oil

Jus de Mer

1 tablespoon olive oil
2 teaspoons minced garlic
Pinch of crushed red pepper flakes
½ cup chopped onion
22 black mussels, scrubbed and debearded (page 15)
22 Manila clams, scrubbed (page 85)
¼ cup dry white wine
¼ cup tomato puree
1 cup fish stock (page 211)
   or chicken stock (page 208)
½ teaspoon saffron threads
Salt and freshly ground white pepper to taste

4 (6-ounce) halibut fillets, about 1¼ inches
   by 2½ inches by 4 inches
Salt and freshly ground white pepper
½ cup all-purpose flour
2 tablespoons clarified butter (page 200)

2 cups hot garlic mashed potatoes (page 206)
2 teaspoons chopped fresh flat-leaf parsley
2 tablespoons aioli (page 201)

To make the croutons, preheat the oven to 350°. Brush the baguette slices with the olive oil, place them on a rimmed baking sheet pan, and bake until golden brown, about 3 minutes. Set aside. Increase the oven temperature to 500° for the halibut.

to make the jus de mer, heat the olive oil, garlic, and chili flakes in a large saucepan over medium heat and sauté until the garlic is golden brown. Add the onion, increase the heat to high, and sauté until soft, about 3 minutes. Add the mussels and clams and sauté for 1 minute. Add the wine, bring to a boil, then add the tomato puree, stock, and saffron. Bring to a boil, cover, and cook the mussels and clams for 3 minutes, or until the mussels and clams open; shake the pan once or twice to evenly distribute the heat. Discard any mussels or clams that don't open. Season with salt and pepper. Set aside and keep warm.

meanwhile, to cook the halibut, season the fillets with salt and pepper and dust with flour.

Melt the butter in a large ovenproof sauté pan or skillet over high heat, add the fillets, and cook until golden brown, 2 to 3 minutes. Turn the fillets over, put the pan in the oven, and roast for 2 to 3 minutes, or until opaque throughout.

TO SERVE, mound ½ cup mashed potatoes in the center of 4 warmed shallow bowls. Spoon the jus de mer around the potatoes, evenly distributing the mussels and clams. Place a halibut fillet on top of the potatoes and sprinkle with chopped parsley. Put some aioli on each crouton and place one in each bowl, sticking out from the potatoes.

How to Clean Clams

AS SOON AS YOU GET THE CLAMS HOME, PUT THEM IN A LARGE BOWL, TOSS IN A HANDFUL OF SALT, AND SHAKE THE BOWL TO BEGIN CLEANING THE SHELLS. RINSE THE CLAMS UNDER COLD WATER. CHECK EACH CLAM BY TWISTING THE SHELLS APART BETWEEN YOUR THUMB AND FOREFINGER (LIKE SNAPPING YOUR FINGERS). IF ANY CLAMS OPEN, DISCARD THEM; LIVE CLAMS WILL BE STRONG ENOUGH TO HOLD THEIR SHELLS CLOSED. FILL THE BOWL WITH COLD WATER AND ADD A LIBERAL AMOUNT OF SALT. PUT THE CLAMS IN THE WATER AND REFRIGERATE 1 HOUR TO PURGE THEM OF ANY DIRT OR SAND THEY MAY CONTAIN. DRAIN THE CLAMS, RINSE THEM IN COLD WATER, PUT THEM BACK IN THE BOWL, AND COVER THEM WITH A DAMP CLOTH. REFRIGERATE THE CLAMS UNTIL YOU'RE READY TO USE THEM. WHEN YOU COOK THE CLAMS, ANY THAT DON'T OPEN ARE DEAD AND SHOULD BE DISCARDED.

Roasted Risotto-Stuffed Monterey Squid with Black Olive—Balsamico Vinaigrette

Serves 4

This is our twist on seafood risotto, and the squid bodies make the perfect casing for the stuffing. We use Monterey squid for this dish because they're small and tender. Any small fresh squid will work, as will high-quality frozen squid. Avoid larger, thicker squid, which will become tough when cooked in this way.

Risotto

1 tablespoon unsalted butter

2 tablespoons finely chopped onion

½ teaspoon minced garlic

½ cup arborio rice

Tentacles from squid, below, coarsely chopped
(reserve 4 tentacles for garnish, optional)

3 tablespoons dry white wine

1 cup chicken stock (page 208)

3 tablespoons tomato concassée (page 199)

Pinch of saffron threads

Salt and freshly ground white pepper to taste

½ teaspoon chopped fresh basil

Black Olive—Balsamico Vinaigrette

2 tablespoons minced kalamata olives

2 teaspoons balsamic vinegar

1 teaspoon soy sauce

2 tablespoons extra virgin olive oil

Salt and freshly ground black pepper to taste

8 Monterey squid, each about 5 inches long,
cleaned and skinned

Fried Squid Tentacles (optional)

Vegetable oil for deep-frying

4 squid tentacles, reserved above

½ cup all-purpose flour

Salt and freshly ground black pepper to taste

2 tablespoons olive oil

Salt and freshly ground white pepper

3 large red or yellow bell peppers, roasted,
peeled, and cut into ½-inch strips (page 198)

TO MAKE THE RISOTTO, preheat the oven to 400°. In a small, heavy ovenproof saucepan or Dutch oven, melt the butter over high heat and sauté the onion and garlic until translucent, 2 to 3 minutes. Add the rice and sauté until opaque, 2 to 3 minutes. Add the squid tentacles and sauté until they turn white. Add the wine, stock, tomato concassée, and saffron and bring to a boil. Season with salt and pepper. Cover and cook in the oven for about 14 minutes, or until tender but firm. Spread the risotto out on a rimmed baking sheet pan and let cool, then mix the basil into the risotto. Increase the oven temperature to 450° for the squid.

MEANWHILE, TO MAKE THE VINAIGRETTE, combine the olives, vinegar, soy sauce, and olive oil in a small bowl. Season with salt and pepper and set aside.

TO STUFF THE SQUID BODIES, use a spoon or pastry bag (or your fingers) to fill each body with the risotto. Don't stuff them too tight; as they cook the squid will shrink a little bit and can burst. Close the opening with a toothpick by squeezing the open end flat; push the toothpick through at the end of one side, then bring it back down and through the end of the other side, like using a pin to hold a hem.

TO MAKE THE FRIED TENTACLES, heat 2 inches of oil in a deep, heavy pot to 360°. Dredge the reserved tentacles in the flour; shake off the excess. Add the tentacles to the hot oil and deep-fry until crisp, 45 to 60 seconds. Using a wire-mesh

skimmer or a slotted metal spoon, transfer the tentacles to paper towels to drain. Season with salt and pepper. Set aside and keep warm.

TO ROAST THE SQUID, heat the olive oil in a large ovenproof, nonstick pan over high heat until hot. Season the stuffed squid with salt and pepper and carefully put them in the pan. Lower the heat to medium and cook for about 1 minute, then turn the squid over, put the pan in the oven, and roast for 3 minutes. Remove from the oven and turn the squid again, then cover and let rest for 1 minute. (This is to let the risotto get hot without overcooking the squid.)

TO SERVE, divide the bell pepper strips among 4 warmed plates, mounding them in the center. Place 2 squid on each mound of bell pepper strips, then drizzle the vinaigrette over and around the squid. Garnish with a fried squid. ♪♪♪

Acqua Pazza

"Acqua Pazza" means "crazy water," and we're crazy about this classic southern Italian-style whole fish that's as flavorful as it is beautiful. The fish is first lightly sautéed, then poached in water flavored with garlic, tomato, and wine. This rich broth becomes the sauce for the moist, tender fish. If you'd rather make this dish with boneless fish, choose fillets with the skin on, which will be less likely to fall apart. (See photo on pages 88–89.)

Acqua Pazza Broth
3 tablespoons olive oil
4 large cloves garlic, smashed
Pinch of crushed red pepper flakes
2 cups dry white wine
2 teaspoons capers
4 cups water
Salt and freshly ground black pepper to taste

4 (1-pound) whole Tai snapper or striped bass,
   cleaned, scales, gills, and fins removed
Salt and freshly ground black pepper
½ cup all-purpose flour
½ cup olive oil
24 oven-dried tomatoes (page 199)
½ cup cherry tomatoes, stemmed and halved
20 kalamata olives
1½ pounds Manila clams, cleaned (page 85)
2 heads escarole, halved and stemmed
2 tablespoons chopped fresh flat-leaf parsley
1 tablespoon chopped fresh basil

Preheat the oven to 400°.

TO MAKE THE BROTH, heat the olive oil and garlic over medium heat in an ovenproof saucepan or baking dish large enough to hold the 4 fish; sauté the garlic until it is lightly browned. Add the pepper flakes, wine, and capers, and bring to a boil. Add the water, bring the broth back to a boil, then lower the heat to a simmer and season with salt and pepper.

While the broth is simmering, season the fish with salt and pepper, including the inside of the cavities, then dredge in the flour. Heat the olive oil in a large sauté pan or skillet over high heat until almost smoking. Working in batches, if necessary, add the fish and sauté until golden brown, about 3 minutes per side.

Transfer the fish to the simmering broth and add the oven-dried tomatoes, cherry tomatoes, and olives. Bring to a boil, then cook in the oven for 10 minutes. Put the pan back on the stove. Add the clams and cook over medium heat to reduce the broth to 4 cups, gently shaking the pan so that the fish don't stick to the bottom and occasionally using a ladle to baste the fish with the broth.

Meanwhile, bring a large pot of salted water to boil. When the broth has reduced, add the escarole to the boiling water and blanch for 1 to 1½ minutes. Drain, then gently squeeze the excess water out with tongs.

TO FINISH THE DISH, divide the escarole among 4 warmed large plates as a bed for the fish. Carefully place a fish on top of each escarole bed, using 2 slotted metal spatulas if necessary so the fish does not break. Taste the broth and adjust the seasoning. Add the parsley and basil to the broth. Divide the broth, oven-dried tomatoes, clams, olives, and cherry tomatoes evenly among the plates. ♪♪

Bottom: Discussing olive oil with Osvaldo

Sautéed Pesto-Marinated Tai Snapper with Grilled Langoustines and Tomato—Black Olive Vinaigrette

Serves 4

Tai snapper is the snapper of choice in Japan, because its flavor is mild and sweet and its flesh firm. That's what makes it a good choice for marinating in a flavorful coating of pesto, then sautéeing in olive oil. If you can't find Tai snapper, any small snapper will work well. Don't leave the fish in the pesto for more than 24 hours, or it will take on too much pesto flavor. This is a perfect warm-weather dish, with the summery flavors of the Mediterranean.

4 (5- to 6-ounces each) Tai snapper fillets, boned, and skin on
⅓ cup pesto (page 203)
4 (3- to 4-ounces each) langoustines or large tiger shrimp, head on if possible
1 tablespoon olive oil

Tomato—Black Olive Vinaigrette
½ cup tomato concassée (page 199)
1 teaspoon chopped shallots
2 teaspoons sherry wine vinegar
¼ teaspoon paprika
Pinch of cayenne pepper
2 tablespoons extra virgin olive oil
1 teaspoon coarsely chopped kalamata olives
Salt to taste

Salt
1 tablespoon olive oil
Freshly ground white pepper to taste
12 asparagus, trimmed and peeled
2 cups hot mashed potatoes (page 206)
4 fresh basil sprigs, for garnish

 Marinating

TO MARINATE THE SNAPPER AND LANGOUSTINES, first score the skin of the snapper with a sharp knife, making 2 to 3 shallow diagonal slits in the skin so that the fillets will not curl when cooking. Spread the pesto on both sides of the fillets and put the fish in a glass baking dish, skin side down. Cover and refrigerate for at least 1 hour or up to 5 hours. To marinate the langoustines, butterfly them by cutting from the top of the head down to the tail in a straight line, being careful not to cut all the way through, and devein. Open them up and lay them flat on a plate. Drizzle the olive oil over them, turning to coat both sides. Cover and refrigerate until ready to cook.

Prepare a fire in a charcoal grill or preheat a gas grill.

TO MAKE THE VINAIGRETTE, combine all the ingredients in a small bowl. Set aside.

TO COOK THE SNAPPER AND LANGOUSTINES, season the snapper with salt. In a large nonstick sauté pan, heat the olive oil over high heat, add the snapper, skin side down, and sauté until crisp and golden brown, 2 to 3 minutes; using a spatula, gently press on the fillet as it cooks so that the entire skin gets caramelized. Turn it over and cook for about 2 minutes, or until opaque throughout.

At the same time, season the langoustines with salt and pepper. Grill the langoustines, shell side down, until the shell color changes to a pinkish white and smells toasty, about 1 minute. Flip over

and grill the other side for about 1 minute. Or, heat a skillet or grill pan over high heat until very hot and cook the langoustines, shell side down, until the shell color changes to a pinkish white, about 1 minute; cook the other side for about 1 minute.

Meanwhile, bring a pot of salted water to boil. Add the asparagus and blanch for 2 minutes.

TO SERVE, put ½ cup mashed potatoes into the center of each of 4 warmed plates. Drizzle the vinaigrette around the mashed potatoes and put the snapper, skin side up, on top of the mashed potatoes. Position the langoustines, meat side up, on the snapper at an angle to the fillet. Arrange the asparagus, tips up, in a triangular pattern against the langoustines. Garnish with a basil sprig.

Grilled Tournedos of Tuna
and Fried Miyagi Oysters with Lemon-Caper Aioli

Serves 4

Tuna is best when it's cooked no more than medium-rare and served with clean, simple flavors. In this luxurious presentation, its steak-like taste and texture make a nice counterpoint to the crunchiness of fried oysters. On their own, the oysters are also a great first course or passed appetizer, and you'll find all kinds of other uses for the aioli.

4 (6-ounce) tuna steaks, 1½ inches thick
2 teaspoons olive oil

Lemon-Caper Aioli
1 cup mayonnaise (page 201)
⅛ teaspoon grated garlic
1 teaspoon chopped capers
1 teaspoon freshly squeezed lemon juice

Black-Olive Oil
2 tablespoons chopped kalamata olives
2 tablespoons extra virgin olive oil

Fried Oysters
Vegetable oil for deep-frying
1 egg
2 tablespoons milk
2 tablespoons all-purpose flour
12 Miyagi or other Pacific oysters, shucked
Salt and freshly ground black pepper
½ cup dry bread crumbs

2 tablespoons unsalted butter
2 bunches green Swiss chard, stemmed
  and blanched (page 198)
12 oven-dried tomatoes (page 199)
1 cup upland cress or watercress sprigs
2 teaspoons chopped fresh chives

COAT BOTH SIDES OF THE TUNA with the olive oil and marinate for 30 minutes.

Preheat the oven to 350°. Prepare a fire in a charcoal grill or preheat a gas grill.

TO MAKE THE AIOLI, whisk together all the ingredients in a small mixing bowl.

TO MAKE THE BLACK-OLIVE OIL, whisk together the olives and the olive oil in a small bowl. Set aside.

TO DEEP-FRY THE OYSTERS, heat 2 inches of oil in a deep, heavy pot to 350°. In a mixing bowl, whisk together the egg, milk, and flour. Lightly season the oysters with salt and pepper. Dip the oysters in the egg mixture, then dredge in the bread crumbs. Add as many oysters as will fit in the pot without overcrowding, and cook until golden brown, about 2 minutes. Using a wire-mesh skimmer or slotted metal spoon, transfer the oysters to paper towels to drain and keep warm.

TO COOK THE TUNA, season the steaks with salt and pepper and grill for 1½ minutes per side for medium rare. Or, heat a grill pan or skillet over high heat until very hot and cook the steaks for 1½ minutes per side. Meanwhile, melt the butter in a large sauté pan or skillet over high heat and sauté the Swiss chard for 2 minutes, or until heated through. Put the oven-dried tomatoes on a baking sheetpan and heat in the oven until hot, about 2 minutes.

TO SERVE, divide the Swiss chard among 4 warmed plates. Place 3 oven-dried tomatoes around the chard, then place a tuna steak on top of the chard. Place 3 fried oysters on top of the tuna. Drizzle the aioli on the oysters and around the Swiss chard. Drizzle the black-olive oil around the Swiss chard. Place a mound of upland cress on top of the oysters and sprinkle with chives. ♪♪♪

Poached Skate Wing
on Napa Cabbage with Ponzu

Serves 4

Skate is the most succulent fish we know. The "wing," or fin, contains a lot of gelatin, making it moist and flavorful. If you're not familiar with skate, eating it can be a bit of a surprise: It has a triangular shape with cartilage running down the middle and meat on either side, which falls away easily when the fish is cooked. It's most often served sautéed or roasted, but we like to poach it to bring out its toothsome texture and sweet flavor. You can make this recipe with fillets from larger wings or whole smaller ones.

½ napa cabbage, cored and
   cut into 2-inch-square pieces (about 8 cups)
4 cups water
1 tablespoon rice vinegar
¼ cup dry sake
Salt and freshly ground white pepper to taste
4 (5-ounce) skate wing fillets, skinned,
   each at least ½ inch thick and 4 by 3 inches
½ cup julienned leek (white part only), soaked
   in ice water for 30 minutes and drained
⅓ cup daikon sprouts, without roots,
   cut into 1-inch-long pieces
1 cup ponzu (page 202)
1 tablespoon Asian (toasted) sesame oil

Garnish
1 tablespoon sesame seeds, toasted (page 68)
2 tablespoons chopped fresh chives

To cook the cabbage, bring a large pot of salted water to boil. Add the cabbage and cook for 3 minutes; drain, reserving a little of the boiling water in the pot. Put the cabbage in a colander suspended over but not touching the water; cover with the lid. Set aside.

At the same time, in a large saucepan, combine the water, rice vinegar, and sake. Bring to a boil, lower the heat to a simmer, and season lightly with salt and pepper. Add the skate wing fillets and gently poach for 2 to 3 minutes, or until opaque throughout. Carefully remove the fillets from the pan and drain on a towel. Keep hot.

TO SERVE, divide the cabbage evenly among 4 warmed shallow bowls. Place a fillet on top of each mound of cabbage. Mix the leek and daikon sprouts together and mound on top of each skate wing. In a small saucepan, combine the ponzu and sesame oil and heat just until warm. Spoon the mixture over the leeks, sprouts, and fillets. Sprinkle with the toasted sesame seeds and chives.

Sautéed Alaskan Spot Prawns with Curry-Shrimp Sauce, Black Trumpet Mushrooms, and Snow Peas

Serves 4

We think crustacean and curry is a natural combination. And when you marry the sweetness of plump spot prawns with the spiciness of a creamy curry sauce enriched with their shells, the result is unbelievable. This dish has a lot of ingredients, but it's not at all tricky to make. Just take the time to measure and prepare everything before you start cooking.

20 (3-ounce) head-on Alaskan spot prawns or
    black tiger shrimp, or 20 (1½-ounce)
    black tiger shrimp without heads

Curry-Shrimp Sauce
3 tablespoons unsalted butter
½ cup sliced onion
⅓ cup sliced carrot
½ teaspoon chopped garlic
Shells (and heads, if available) from
    20 prawns, above
1 tablespoon curry powder
2 tablespoons Cognac
4 cups chicken stock (page 208)
½ cup heavy cream
3 tablespoons tomato paste
2 teaspoons fennel seeds
Salt and freshly ground white pepper to taste

5 tablespoons unsalted butter
Salt and freshly ground black pepper to taste
2 tablespoons minced shallots
2½ ounces black trumpet mushrooms or
    1½ ounces shiitake mushrooms, cleaned,
    stemmed, and cut into ¼-inch-thick slices
40 snow peas, stemmed and blanched (page 198)
2 tablespoons tomato concassée (page 199)

TWIST THE HEADS OFF THE PRAWNS, then shell and devein (page 69). Reserve the head and shells for the sauce; refrigerate the cleaned shrimp.

TO MAKE THE SAUCE, melt the butter in a large saucepan over medium heat and sauté the onion, carrot, and garlic until soft, about 3 minutes. Add the shrimp shells and heads, increase the heat to high, and sauté for 3 minutes, using a wooden spoon to crush the heads and shells so they release their juices. Add the curry powder and sauté for 1 minute. Add the Cognac and carefully ignite it with a long-handled match. When the flames have subsided, add the stock, cream, tomato paste, and fennel seeds. Return the mixture to a boil, skim off any foam that develops, and simmer for 20 minutes. Strain through a fine-mesh sieve. Rinse out the pan and return the sauce to the pan. Cook the sauce over medium heat until reduced to 1 cup. Season with salt and pepper. Set aside and keep warm.

Melt 3 tablespoons of the butter in a large non-stick sauté pan or skillet over high heat. Season the prawns with salt and pepper, and sauté for about 1 minute on each side, or until they turn red. At the same time, melt the remaining 2 tablespoons butter in another large sauté pan or skillet over high heat, and cook the shallots until translucent, about 2 minutes. Add the mushrooms and snow peas and sauté for about 2 minutes, then add the tomato concassée and sauté for 10 seconds. Season with salt and pepper.

TO SERVE, divide three-fourths of the sauce among 4 warmed plates. Evenly distribute the black trumpet mushrooms and snow peas over the sauce. Arrange 5 prawns on top of each serving of mushrooms and snow peas. Drizzle the remaining sauce over the prawns. ♩♩

Grilled Lingcod
with English Peas and Peeky Toe Crab Risotto

We like the depth of flavor and contrasting textures that come from using more than one cooking technique in a single presentation. In this case, the creamy richness of the risotto sets off the smokiness of the grilled lingcod beautifully. Both the fish and the risotto work well on their own, too. You can serve the lingcod with just the sauce and some simple vegetables, and the risotto makes a perfect first course or lunch entrée. If you're lucky enough to find fresh English peas, don't let them sit out or in the refrigerator for long. Their sugar will begin turning to starch, and they'll be less sweet. Instead, shuck and blanch them the minute you get them home; they can then be kept for up to a day. Peeky Toe crabs come from the same family as Dungeness crab, but they're smaller and sweeter.

4 (4-ounce) skinless, boneless lingcod fillets
1 tablespoon extra virgin olive oil

Sauce
2 teaspoons olive oil
1/8 teaspoon crushed red pepper flakes
1 teaspoon minced garlic
2 tablespoons dry white wine
1/3 cup tomato concassée (page 199)
2/3 cup fish stock (page 211)
   or chicken stock (page 208)
1/4 teaspoon saffron threads
Salt and freshly ground white pepper to taste

Risotto
3 to 4 cups chicken stock
1 tablespoon unsalted butter
1/2 cup chopped onion
1 teaspoon minced garlic
1 cup arborio rice
1/4 cup dry white wine
Salt and freshly ground white pepper to taste
1/4 cup English peas
1/2 cup fresh lump Peeky Toe, Dungeness,
   or Blue crabmeat, picked over for shell
1/8 teaspoon chopped fresh tarragon
1/4 cup freshly grated Parmesan cheese
2 tablespoons mascarpone cheese

12 oyster mushrooms, each about
   3 inches long, cleaned
1 tablespoon extra virgin olive oil
Salt and freshly ground white pepper to taste

Garnish
12 sugar snap peas, stemmed
4 fresh tarragon sprigs

MARINATE THE LINGCOD in the olive oil for at least 1 hour. If grilling, prepare a fire in a charcoal grill or preheat a gas grill. If pan-roasting, preheat the oven to 350°.

TO MAKE THE SAUCE, heat the olive oil, chili flakes, and garlic in a small saucepan over medium heat until the garlic is golden brown. Add the wine and bring to a boil. Add the tomato concassée, stock, and saffron, and return the mixture to a boil. Lower the heat to a simmer and cook for about 3 minutes. Season with salt and pepper and set aside.

TO MAKE THE RISOTTO, bring the stock to a simmer. In a medium, heavy saucepan over medium heat, melt the butter, add the onion and garlic, and sauté until translucent, about 4 minutes. Add the rice and sauté for about 3 minutes, stirring with a wooden spoon until the outside of the rice becomes opaque. Add the wine, bring to a boil, and season lightly with salt and pepper. Stir constantly, scraping the entire bottom of the pan until almost all the wine is absorbed by the rice. Add 1 cup of the simmering chicken stock. The rice should be kept at a fast simmer and not a boil as you stir and add stock. Stir the rice constantly until almost all the stock has been absorbed. Add ½ cup of the simmering stock, stirring constantly, until almost all the stock has been absorbed. Repeat the process until the rice is almost tender yet firm, 10 to 12 minutes (the amount of stock added may be decreased to ¼ cup as the cooking progresses). Add the peas and crabmeat and cook, stirring constantly, until the risotto is tender but firm. Add the tarragon, Parmesan, and mascarpone, and mix well. Taste and adjust the seasoning if necessary. Remove from the heat and keep warm.

Just before the risotto is ready, season the lingcod with salt and pepper, then grill for about 2 minutes per side, or until lightly browned on the outside and opaque throughout. Or, heat an ovenproof sauté pan or skillet over high heat until very hot. Add the lingcod, and cook for 2 minutes on one side or until lightly browned, then turn it over and put the pan in the oven to roast for 3 to 4 minutes, or until opaque throughout.

Meanwhile, coat the oyster mushrooms with the olive oil, season with salt and pepper, and grill or sauté for 2 to 3 minutes.

Bring a pot of salted water to boil. Add the sugar snap peas and blanch for 1 minute or until crisp-tender (page 198).

TO SERVE, reheat the sauce. Divide the risotto among 4 warmed shallow bowls. Place a piece of lingcod on top of the risotto. Arrange the oyster mushrooms and sugar snap peas around the lingcod, then spoon the sauce on top of the fish and around the risotto. Place a tarragon sprig on top of each serving of lingcod. ♪♪♪

Pan-Roasted California White Bass with Preserved-Lemon Beurre Blanc and Roasted Shad Roe

Serves 4

Shad roe is the holy grail of seafood. True aficionados will go to any lengths to get their hands on these succulent eggs of the small North American shad herring, available only in the late spring. If you can't find it, don't let that stop you from trying this recipe; just leave the roe out. We love the mild flavor and succulent texture of California white bass, and even without the shad roe it's a beautiful dish.

Preserved-Lemon Beurre Blanc

1 cup dry white wine

2 teaspoons chopped shallot

⅓ cup heavy cream

½ cup (1 stick) cold unsalted butter, cut into small cubes

2 teaspoons chopped preserved lemon rind (page 203)

Salt and freshly ground white pepper to taste

4 (5-ounce) California white bass fillets, at least 1 inch thick, skin on

Salt and freshly ground black pepper

Flour for dredging

2 tablespoons clarified butter (page 200)

½ cup (1 stick) unsalted butter

2 (8-ounce) shad roe

4 cloves garlic, smashed

3 tablespoons tomato concassée (page 199)

¼ cup veal stock (page 207) or brown chicken stock (page 209)

1 teaspoon chopped fresh flat-leaf parsley

2 tablespoons unsalted butter

1 ounce shiitake mushrooms, cleaned, stemmed, and sliced

8 cups spinach leaves

⅛ teaspoon minced garlic

¼ cup water

To make the beurre blanc, combine the wine and shallot in a small nonreactive saucepan, and cook over high heat until reduced to about 1 tablespoon. Add the cream and cook until reduced by two thirds. Decrease the heat to low and whisk in the butter a few pieces at a time. If the butter starts to melt instead of incorporating into the cream, remove the pan from the heat for a minute and continue whisking. Add the lemon, salt, and pepper (preserved lemon is salty, so go lightly on the salt). Keep warm in a double boiler.

To cook the bass, preheat the oven to 500°. With a small, sharp knife, make 2 to 3 slits across the width on the skin side of the fillets; this will keep them from curling. Season them with salt and pepper and lightly dredge in flour. Heat the clarified butter in a large ovenproof sauté pan or skillet over medium heat until hot. Add the bass, skin side down, and cook until the skin is crisp and golden brown, 2 to 3 minutes. Turn the fillets over, put the pan in the oven, and roast for 2 to 3 minutes, or until opaque throughout. Remove from the oven and keep warm.

To cook the shad roe, season them with salt and pepper, then lightly dredge in flour. Melt the butter in a medium nonstick sauté pan or skillet over low heat. When the butter starts to bubble, add the shad roe and garlic and cook until the shad roe are golden brown, 2 to 3 minutes per side. Be sure to keep the butter temperature low, because if the temperature gets too high, the eggs will explode. When the garlic is brown, remove it with

a slotted spoon. Once the shad roe are cooked, add the tomato concassée and veal stock, and bring to a boil. Remove the pan from the heat, season with salt and pepper, then add the parsley and gently mix in. Set aside and keep warm.

TO COOK THE VEGETABLES, melt the butter in a large sauté pan or skillet over high heat. Add the mushrooms, spinach, and garlic and sauté for 1 minute. Add the water, cover the pan, and steam just until the spinach has wilted, about 2 minutes. Season with salt and pepper.

TO SERVE, mound the mushroom and spinach mixture on 4 warmed plates. Top each mound with a piece of bass. Spoon the sauce around the bass, then cut the shad roe into 12 pieces and place 3 pieces of roe around the mushrooms on the sauce on each plate. Top each piece of roe with the roe sauce.

"Mounting" a Sauce with Butter

THIS FINISHING TECHNIQUE, KNOWN IN FRENCH AS *MONTER AU BEURRE*, IS USED TO ROUND OUT THE FLAVOR OF A SAUCE, THICKEN IT SLIGHTLY, AND GIVE IT AN ATTRACTIVE SHEEN. IT'S DONE RIGHT AT THE LAST MINUTE. ONCE THE SAUCE HAS FINISHED COOKING AND YOU'RE READY TO SERVE, REDUCE THE HEAT TO VERY LOW OR REMOVE THE PAN FROM THE HEAT ALTOGETHER. THE BUTTER SHOULD BE COLD AND IN SMALL PIECES THE SIZE OF ALMONDS. ADD THE BUTTER AND GENTLY SHAKE THE PAN OR STIR THE BUTTER IN WITH A WHISK. YOU WANT THE BUTTER TO MELT SLOWLY SO IT BECOMES EMULSIFIED INTO THE SAUCE. IF IT MELTS TOO FAST, IT WILL SEPARATE AND COAT THE TOP OF THE SAUCE. ONCE FINISHED IN THIS WAY, A SAUCE CANNOT BE REHEATED (THE BUTTER WILL SEPARATE), BUT IT CAN BE KEPT WARM FOR A SHORT WHILE OVER A WATER BATH.

Broiled Sake-Marinated Chilean Sea Bass with Shrimp Dumplings in Shiso Broth

Serves 4

We like to joke that this dish doesn't need us any more. It's so popular, it can have a restaurant of its own. In fact, we could never take it off our menu because people ask for it year after year. The fish takes on a deep mahogany glaze and it sits in a beautiful broth with shiso leaves and delicate shrimp dumplings. It's a great choice for entertaining because you can prepare everything ahead of time and finish the dish in just a few minutes.

4 (6- to 7-ounce) Chilean sea bass fillets,
about 2 by 2 by 4 inches each
¾ cup sake marinade (page 202)

Shrimp Filling
5½ ounces rock shrimp, deveined (page 69)
2½ ounces scallops
1 tablespoon beaten egg
¼ teaspoon grated peeled fresh ginger
¼ teaspoon grated fresh garlic
2 teaspoons sugar
2 teaspoons mirin
2 teaspoons soy sauce
Pinch of freshly ground white pepper
1 tablespoon Asian (toasted) sesame oil

1 egg yolk
¼ teaspoon water
20 wonton wrappers

Shiso Broth
2 cups chicken stock (page 208) or water (really)
1 tablespoon soy sauce
2 teaspoons mirin
2 teaspoons rice vinegar
⅛ teaspoon grated garlic
⅛ teaspoon grated peeled fresh ginger
½ teaspoon sugar
½ teaspoon Asian (toasted) sesame oil

¾ ounce shiitake mushrooms, cleaned,
stemmed, and thinly sliced
20 thin slices peeled carrot

¼ cup julienned leek (white part only)
1 cup spinach leaves

Garnish
4 shiso leaves, cut into chiffonade
1½ teaspoons white sesame seeds, toasted (page 68)

To marinate the sea bass, put the fillets in a nonreactive container and pour the marinade over the tops, making sure the fillets are completely covered by the marinade. Cover and refrigerate for at least 3 hours or up to overnight.

To make the filling, combine all the ingredients except the sesame oil in a food processor and process until smooth. With the machine running, gradually add the sesame oil through the feed tube and process to mix.

In a small bowl, combine the egg yolk with the water to make an egg wash for the wonton wrappers. To assemble the dumplings, follow the directions on page 212 for ravioli. Use 1 scant tablespoon of the filling for each dumpling.

To make the broth, whisk together all the ingredients in a medium bowl.

To cook the sea bass, preheat the broiler. Take the sea bass fillets out of the marinade and place on a baking sheet pan. Broil 3 inches from the heat source for about 10 minutes, or until

102 | Fish and Shellfish

a deep mahogany in color outside and opaque throughout. Set aside and keep warm.

Meanwhile, being a large pot of salted water to boil. Add the shrimp dumplings and cook for 3 minutes, or until translucent; drain. In a medium saucepan, bring the broth to a boil and add the shiitake mushrooms, carrots, and leek. Lower the heat to a simmer, then add the spinach and dumplings and simmer just to warm, about 5 seconds.

TO SERVE, divide the dumplings, vegetables, and broth among 4 warmed large shallow bowls and sprinkle with the shiso. Place a fillet in the center of each bowl and sprinkle with the toasted sesame seeds. ♫♫♫

Pan-Roasted Medallions of Salmon on Brandade
with Cabernet Sauvignon Sauce

Serves 4

All over Europe, a favorite way to prepare salt cod is to soak it in water, then whip it with olive oil and other ingredients into a fluffy purée. It's baccalà in Italy, brandade in southern France. And in St. Helena, we like to make our own version using fresh Chilean sea bass, which we salt overnight, then poach and purée with mashed potatoes. Our brandade makes an ideal base for grilled or broiled fish, and we love how it tastes with these peppered salmon medallions. The hearty cabernet sauce that finishes this dish gives you the perfect excuse to break out a nice bottle of Cabernet Sauvignon to serve with it.

Brandade

8 ounces Chilean sea bass fillet,
  cut into 1-inch cubes

2 teaspoons salt

⅔ cup hot mashed potatoes (page 206)

Cabernet Sauvignon Sauce

2 cups Cabernet Sauvignon

1 teaspoon minced shallot

½ cup veal stock (page 207)

2 tablespoons tomato puree

2 teaspoons cold unsalted butter

Salt and freshly ground black pepper to taste

Sugar to taste (optional)

28 ounces center-cut salmon fillet, skinned
  and pin bones removed (page 105)

½ teaspoon cracked black peppercorns

Salt

4 tablespoons unsalted butter

1 teaspoon minced shallot

1 ounce morel, chanterelle, or
  oyster mushrooms, cleaned

12 yellow wax beans, stemmed and
  blanched (page 198)

1 tablespoon tomato concassée (page 199)

12 fresh chervil sprigs

TO START THE BRANDADE, put the sea bass in a small bowl, toss with the salt, then cover and refrigerate overnight.

TO PREPARE THE SAUCE, combine the wine and shallot in a small, heavy nonreactive saucepan and cook over medium heat until reduced to 2 tablespoons. Add the veal stock and tomato puree and cook until reduced to ½ cup. Strain through a fine-mesh sieve and return to the saucepan. Just before serving, bring the sauce to a simmer and remove it from the heat. Add the butter and incorporate it by gently shaking the pan. Season with salt and pepper. Taste and adjust the seasoning with a pinch of sugar if the sauce is too acidic.

TO FINISH THE BRANDADE, bring a medium pot of water to boil. Add the sea bass and cook for 2 to 3 minutes, or until white throughout; drain well. Place it in a heavy-duty electric mixer fitted with the paddle attachment. Add the hot mashed potatoes and beat until well blended. Set aside and keep warm.

TO COOK THE SALMON, preheat the oven to 400°. Cut the salmon fillet crosswise into 4 equal strips. Roll each strip into a medallion, starting with the thicker end and moving towards the thin end, with the former skin side inside. Tie each medallion with a piece of kitchen string. Sprinkle one side of each medallion with the cracked peppercorns and press gently. Season with salt.

Melt 2 tablespoons of the butter in an ovenproof nonstick sauté pan or skillet over medium heat, add the salmon, pepper side down, and cook until golden brown, 2 to 3 minutes. Turn the salmon over, put the pan in the oven, and roast for 2 to 3 minutes for medium rare. Set aside and keep warm.

Melt the remaining 2 tablespoons butter in a medium sauté pan or skillet over medium heat and sauté the shallot and morel mushrooms for 2 minutes, or until the shallot is translucent. Add the beans and tomato concassée, and cook for 1 minute longer. Season with salt and pepper.

TO SERVE, divide the brandade among 4 warmed plates and place a salmon medallion on top of the brandade. Drizzle 2 tablespoons of the sauce around each medallion. Arrange the mushroom mixture over the salmon and garnish with 3 sprigs of chervil. ♪♪♪

Boning Salmon

TO REMOVE THE PIN BONES FROM A SIDE OF SALMON, START BY RUNNING YOUR HAND DOWN THE ENTIRE SIDE FROM THE HEAD END. YOU'LL FEEL SMALL BONES PROTRUDING IN A LINE DOWN THE CENTER OF THE FISH AT ABOUT ½ -INCH INTERVALS. THESE ARE THE PIN BONES. TO REMOVE THEM, USE FISH BONE TWEEZERS OR NEEDLE-NOSE PLIERS. GRASP THE END OF THE BONE WITH THE PLIERS, HOLDING THE FISH DOWN WITH YOUR OTHER HAND, AND PULL FORCEFULLY. YOU WILL PULL OUT A BONE ABOUT 2½ INCHES LONG. WORK YOUR WAY DOWN THE SALMON IN THIS MANNER UNTIL THE BONES ARE TOO SMALL OR SOFT TO FEEL WITH YOUR HAND. ATLANTIC SALMON HAVE SHORTER, MORE EASILY REMOVED BONES THAN PACIFIC KING SALMON. IN GENERAL, THE FRESHER THE FISH, THE MORE DIFFICULT IT WILL BE TO REMOVE THE BONES.

Top left: Peter and Genna of Forni Brown

Grilled Swordfish Steak on Caponata with Tuscan White Beans

Serves 4

Caponata is a big-flavored Sicilian relish made with zucchini and eggplant. Together with the pistou, it makes an exciting counterpoint to the mild meatiness of grilled swordfish. This is an easy dish for entertaining because you can make the caponata and the pistou in advance, then simply grill the fish and put the plates together at the last minute. It's best to serve the caponata just warm, not piping hot.

Caponata

2 tablespoons olive oil
1 teaspoon chopped garlic
Pinch of crushed red pepper flakes
½ cup ½-inch-diced onion
½ cup ½-inch-diced zucchini
½ cup ½-inch-diced red bell pepper
1 cup ½-inch-diced eggplant
1 cup 1½-inch-diced peeled tomatoes
⅓ cup tomato puree
1 teaspoon sugar
1 tablespoon chopped kalamata olives
1 teaspoon chopped fresh basil
Salt and freshly ground black pepper to taste
2 teaspoons capers, rinsed

1 tablespoon olive oil
½ teaspoon chopped fresh basil
1 tablespoon freshly squeezed lemon juice
4 (6-ounce) swordfish steaks, about ¾ inch thick
Salt and freshly ground black pepper
⅓ cup cooked white beans
1 cup chicken stock (page 208)
2 tablespoons Pistou (page 52)
4 fresh basil sprigs, for garnish

Preheat the oven to 300°. Prepare a fire in a charcoal grill or preheat a gas grill.

To MAKE THE CAPONATA, heat the olive oil, garlic, and chili flakes in a large ovenproof saucepan over medium heat. Sauté until the garlic just starts to caramelize. Add the onion, increase the heat to high, and sauté until the onion is soft, 3 to 4 minutes.

Add the zucchini, bell pepper, and eggplant, and sauté for 3 minutes. Add the tomatoes, tomato puree, sugar, olives, and basil, and bring to a boil. Season with salt and pepper. Cut a circle of parchment paper that just fits inside the pan and cut a hole in the middle about 1 inch across. Place the paper on the caponata to cover, then bake in the oven for about 30 minutes, or until the vegetables are very tender. Remove from the oven, stir in the capers, and keep warm.

While the caponata is baking, mix together the olive oil, basil, and lemon juice in a small bowl. Coat both sides of the fish with the oil mixture and marinate for 30 minutes.

TO COOK THE SWORDFISH, season the steaks with salt and pepper. Grill for 2 minutes, then turn the steaks 45 degrees on the same side so that the grill will make a cross-hatch pattern, and cook 2 minutes longer. Turn over and cook another 2 to 3 minutes, or until opaque throughout. Or, heat a grill pan or skillet over high heat until very hot. Cook the steaks for 4 minutes on the first side, and another 2 to 3 minutes on the second side.

Meanwhile, combine the white beans and chicken stock in a small saucepan. Bring to a boil, lower the heat to a simmer, and just before serving whisk in the pistou.

TO SERVE, place equal amounts of the caponata in the center of 4 warmed plates. Spoon the white beans and sauce around the caponata. Place the grilled swordfish on top of the caponata. Garnish each swordfish steak with a sprig of basil.

MEATS

Grilled Spice-Rubbed Pork Chops
with Yam Puree and Pickled Red Onions

Serves 4

These juicy grilled pork chops get their flavor two ways: from a spicy rub and an onion-garlic "mud." Both are easy ways to add a lot of flavor to grilled foods, and you can vary the spices to suit your taste. Make some extra spice mix and keep it on hand. You'll find it's great on just about anything grilled or broiled—from steak and chicken to swordfish. The "mud" is fun to experiment with, but we recommend it for outdoor grilling only, because it creates quite a bit of smoke.

Da Spice Mix

1 tablespoon black peppercorns
2 teaspoons coriander seeds
½ teaspoon cayenne pepper
½ teaspoon ground cumin
¼ teaspoon ground cinnamon
¼ teaspoon freshly grated nutmeg
5 dried bay leaves

Da "Mud"

1 cup coarsely chopped onion
1 teaspoon chopped garlic
⅔ cup olive oil
1 tablespoon tomato paste

4 (10-ounce) T-bone pork chops, each 1 inch thick

Pickled Red Onions

2 red onions, cut into ¼-inch-thick rings
1 teaspoon salt
⅓ cup rice vinegar
⅛ teaspoon minced jalapeño
2 tablespoons sugar

Yam Puree

1½ pounds jewel or garnet yams,
    peeled and cut into ½-inch discs
⅓ cup heavy cream
1 tablespoon unsalted butter
Salt and freshly ground white pepper to taste

To MAKE THE SPICE MIX, combine all the ingredients in a clean electric coffee grinder or spice grinder and process to a powder. (If you don't have a grinder, use a mortar and pestle.) Set aside.

TO MAKE THE "MUD," puree all the ingredients in a blender until smooth. Set aside.

TO MARINATE THE PORK CHOPS, spread half of the "mud" on the bottom of a glass baking dish large enough to hold all the chops in a single layer. Sprinkle half of the spice mix on one side of the chops and put them, spiced side down, on the "mud." Sprinkle the remaining spice mix evenly over the chops and cover with the "mud." Cover and refrigerate for at least 3 hours or as long as overnight.

TO MAKE THE PICKLED RED ONIONS, separate the onions into individual rings and place in a medium bowl. Sprinkle with the salt, toss gently for 30 seconds, then set aside for 30 minutes. Put the onion rings in a clean towel and squeeze tightly to remove all the moisture. In a clean bowl, whisk together the vinegar, jalapeño, and sugar. Add the onion rings, toss well, and marinate in the refrigerator for 1 hour.

Prepare a fire in a charcoal grill or preheat a gas grill to medium. Preheat the oven to 250°.

TO MAKE THE YAM PUREE, bring a large saucepan of salted water to boil. Add the yams and cook until soft, about 10 minutes. Drain and return

to the pan over high heat, shaking the pan to help evaporate the excess water (be careful not to burn the yams). Add the cream and butter and bring just to a boil. Remove from the heat. Force the potatoes through a ricer, or mash in the pan with a potato masher. Season with salt and pepper. Set aside and keep hot.

TO GRILL THE PORK CHOPS, season them with salt. Put the chops, along with any of the "mud" that sticks to them, on the grill and cook for about 5 minutes, or until charred. Turn them over and cook 5 minutes longer, or until charred again. (Because of the natural sugar in the marinade, the pork chops will caramelize and get very dark but they will not have a burnt flavor, so don't worry.) Transfer the chops to the oven to rest for about 3 minutes.

TO SERVE, divide the yam puree onto the upper left side of each of 4 warmed plates. Mound the pickled red onions on the right side of the plates. Place a pork chop to the front and center of each plate. ♪♪

Lamb Shanks Braised in Petite Syrah
with Black Mission Figs

Serves 4

We created this tender braised lamb to go with our family's Stag's Leap Petite Syrah, and originally we made it with a whole leg of lamb. We liked it so much that we came up with this scaled-down version made with lamb shanks for our menu. The intensity of the wine is just right with the flavor of the lamb, and the dried figs thicken the sauce, adding a note of sweetness that offsets the acidity of the wine. Serve this dish with the same wine you used to make it.

Braising Broth

2 tablespoons olive oil

2 teaspoons chopped garlic

¾ cup chopped onion

⅓ cup chopped carrot

¼ cup chopped celery

½ teaspoon dried basil

1 fresh thyme sprig

4 cups Petite Syrah or
  another Rhône-style red wine

¾ cup tomato puree

8 cups brown chicken stock (page 209)

20 dried black figs (do not use fresh)

Salt and freshly ground black pepper to taste

4 (1½-pound) lamb shanks

Salt and freshly ground black pepper

⅓ cup all-purpose flour

⅓ cup olive oil

1 tablespoon Petite Syrah

1 tablespoon cold unsalted butter

3 ounces haricots verts or
  baby Blue Lake beans, stemmed

4 cups hot fontina cheese polenta (page 206)

Finely julienned zest of ½ lemon

1 teaspoon chopped fresh flat-leaf parsley

Preheat the oven to 325°.

To MAKE THE BRAISING BROTH, heat the olive oil in a large ovenproof saucepan or Dutch oven over medium heat and sauté the garlic until it starts to caramelize. Add the onion, carrot, celery, basil, and thyme, and sauté until the onion is translucent, 4 to 5 minutes. Add the wine and bring to a boil. Add the tomato puree, stock, and figs, and return to a boil. Skim off any foam that develops, remove the pan from the heat, and lightly season with salt and pepper. Set aside and keep warm.

TO SAUTÉ THE LAMB SHANKS, season them with salt and pepper, then dredge in flour and pat off any excess. Heat the olive oil in a large skillet over high heat until hot, add the shanks, and sauté until golden brown on all sides, about 5 minutes. Transfer them to the braising pan, and bring the braising broth to a boil. Skim off any foam that develops. Cut a circle of parchment paper that just fits inside the pot and a 1-inch hole in the center. Place the paper on the lamb mixture to cover, and bake in the oven for about 2 hours, or until tender. Remove the pan from the oven and carefully transfer the lamb shanks and figs to another container. Set aside and keep warm. Or, if making ahead, let cool, cover, and refrigerate for up to 3 days.

TO MAKE THE SAUCE, cook the braising liquid over medium-high heat until reduced to about 3 cups. Strain through a fine-mesh sieve. Return the sauce, shanks, and figs to the pan and simmer for 2 to 3 minutes to reheat the shanks. If reheating refrigerated shanks, first bring the dish to a boil on the stove, then cover and heat in a preheated 325° oven for 20 minutes. Check each lamb shank to make sure it is hot by inserting a small knife in the thickest part for 30 seconds. Remove it and check to see if the knife is hot; if it is, so is the lamb. Add the Petite Syrah and butter to the pot and gently shake to incorporate. Season to taste with salt and pepper. Set aside and keep warm.

TO SERVE, blanch the haricots verts (page 198). Ladle the polenta onto the center of 4 warmed plates and place a lamb shank on the polenta. Ladle the sauce and the figs over the shanks. Place an equal amount of haricots verts on top of each lamb shank. Sprinkle with the lemon zest and parsley.

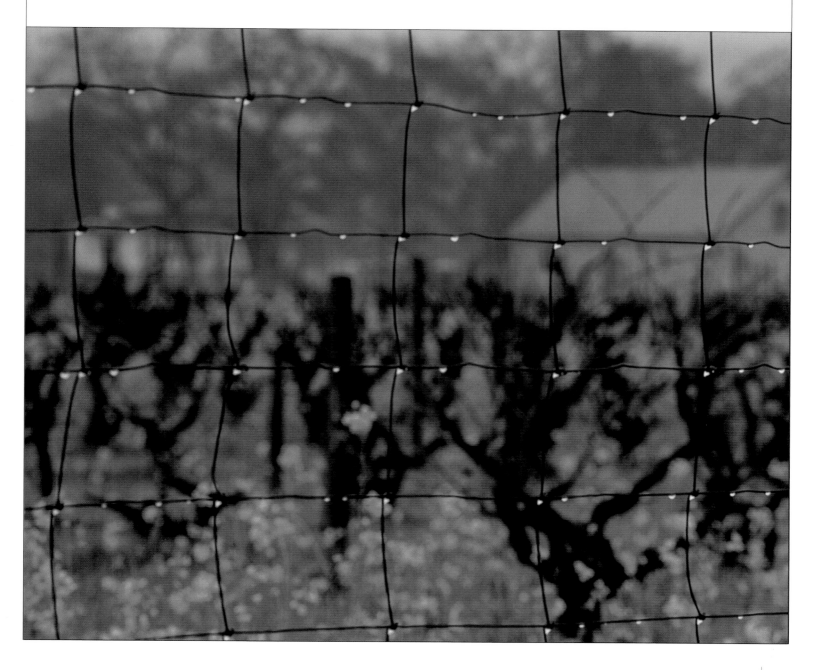

Grilled Duck Breast on Foie Gras and Sourdough Bread Stuffing with Sun-Dried Cherry Sauce

Serves 4

This is one of those dream combinations that takes some work to pull off but is truly worth the effort: grilled duck breast with a sweet-savory dried-cherry sauce, with apple and sweet potato purée and a soul-satisfying bread stuffing. The stuffing is Hiro's take on the old-fashioned Thanksgiving variety, with an added special touch: a luscious slice of foie gras terrine nestled on top. If you're not up to making the terrine from scratch, buy a smooth, silky duck or goose liver terrine, not a chicken liver pâté.

4 (8- to 9-ounce) duck breasts
1 tablespoon verjus or red wine
2 teaspoons sake marinade (page 202)

Sun-Dried Cherry Sauce
2½ cups Cabernet Sauvignon
2 cups duck stock (page 209) or
   brown chicken stock (page 209)
2 teaspoons sake marinade (page 202)
1 tablespoon plus 1 teaspoon sun-dried sour cherries
⅛ teaspoon cracked black peppercorns
2 teaspoons cold unsalted butter
Salt and freshly ground black pepper to taste
Sugar to taste (optional)

Stuffing
2 cups ¾-inch-cubed sourdough bread
1 to 1½ cups chicken stock (page 208)
2 tablespoons unsalted butter
2 tablespoons coarsely chopped bacon
½ teaspoon minced garlic
⅓ cup chopped celery
½ cup chopped onion
¼ teaspoon chopped fresh oregano
Salt and freshly ground black pepper to taste

Apple and Sweet Potato Puree
3 teaspoons unsalted butter
½ Granny Smith apple, peeled, cored,
   and sliced ¼ inch thick
14 ounces sweet potatoes, peeled
   and sliced ¼ inch thick
¼ cup heavy cream
Salt and freshly ground white pepper to taste

1 tablespoon unsalted butter
16 snap peas, stemmed and blanched for 1 minute
   (page 198)
Salt and freshly ground white pepper to taste
4 ounces Foie Gras Terrine (page 40) or
   a high-quality commercial foie gras terrine,
   cut into 4 sticks
4 fresh oregano sprigs, for garnish

Glass of verjus

To marinate the duck breasts, trim off the silver skin and cut away half of the thickness of

continued page 116

the duck skin (fat) from the top of the breast. Score the skin in a cross-hatch pattern. Put the duck breasts in a medium bowl with the verjus and sake marinade and mix well. Cover and refrigerate for at least 3 hours or up to overnight.

TO MAKE THE SAUCE, cook the wine in a medium, nonreactive saucepan over high heat until reduced to ¼ cup. Add the duck stock and sake marinade, and cook until reduced to 1 cup. Add the cherries and peppercorns, and simmer for 1 minute. Set aside and keep warm. Just before serving, add the butter and incorporate it into the sauce by shaking the pan, and season with salt and pepper. Taste the sauce; if it is too sour, add a pinch of sugar. Taste and adjust the seasoning again if necessary.

Prepare a fire in a charcoal grill or preheat a gas grill.

TO MAKE THE STUFFING, preheat the oven to 350°. Spread the bread cubes on a rimmed baking sheet pan and toast in the oven until golden, 3 to 4 minutes. Bring the chicken stock to a boil in a small saucepan, then decrease the heat to a simmer. Melt the butter in a large saucepan over medium heat, add the bacon, and cook until lightly browned. Add the garlic, celery, onion, and oregano, and sauté until the onion is translucent, about 3 minutes. Lightly season with salt and pepper. Add the croutons and sauté for 2 to 3 minutes, then add one half of the simmering chicken stock to evenly moisten (adding more chicken stock if necessary). Bring to a boil, then remove from the heat. Taste and adjust the seasoning. Set aside and keep warm.

TO MAKE THE PUREE, bring a saucepan of salted water to boil. Melt 1½ teaspoons of the butter in a small sauté pan or skillet over low heat. Add the apple and mix with the butter, then cover and cook until the apples are soft, about 5 minutes.

Meanwhile, cook the sweet potatoes in the boiling water until tender, 8 to 10 minutes; drain. Return the sweet potatoes to the pan and add the cream, remaining 1½ teaspoons butter, and the apple. Return to a boil. Press the mixture through a food mill or mash it in the pan with a potato masher. Season with salt and pepper. Transfer to a double boiler to keep hot.

TO GRILL THE DUCK, place the duck breasts skin side down and grill until the skin is crisp and golden brown, 5 to 6 minutes. Turn and cook on the other side for about 3 minutes for medium rare. Or, to pan-roast the duck, increase the oven temperature to 500°. Heat a large ovenproof sauté pan or skillet over high heat until hot, add the duck, skin side down, and cook for 5 to 6 minutes. Turn the duck over, place the pan in the oven, and roast the duck for 3 minutes. Remove the duck breast from the grill or oven and let rest for 3 minutes.

Meanwhile, to cook the snap peas, melt the butter in a small sauté pan or skillet over medium heat, add the peas, and sauté for 1 minute. Season with salt and pepper.

TO SERVE, finish the sauce by adding butter and adjusting the seasoning. Spoon the stuffing onto the center of each of 4 warmed plates. Place a stick of foie gras on top of the stuffing as in a nest. Spoon the puree next to the stuffing on the top side of the plate. Cut each duck breast lengthwise into 6 or 7 diagonal slices. Fan the slices over the stuffing. Spoon the sauce around the bottom edge of the plate all around the duck. Arrange 2 snap peas on either side of the duck and puree. Top the plate with oregano sprigs. If necessary, return the plates to the oven for 2 to 3 minutes to heat before serving. ♪♪

Paillards of Venison
with French Fries

Serves 4

This is a simple, bistro-style presentation—a thinly pounded paillard of grilled venison with garlic-parsley compound butter and a mound of crispy fries. Every component of this recipe has plenty of other uses. The paillard technique works with chicken, beef, pork, lamb, and other meats. The compound butter goes with many dishes, and the fries, well, they're just always good. The secret to sensational French fries is the restaurant double-frying technique we describe here—frying first at a low temperature to blanch and cook the potatoes, then at a higher temperature to crisp and color them. They'll be soft in the center and crisp on the outside. A second tip: Look for Kennebec potatoes. They're white-skinned and oblong, and we prefer them for frying because their low sugar and moisture content means you can fry them longer, so they get crispy before they get too dark.

French Fries

Vegetable oil for deep-frying

3 pounds large Keñebec or russet potatoes

Salt to taste

2 pounds venison leg without sinew

Salt and freshly ground black pepper

4 tablespoons garlic-parsley compound butter
   (page 200)

1 bunch watercress, cleaned

2 lemons, halved

To START THE FRENCH FRIES, heat 3 inches of the oil in a deep, heavy pot to 300°. Meanwhile, peel and cut the potatoes into sticks ¼ inch square and 3 inches long; keep them in cold water until ready to fry.

TO FRY, drain the potato sticks and pat them dry with a towel. Add as many potato sticks as will fit in the oil without overcrowding. Deep-fry until soft but not colored or crisp, about 5 minutes. Using a wire-mesh skimmer of slotted metal spoon, transfer to paper towels to drain. Repeat with remaining potatoes. Set aside.

TO PREPARE THE VENISON PAILLARDS, slice the meat against the grain into 4 equal pieces. Brush a large piece of plastic wrap with olive oil, then place the venison in the center and cover, oil side down, with another large piece of plastic wrap that has been brushed with oil. Use a smooth-surfaced meat mallet to pound the meat evenly to a ¼-inch thickness. Repeat with all the pieces. Keep each one in the plastic wrap for easier handling. Set aside.

TO FINISH COOKING THE FRIES, heat the oil to 360° and deep-fry the potato sticks again until golden brown and crispy, 2 to 3 minutes. Drain on paper towels and season with salt.

TO COOK THE PAILLARDS, heat a grill pan or sauté pan over high heat until very hot. Season each paillard with salt and pepper, then grill for about 1 minute per side.

TO SERVE, divide the French fries among 4 warmed plates. Place a paillard on each plate, half on top of the French fries. Top each paillard with 1 tablespoon compound butter. Arrange the watercress next to the fries with a lemon half. ♪♪♪

"Cassoulet" of Quail Confit
with Pancetta and Lentils

Serves 4

Quail cooked confit-style in duck fat is meltingly tender and rich tasting. We serve it in a presentation inspired by cassoulet, the slow-cooked French casserole of beans, sausage, and duck or goose confit. In our version, the quail gets topped with pancetta-scented green lentils and garlic bread crumbs and is finished in a hot oven. Many butchers sell rendered duck fat, but it's usually a special order.

Quail Confit

⅓ cup salt
1 tablespoon black peppercorns
2 tablespoons sugar
6 bay leaves
5 fresh thyme sprigs
8 cups water
8 bone-in quail
8 cups duck fat
1 head garlic, halved crosswise

Lentils with Pancetta

1 tablespoon olive oil
1 cup ½-inch-diced pancetta
1½ cups ½-inch-diced onion
1 cup ½-inch-diced peeled carrot
½ cup ½-inch-diced celery
1 tablespoon chopped garlic
Pinch of chopped fresh thyme
2 cups green French lentils (lentilles de Puys)
5 cups chicken stock (page 208)
Salt and freshly ground black pepper to taste

Bread Crumb Crust

1 cup dry bread crumbs
2 tablespoons chopped fresh flat-leaf parsley
½ teaspoon minced garlic
3 tablespoons freshly grated Parmesan cheese

TO MAKE THE CONFIT, combine the salt, peppercorns, sugar, bay leaves, thyme, and water in a large stockpot. Bring to a boil, lower the heat to a simmer, and cook for 5 minutes. Remove from the heat and set the pot in an ice bath until cold. Add the quail. Put a dish that just fits inside the pot on top of the quail to hold them under the liquid and cure in the refrigerator for at least 6 hours or as long as overnight.

Preheat the oven to 325°. Combine the duck fat and the garlic bulb in a large ovenproof saucepan or Dutch oven and heat to 290° on the stove. Remove the quail from the cure and pat dry with paper towels. Add the quail to the duck fat and heat until the oil temperature increases back to 290°. Partially cover to leave a little space for steam to escape. Put in the oven and cook for 1 hour to 1 hour 15 minutes, or until the quail are tender. Set aside and keep warm.

TO MAKE THE LENTILS, increase the oven temperature to 350°. Heat the oil in a large ovenproof saucepan or Dutch oven over high heat until hot, and cook the pancetta until lightly browned, about 2 minutes. Add the vegetables and garlic and sauté until soft, 3 to 4 minutes. Add the thyme, lentils, and stock, and bring to a boil. Season with salt and pepper. Cover, put it in the oven, and bake for 30 to 35 minutes, or until the lentils are tender but firm. Set aside.

TO MAKE THE CRUST MIXTURE, combine all the ingredients in a medium bowl.

TO ASSEMBLE AND SERVE, increase the oven temperature to 450°. Drain the quail and transfer to a large baking dish. (Strain, then cool the duck fat. Refrigerate for up to 6 months and use as many times as you like.) Spoon the lentil mixture over the quail. Sprinkle the entire surface with the crust mixture and put in the oven to bake until the crust is golden brown and the liquid starts to bubble, about 5 minutes. (If you are starting with cold ingredients, this will take longer.) Serve in the baking dish, or serve 2 quail with the pancetta and lentils and crust on each of 4 warmed plates. 🍳

Daube of Lamb Shoulder and Artichokes

Serves 6 with a little extra

*A daube is a slow-cooked French stew, sometimes made in a pot that has been sealed with dough. In the days before home ovens, housewives would bring their **daubières** to the local baker in the morning after the bread baking was finished. The daube would braise in the still-warm oven all day, to be picked up just before dinnertime. This daube works on a similar principle. Once you get it into the oven, it requires no attention, and a few hours later, you can sit down to a hearty, wonderfully aromatic lamb stew. It's even better the second day.*

1 lamb shoulder with bones (about 10 pounds)
Salt and freshly ground black pepper
1/3 cup olive oil
2 onions, coarsely chopped
2 carrots, peeled and coarsely chopped
1 cup dry white wine
3 quarts chicken stock (page 208)
3 large ripe tomatoes, coarsely chopped
  (about 3 cups)
2 cups tomato puree
2 teaspoons black peppercorns
1 fresh rosemary sprig
1/2 ounce dried porcini mushrooms
1 head garlic, halved crosswise
5 bay leaves

Bread Crumbs
1/2 cup dry bread crumbs
1/2 teaspoon minced garlic
2 teaspoons olive oil

8 large artichokes, cooked and quartered (page 197)
24 oven-dried tomatoes (page 199)
1/2 cup kalamata olives
1 tablespoon chopped fresh flat-leaf parsley
6 cups hot fontina cheese polenta (page 206)
6 to 8 fresh rosemary sprigs

PREHEAT THE OVEN to 350°. Cut the meat from the bone of the lamb shoulder and set aside. Put the bone in a roasting pan and roast for 20 minutes, or until golden brown. Set the bone aside.

TO BRAISE THE LAMB, cut the lamb shoulder meat into 2-inch cubes and season with salt and pepper. Heat the olive oil in a large ovenproof saucepan or Dutch oven large enough to hold 13 quarts over high heat until hot. Add the lamb and brown, in batches if necessary. Remove the lamb and keep warm. Spoon off all but 2 tablespoons of the fat from the pan, then add the onions and carrots and sauté until browned, 3 to 4 minutes. Return the lamb and bones to the pan and add the wine. Bring to a boil and add the stock, tomatoes, tomato puree, peppercorns, rosemary, mushrooms, garlic, and bay leaves. Return to a boil, decrease the heat to a simmer, and skim off any foam that develops. Season with salt. Cut

a circle of parchment paper that just fits inside the pot and a 1-inch hole in the center. Place the paper on the stew to cover, and bake in the oven for 2 to 2½ hours, or until the lamb is tender.

Meanwhile, combine all the ingredients for the bread crumbs in a medium sauté pan or skillet over medium heat and stir until golden brown, about 3 minutes. Transfer to a rimmed baking sheet pan to cool, then set aside.

Remove the lamb from the oven and discard the bones. Gently take the lamb pieces out, let the liquid settle, and skim off any fat from the top. Transfer the liquid to a blender and puree for 1 minute, working in batches if necessary. Strain

through a medium-mesh sieve. Rinse out the pan, then return the sauce and the lamb to the pan. Set aside and keep warm. Or, if making ahead, let cool and refrigerate for up to 3 days.

TO COMPLETE THE DAUBE, add the artichokes, tomatoes, olives, and parsley to the pan with the lamb and bring to a boil. Lower the heat to a simmer and cook for 5 minutes, or until all the ingredients are heated through.

TO SERVE, divide the polenta among 6 to 8 warmed shallow bowls, then spoon the daube over the polenta and sprinkle with the bread crumbs. Insert a rosemary sprig in the center of each serving.

Malfatti
with Rabbit and Forest Mushrooms Cacciatore

Serves 4

You can make these tender rabbit legs, braised "hunter's-style" in a tomato–white wine sauce with woodsy wild mushrooms, a day ahead of time, but make the malfatti the day you're serving the dish. Malfatti literally means "badly made" or "mistake," a reference to their irregular shape. Think of ravioli filling without the pasta. They turn up here and there in the Napa Valley, where Italian families brought them around a hundred years ago. We first tried them at the takeout window of a local liquor store that has been run by an Italian family for the last 30 years. Malfatti are also wonderful on their own, tossed in a slow-cooked tomato sauce or a mushroom sauce and topped with a sprinkling of Parmesan cheese. You can use chicken thighs for this recipe instead of the rabbit.

6 ounces spinach, cleaned and stemmed

1 egg

1 cup ricotta cheese

Pinch of nutmeg

½ cup freshly grated Parmesan cheese

½ cup plus ⅓ cup pastry flour

1 cup rice flour

Cacciatore

8 tablespoons olive oil

2 teaspoons minced garlic

½ cup finely diced onion

¼ cup finely diced carrot

¼ cup finely diced celery

¼ teaspoon coarsely chopped fresh oregano

1 cup dry white wine

1 cup tomato puree

6 cups chicken stock (page 208)

⅓ ounce (about ⅓ cup) dried porcini mushrooms, tied in cheesecloth to make a packet

Salt and freshly ground black pepper to taste

4 (12-ounce) bone-in rabbit legs

½ cup all-purpose flour

2 tablespoons unsalted butter

2 teaspoons minced shallots

6 ounces fresh wild mushrooms such as chanterelles, porcini, oysters, or shiitake, or button or portobello mushrooms, cleaned and cut into ½-inch-thick slices

3 tablespoons freshly grated Parmesan cheese

TO MAKE THE MALFATTI, bring a large pot of salted water to boil. Blanch the spinach for a second; as soon as the spinach wilts, remove it and shock (page 198) in ice water, then drain. Squeeze the spinach to remove any excess water (if you don't remove all the water in the spinach, it will make the malfatti too soft). The spinach should weigh 2½ ounces, about ⅓ cup. Coarsely chop the spinach and transfer it to a food processor. Beat the egg and measure 1 tablespoon into the food processor; use the remaining egg for something else. Add the ricotta cheese and nutmeg, and process until smooth. Transfer the spinach mixture to a medium bowl and add the Parmesan cheese and pastry flour; mix well. Knead lightly and check the texture—the mixture should feel as firm as your earlobe.

TO FORM THE MALFATTI, dust a flat work surface (wood is perfect) with some rice flour so the malfatti won't stick. Take a baseball-size piece of the dough and roll it into a rope ⅝ inch in diameter, then cut the rope into 1½-inch pieces. Transfer to a baking sheet pan lined with parchment paper sprinkled with rice flour; cover with a clean towel.

Repeat with the remaining dough. Refrigerate. The malfatti can be made up to one day in advance, or it can be wrapped in plastic wrap and frozen for up to one month.

continued page 124

Malfatti with Rabbit, continued

TO PREPARE THE CACCIATORE, preheat the oven to 350°. In an ovenproof saucepan or Dutch oven just large enough to hold the rabbit legs in a single layer, heat 2 tablespoons of the olive oil over medium heat and sauté the garlic until lightly browned. Add the onion, carrot, celery, and ⅛ teaspoon of the oregano, and sauté until the vegetables start to brown, about 3 minutes. Add the wine, tomato puree, chicken stock, and dried porcini in cheesecloth. Bring to a boil, skim off any foam that develops, season lightly with salt and pepper, and decrease the heat to a simmer.

Meanwhile, season the rabbit legs with salt and pepper, then dredge in the flour; pat off any excess. Heat the remaining 6 tablespoons olive oil in a large sauté pan over medium-high heat until hot. Add the rabbit and cook until golden brown, about 2½ minutes per side. Transfer the rabbit to the sauce. Return the sauce to a simmer and skim off any foam that develops. Cut a circle of parchment paper that just fits inside the pot and a 1-inch hole in the center. Place the paper on the cacciatore to cover and bake in the oven, for 45 to 60 minutes, or until the legs are fork tender. Remove the pan from the oven. Transfer the rabbit legs to a dish and keep warm. Remove the porcini mushroom packet and take the mushrooms out of the cheesecloth.

Transfer them to a blender with 1 cup of the sauce and puree until smooth, then return the puree to the sauce. Cook over high heat until the sauce is reduced to 5 cups.

Return the rabbit to the sauce and keep warm. To cook the mushrooms, melt the butter in a large sauté pan or skillet over high heat, add the shallots, and sauté until the shallots start to caramelize. Add the mushrooms and sauté for about 2 minutes, or until tender. Season with salt and pepper, transfer to a rimmed baking sheet pan, and spread in a thin layer to cool.

TO COOK THE MALFATTI, being a large pot of salted water to boil. Add the malfatti and cook for about 3 minutes, or until they all float to the surface. Meanwhile, add the mushrooms to the sauce with the rabbit and bring to a boil. Using a slotted spoon, transfer the malfatti to the sauce. Bring back to a boil and cook for 1 minute. Add the remaining ⅛ teaspoon oregano and stir. (Be careful when you stir the malfatti, as they are fragile.) Taste and adjust the seasoning.

TO SERVE, put 1 rabbit leg on each of 4 warmed plates, then divide the malfatti and sauce among the plates, and sprinkle with the Parmesan cheese. 🦌

Daube of Oxtail
in Cabernet Sauvignon Sauce

Serves 4

We love putting this dish on the menu and hearing customers—almost always men, for some reason—say, "Oxtails! I haven't had those since I was a little boy and my mother made oxtail soup." A daube is a classic French dish made by slowly braising meat with red wine and vegetables, and oxtails are a perfect candidate for this style of cooking. As they braise, their flavor intensifies and they release gelatin, which naturally thickens the cooking liquid. Like most braised dishes, this one is even better the day after you make it. If you have any left over, remove the meat from the bone, shred it, and use it to fill ravioli, which you can serve with the strained braising liquid and a little Parmesan cheese.

8 oxtail pieces (8 to 10 ounces each)
  from the large end of the tail
Salt and freshly ground black pepper
1 cup all-purpose flour
1 cup vegetable oil
1 cup coarsely chopped onion
½ cup coarsely chopped carrot
⅓ cup coarsely chopped celery
4 cups Cabernet Sauvignon
1 cup coarsely chopped tomatoes
1 bulb garlic, halved crosswise
8 cups chicken stock (page 208)
1 fresh thyme sprig
1 teaspoon black peppercorns
2 bay leaves
2 tablespoons cold unsalted butter
Pinch of sugar (optional)
4 cups hot mashed potatoes (page 206)

PREHEAT THE OVEN TO 350°. Season the oxtails with salt and pepper, dredge in flour, and pat off the excess. Heat ¾ cup of the oil in a large, heavy sauté pan or skillet over high heat. Add the oxtails, lower the heat to medium, and sauté until golden brown on all sides, about 2 minutes per side. Set aside.

Meanwhile, in a large ovenproof saucepan or Dutch oven large enough to hold the oxtails in a single layer, heat the remaining ¼ cup oil and sauté the onion, carrot, and celery until the onion is golden brown, 3 to 4 minutes. Add all but 2 tablespoons of the wine, the tomatoes, garlic, stock, thyme, peppercorns, and bay leaves. Bring to a boil and add the oxtails. Return to a boil and skim off any foam that develops. Lower the heat to a simmer and lightly season with salt and pepper. Cut a circle of parchment paper that just fits inside the pan and a 1-inch hole cut in the center. Place the paper on the oxtail mixture to cover. Put into the oven and bake for 2½ hours, or until the meat is tender.

Remove from the oven and carefully transfer the oxtails to a rimmed baking sheet pan. Set aside and keep warm. Skim any fat off the top of the sauce. Transfer the sauce to a blender, in batches if necessary, and puree for 10 seconds; the sauce is extremely hot, so be careful. Strain through a fine-mesh sieve. Return the sauce to the pan and cook over high heat until reduced to 3 cups. Return the oxtails back in the sauce and simmer until they are heated through. Add the reserved 2 tablespoons wine, return to a boil, decrease the heat to a simmer, and add the butter. Gently shake the pan to incorporate the butter into the sauce. Taste and adjust the seasonings. If the sauce tastes too acidic, add a pinch of sugar to balance the acid; taste and adjust the seasoning again if necessary.

TO SERVE, place 1 cup of the mashed potatoes to one side of each of 4 warmed shallow bowls. Place 2 oxtails alongside of the mashed potatoes, then ladle the sauce over the oxtails. ♪♪♪

Pan-Roasted Quail on Braised Endive
with Sultanas and Napa Valley Verjus Sauce

Serves 4

We love this simple, pan-roasted quail (you can also use chicken or pork) in a complex-tasting, sweet-and-tangy sauce. Much of that complexity comes from verjus (pronounced "vair-zhoo"), the unfermented juice of unripe grapes, which is used in cooking like vinegar. We enjoy using verjus because sauces made with it can be much more successfully paired with wine than those made with vinegar. This is because verjus gets its tartness from natural fruit acids—the same acids present in wine—as opposed to the "wine-hostile" acetic acid found in vinegar. The verjus we use is made by our dear friend and former sous chef, Jim Neal, who now devotes his energies to producing and bottling both red and white verjus under the Fusion label here in the Napa Valley (707-963-0206). We encourage you to give verjus a try; you'll find all kinds of ways to use it. One of our favorites is to toss Jim's red verjus with fresh berries as a quick, easy dessert.

1 tablespoon plus 1 teaspoon sultana raisins
   or golden raisins
1 tablespoon Cognac
8 partially boned quail (leg and wing bones left in)
¼ teaspoon chopped fresh thyme
1 tablespoon olive oil
¼ teaspoon grated garlic

Braised Endive
3 tablespoons unsalted butter
4 heads Belgian endive, halved lengthwise
2 tablespoons dry white wine
2 cups chicken stock (page 208)
Salt and freshly ground white pepper to taste

Verjus Sauce
⅓ cup white verjus
1 cup game stock (page 209) or
   brown chicken stock (page 209)
⅓ cup Red Flame grapes or other seedless red grapes
1 tablespoon cold unsalted butter
Salt and freshly ground white pepper to taste
Pinch of sugar (optional)

3 tablespoons clarified butter (page 200)
Salt and freshly ground white pepper
2 cups hot mashed potatoes (page 206)
2 ounces Foie Gras Terrine (page 40),
   cut into ¼-inch cubes (optional)

In a small bowl, soak the raisins in the Cognac for 2 hours or up to overnight.

To marinate the quail, make a small incision through the skin on the end of one leg of each quail. Slide the end of the other leg through the small hole to keep the legs together. In a large bowl, combine the thyme, olive oil, and garlic. Add the quail, turning to completely coat. Cover and refrigerate for 2 hours or up to overnight.

To braise the endives, melt the butter in a sauté pan or skillet over medium heat, add the endives, cut side down, and sauté until golden brown, 2 to 3 minutes per side. Add the wine and bring to a boil, then add the chicken stock and return to a boil. Lightly season with salt and pepper, lower the heat to a simmer, cover, and cook for about 30 minutes, or until tender. Keep warm.

To start the verjus sauce, cook the verjus in a small nonreactive saucepan over high heat until reduced to 1 tablespoon. Add the game stock and cook until reduced to ⅔ cup. Set aside. Just before serving, add the soaked raisins and grapes to the verjus sauce and heat through. On low heat, whisk in the butter, then season with salt and pepper. If the sauce tastes too acidic, add a pinch of sugar to balance the acid; taste and adjust the seasoning again if necessary.

TO COOK THE QUAIL, preheat the oven to 500°. Heat the clarified butter in a large ovenproof sauté pan or skillet over high heat until hot. Season the quail with salt and pepper and cook, breast side down, until golden brown, 2 to 3 minutes. Turn the quail over, place the pan in the oven, and roast for 2 to 3 minutes, or until the juices run clear when the breast is pierced. Remove the quail from the oven and let rest in the pan for about 2 minutes before serving.

Meanwhile, cook the endives and the cooking liquid over high heat until the liquid is reduced to a syruplike consistency, basting the endives with it.

TO SERVE, finish the verjus sauce and divide the mashed potatoes among 4 warmed shallow bowls. Place 2 halves of endive, cut side up and parallel, on either side of the mashed potatoes. Place 2 quail, breast side up, on top of the mashed potatoes. Arrange the foie gras on the quail. Pour off the fat from the sauté pan or skillet that the quail was cooled in, add the verjus sauce, and bring to a boil, stirring to scrape up the browned bits from the bottom of the pan. Spoon the sauce with the grapes and raisins over the quail.

Grilled Lamb Tenderloins on "Tagine" of Riblets with Minted Israeli Couscous

Serves 4

We love to serve—and eat—meat cooked two ways in a single presentation. In this one, we top Moroccan-style braised lamb riblets with grilled lamb tenderloins. This is a great party dish, and you can easily increase the recipe to feed a big crowd. It's not hard to prepare and most of the work can be done a day or two ahead of time, so all you have to do at the last minute is heat the tagine and cook the tenderloins. If you can't find lamb tenderloins, use larger lamb loins. Plan on four loins—one per person— and give them a little extra time on the grill. Israeli couscous isn't really couscous at all. It's a pearl-shaped toasted pasta that's great fun to eat because of its shape and texture. If it's not available, you can use regular couscous as a base for the tagine, but don't stir it in.

Herb Oil

2 tablespoons olive oil

¼ teaspoon minced garlic

1 teaspoon herbes de Provence

12 lamb tenderloins (about 1½ pounds total),
  sinew removed

"Tagine" Base

1 tablespoon olive oil

2 teaspoons chopped garlic

½ cup chopped onion

¼ cup chopped carrot

Pinch of ground cinnamon

1 teaspoon sherry wine vinegar

4 cups chicken stock (page 208)

½ cup tomato puree

1 slab lamb riblets with 8 bones

Salt and freshly ground black pepper to taste

Couscous

2 tablespoons unsalted butter

⅓ cup chopped onion

½ teaspoon minced garlic

⅓ cup Israeli couscous

1 cup chicken stock (page 208)

Minted Yogurt

⅓ cup plain yogurt

⅛ teaspoon grated garlic

1 large fresh mint leaf, minced

Salt and freshly ground black pepper to taste

2 tablespoons unsalted butter

20 white pearl onions, peeled

Pinch of sugar

½ cup water

Salt and freshly ground black pepper to taste

1 carrot, peeled and obliquely cut (pages 204–205)

Pinch of curry powder

1 tablespoon finely diced preserved lemon rind
  (page 203)

1 tablespoon chopped fresh flat-leaf parsley

Garnish

1 tablespoon sliced almonds, toasted (page 68)

12 kalamata olives

4 fresh cilantro sprigs

To make the herb oil, whisk together all the ingredients in a small bowl.

To marinate the lamb, place the tenderloins in a nonreactive baking dish and coat with the oil mixture. Cover and refrigerate for an hour or up to overnight.

To make the "tagine" base, preheat the oven to 350°. Heat the olive oil and garlic in an ovenproof pan or Dutch oven over high heat and sauté until the garlic just starts to caramelize, about 4 minutes. Add the onion, carrot, and cinnamon, and sauté until soft, 4 to 5 minutes. Add the remaining ingredients except salt and pepper, bring to a boil, and skim off any foam that develops. Remove the pan from the heat and season with salt and pepper. Cut a circle of parchment paper that just fits inside the pan and a 1-inch hole in the center. Place the paper on the tagine to cover, then bake in the oven for about 1 hour, or until the riblets are tender. Remove the pan from the oven and gently remove the lamb riblets, supporting the slab so it comes out in one piece, and transfer it to a plate. Spoon off any fat from the surface of the sauce, then transfer the sauce to a blender and puree for 1 minute, or until smooth. You may need to do this in batches. Strain through a fine-mesh sieve. Rinse the pan, then return the sauce to the pan and cook over medium-high heat until reduced to 3 cups. Cut the riblets into 8 pieces and add them to the sauce. Set aside and keep warm.

TO MAKE THE COUSCOUS, melt the butter in a small saucepan over high heat and sauté the onion and garlic until soft, about 3 minutes. Add the couscous and sauté for 1 minute. Add the stock, bring to a boil, cover, and bake in the oven for 12 to 15 minutes, or until tender but firm. Spread out on a baking sheet pan and let cool.

MEANWHILE, TO MAKE THE MINTED YOGURT, whisk together the yogurt, garlic, and mint in a small bowl. Season with salt and pepper. Cover and refrigerate for at least 30 minutes to let the flavors mingle.

Prepare a fire in a charcoal grill or preheat a gas grill.

TO COOK THE PEARL ONIONS AND CARROT, melt 1 tablespoon of the butter in a small sauté pan or skillet over medium-high heat, add the onions and the sugar, and sauté until caramelized, 4 to 5 minutes. Add ¼ cup of the water and bring to a boil, decrease the heat to a simmer, cover, and cook until the onions are soft, about 2 minutes. Season with salt and pepper and transfer to a small dish. Rinse and dry the pan. In the same pan, melt the remaining 1 tablespoon butter over medium heat, add the carrot and curry powder, and sauté for 1 minute. Add the remaining ¼ cup water and bring to a boil, lower the heat to a simmer, cover, and cook until crisp-tender, about 2 minutes. Season with salt and pepper and transfer to a small dish.

TO COOK THE LAMB, season the tenderloins with salt and pepper. Grill for about 2 minutes per side for medium rare. Or, heat a large sauté pan or skillet over high heat until very hot and cook the tenderloins for 2 minutes per side. (They are very thin and cook quickly, so be careful.) Let rest for 3 minutes in a warm place.

Meanwhile, to finish the tagine, heat the sauce and riblets and add the couscous, pearl onions, carrot, preserved lemon, and parsley. Bring to a boil, then remove from the heat. Taste and adjust the seasoning.

TO SERVE, divide the tagine among 4 warmed plates, giving each plate 2 riblets, then drizzle the minted yogurt around and a little over the tagine. Place 3 lamb tenderloins on each plate on top of the tagine and sprinkle with the almonds. Put 3 kalamata olives around the tangine and a sprig of cilantro on top. 🌶🌶🌶

How to Peel Pearl Onions

BLANCH THE PEARL ONIONS IN BOILING WATER FOR 1 MINUTE, THEN PLUNGE THEM INTO A BOWL OF ICE WATER TO COOL. PEEL WITH A SHARP PARING KNIFE AND CUT OFF THE ROOT END.

Grilled Dry-Aged New York Steak
with Potatoes Aligot and Cabernet Sauvignon Sauce

Serves 4

Aligot (a young Cantal cheese) is reputed to be the oldest cheese in France, first made by monks in Auvergne. This traditional French dish is about as simple as stirring the cheese into warm mashed potatoes until they become stringy and wonderfully rich. These potatoes are divine with steak, roast chicken, and pork. Actually they're divine all by themselves, too.

1 teaspoon herbes de Provence
2 tablespoons olive oil
1 teaspoon minced garlic
4 (12 ounces each) dry-aged New York strip steaks

Cabernet Sauvignon Sauce
3 cups Cabernet Sauvignon
1½ cups veal stock (page 207) or
   brown chicken stock (page 209)
1 tablespoon cold unsalted butter
Salt and freshly ground pepper to taste
Pinch of sugar (optional)

Potatoes Aligot
3 cups mashed potatoes (page 206)
⅔ to 1 cup shredded Aligot or Cantal cheese, or
   ½ cup fontina cheese and ½ cup mozzarella cheese
½ teaspoon minced garlic
Heavy cream (optional)

Salt and freshly ground black pepper
2 tablespoons unsalted butter
2 tablespoons chopped shallots
2 cups haricots verts or baby Blue Lake green beans,
   blanched (page 198)

To MARINATE THE STEAKS, mix together the herbes de Provence, olive oil, and garlic in a small bowl. Coat both sides of the steaks with the marinade, place in a nonreactive baking dish, and refrigerate for at least 30 minutes or up to 1 day.

TO MAKE THE SAUCE, cook the wine in a medium nonreactive saucepan over high heat until reduced to ½ cup. Add the veal stock, bring to a boil, and cook to reduce to about 1 cup. Set aside and keep warm. Just before serving, whisk in the butter and season with salt and pepper. Taste the sauce; if it is too acidic, add a pinch of sugar. Taste and adjust the seasoning again if necessary. (The sauce should not be sweet, but the sugar will cut the acid in the wine if it is too high.) Meanwhile, prepare a fire in a charcoal grill or preheat a gas grill.

TO MAKE THE POTATOES ALIGOT, heat the mashed potatoes in a saucepan over medium-high heat, add the Aligot and the garlic, and stir continuously until it starts to bubble. The potatoes should be a smooth puree and the cheese should make them stringy; if not, add a little more Aligot. If it is too thick, adjust with a little cream. Transfer to a double boiler to keep hot.

TO COOK THE STEAKS, season them with salt and pepper. Grill for 3 to 4 minutes per side for medium rare, then let rest in a warm place for 3 to 4 minutes. Or, heat a large sauté pan, skillet, or grill pan over high heat until very hot and cook the steaks for 3 to 4 minutes per side. Meanwhile, melt the butter in a large sauté pan or skillet over medium heat, add the shallots, and sauté until translucent, about 2 minutes. Add the haricots verts and sauté for about 2 minutes; season with salt and pepper.

TO SERVE, finish the sauce by adding butter and adjusting the seasoning. Divide the potatoes among 4 warmed plates, then place a steak on each serving of potatoes. Top with the haricots verts and spoon ¼ cup sauce around each steak.

Ossobuco
with Risotto Milanese

One of the all-time great combinations of Italian cooking is braised veal shanks with saffron risotto and lemon-parsley gremolata. And that's just the way we serve it at Terra. Nothing could be more gratifying to us than the telltale sound of a happy customer sucking the marrow out of the bone. Of course, you can offer your guests long, thin marrow spoons or even those all-purpose lobster picks with a scoop at one end to make the marrow retrieval easier. But for the truly passionate, ossobuco is best enjoyed as a "hand-to-mouth" experience.

Save any leftovers to make Bone Marrow Risotto (page 62).

Ossobuco

5 tablespoons olive oil
2 tablespoons minced garlic
1 cup diced onion
½ cup diced carrot
½ cup diced celery
1½ teaspoons minced fresh basil
1 teaspoon fennel seed
⅛ teaspoon crushed red pepper flakes
½ cup dry white wine
4 cups chicken stock (page 208)
1 cup tomato puree
Salt and freshly ground black pepper to taste
4 (1-pound) veal shanks, each cut into 1½-inch-
   to 2-inch-thick pieces
¼ cup all-purpose flour

Gremolata

⅛ teaspoon minced garlic
2 teaspoons chopped fresh flat-leaf parsley
⅛ teaspoon minced lemon zest

Risotto Milanese

4 cups chicken stock (page 208)
½ teaspoon saffron threads
3 tablespoons unsalted butter
½ cup finely chopped onion
1 teaspoon minced garlic
1 cup arborio rice
⅓ cup dry white wine
¾ cup freshly grated Parmesan cheese

To make the ossobuco sauce, preheat the oven to 325°. In a large ovenproof saucepan or Dutch oven just large enough to hold the shanks in 1 layer, heat 2 tablespoons of the olive oil over high heat and sauté the garlic, onion, carrot, and celery until tender, about 5 minutes. Add the basil, fennel seed, and pepper flakes, and sauté for 1 minute. Add the wine, chicken stock, and tomato puree and bring to a boil. Season with salt and pepper and decrease the heat to a simmer.

Season the veal shanks with salt and pepper, and lightly dust with flour. In a large sauté pan or skillet, heat the remaining 3 tablespoons olive oil over high heat until smoking. Add the veal shanks and brown well on each side. Transfer them to the simmering sauce, placing them in a single layer. Bring to a boil and skim off any foam that develops. Cut a circle of parchment that just fits inside the pan and a 1-inch hole in the center. Place the paper on the ossobuco to cover and braise in the oven for about 2½ hours, or until the veal shanks are very tender. Remove the pan from the oven and transfer the shanks to an ovenproof plate or roasting pan and keep warm. Place the pan over high heat and cook until the sauce is reduced to 3 cups. Return the shanks to the sauce and heat through.

To make the gremolata, mix together all the ingredients in a small bowl. Cover and refrigerate.

TO MAKE THE RISOTTO, combine the chicken stock and saffron in a saucepan, and bring to a simmer. In a medium, heavy saucepan over medium heat, melt 2 tablespoons of the butter, and sauté the onion and garlic until translucent, about 4 minutes. Add the rice and sauté for about 3 minutes, stirring with a wooden spoon until the outside of the rice becomes opaque. Add the wine and bring to a boil. Stir constantly, scraping the entire bottom of the pan until almost all the wine is absorbed by the rice. Add 1 cup of the simmering chicken stock. The rice should be kept at a fast simmer and not a boil as you stir and add stock. Stir the rice constantly until almost all the stock has been absorbed. Add ½ cup of the simmering stock and repeat the process until the rice is tender but firm. Stir in the remaining 1 tablespoon butter and the Parmesan cheese.

TO SERVE, put a portion of the risotto to one side of each of 4 warmed shallow bowls. Put one veal shank in each bowl to the side of the risotto, spoon the sauce over the shanks, and sprinkle with the gremolata.

Using Parchment Paper as a Lid

WE USE PARCHMENT PAPER INSTEAD OF A LID SO THAT THE INGREDIENTS IN THE POT CAN LOSE SOME OF THEIR MOISTURE WHILE COOKING. IF YOU COVER THE POT WITH A LID, THE STEAM THAT IS RELEASED FROM THE FOOD RECIRCULATES INTO THE SAUCE OR BRAISING LIQUID, AND DILUTES IT. THE PARCHMENT PAPER ALSO HELPS TO HOLD TOGETHER THE INGREDIENTS SO THERE IS LESS DAMAGE TO A FRAGILE PIECE OF MEAT OR VEGETABLE.

Bottom: Connie Green of Wine Country Forest, our mushroom forager

Merlot-Braised Duck Legs
with Wild Mushroom and Bacon Vol-au-Vent

Serves 4

A few years ago, we were asked to do a special dinner for Duckhorn Vineyards, just north of St. Helena. We took our cue from the name of the winery and its renowned Duckhorn Merlot, and came up with these succulent Merlot-braised duck legs. We like the earthy flavor that the root vegetable, salsify, brings to this dish. If it's not in season, or you can't find it, you can substitute baby turnip, rutabaga, or parsnip.

Braised Duck Legs

1 tablespoon vegetable oil

4 large duck legs, trimmed of extra fat
    and the skin scored

Salt and freshly ground black pepper

⅓ cup chopped onion

⅓ cup chopped carrot

¼ cup chopped celery

4 garlic cloves, smashed

¼ teaspoon chopped fresh thyme

1 tablespoon all-purpose flour

4 cups Merlot

2 cups game stock (page 209) or
    brown chicken stock (page 209)

⅓ cup chopped tomato

½ teaspoon black peppercorns

4 bay leaves

1 cup milk

3 cups water

4 salsify, about ¾ inch thick and 8 inches long,
    or 4 baby turnips, 2 inches in diameter

Wild Mushroom and Smoked Bacon Vol-au-Vent
    (page 11)

To BRAISE THE DUCK LEGS, preheat the oven to 325°. Heat the oil in a large ovenproof saucepan or Dutch oven over high heat. Season the duck legs with salt and pepper, then place in the pan, skin side down, and cook until golden brown on each side. Transfer the duck legs to a plate and keep warm. Discard all but 1 tablespoon of the fat in the pan. Add the onion, carrot, celery, garlic, and thyme, and sauté until browned. Add the flour and stir for 1 minute, then add the Merlot, stock, tomato, peppercorns, and bay leaves, and bring to a boil. Lightly season with salt and pepper; add the duck legs and decrease the heat to a simmer. Cut a circle of parchment paper that just fits inside the pan and a 1-inch hole in the center. Place the paper on the duck legs and braise in the oven for about 1 hour, or until tender. Carefully transfer the legs to a plate and keep warm. Strain the sauce through a fine-mesh sieve. Rinse the pan and return the sauce to the pan. Cook over high heat until reduced to 2 cups. Return the duck legs to the pan and keep warm.

Combine the milk and water in a medium saucepan and bring to a boil. Meanwhile, peel the salsify and cut it into 3-inch-long pieces. Put the salsify into the boiling milk and cook until tender, about 3 minutes. (If using turnips instead, cut each into 6 wedges and cook in boiling water, omitting the milk, until tender, about 3 minutes.) Drain and add to the hot mushroom cream sauce for the vol-au-vent.

TO SERVE, place a warm vol-au-vent on the upper side of each of 4 warmed plates and spoon the mushroom and salsify cream sauce into each vol-au-vent. Place a duck leg in front of each vol-au-vent and spoon the Merlot sauce over the duck legs. ♪♪♪

Roasted Rack of Lamb
with Ratatouille, Hummus, Tabbouleh, and Raita

Serves 4

This dish presents several of our favorite Middle Eastern flavors in a contemporary style that lets each element shine on its own alongside succulent roasted lamb chops. The ratatouille, hummus, tabbouleh, and raita are all better when made a day in advance. Ask your butcher to "french" the racks of lamb; this refers to trimming the meat and fat away from the top of the bones and trimming excess fat from the rack. This makes it easier to cut the rack into individual chops and makes for a neater, more refined presentation.

1 tablespoon olive oil

¼ teaspoon minced garlic

¼ teaspoon chopped fresh rosemary

2 racks of lamb (about 1½ pounds each before frenching, 1 pound each after)

Ratatouille

1 tablespoon olive oil

1 teaspoon chopped garlic

½ cup ½-inch-diced onion

⅓ cup ½-inch-diced red bell pepper

⅓ cup ½-inch-diced zucchini

½ cup ½-inch-diced eggplant

½ teaspoon chopped fresh basil

1 cup tomato concassée (page 199)

Salt and freshly ground black pepper to taste

Hummus

1 cup cooked garbanzo beans (if canned, rinse well)

⅓ cup tahini paste (mix the oil and paste together before using)

4 tablespoons freshly squeezed lemon juice

⅛ teaspoon minced garlic

⅓ cup hot water, plus 3 tablespoons more if needed

Salt to taste

Tabbouleh

2 tablespoons fine bulgur (cracked wheat)

½ cup chopped fresh flat-leaf parsley

2 tablespoons tomato concassée (page 199)

2 teaspoons chopped green onion

1 large fresh mint leaf, chopped

1 tablespoon freshly squeezed lemon juice

1 teaspoon extra virgin olive oil

Salt and freshly ground black pepper to taste

Raita

¼ hothouse cucumber, peeled, quartered lengthwise, and sliced ⅛ inch thick

⅔ cup plain yogurt

2 fresh mint leaves, chopped

⅛ teaspoon grated garlic

Salt and freshly ground black pepper to taste

Curry Oil

2 tablespoons vegetable oil

½ teaspoon curry powder

⅛ teaspoon paprika

2 tablespoons olive oil

Salt and freshly ground black pepper

2 popadams (lentil crackers), halved and deep-fried in 2 inches oil for 2 to 3 minutes or until golden, for garnish (optional)

8 fresh cilantro sprigs, for garnish

To marinate the lamb, combine the olive oil, garlic, and rosemary in a medium bowl. Rub evenly all over the lamb. Cover and refrigerate for 1 hour.

TO MAKE THE RATATOUILLE, preheat the oven to 350°. In an ovenproof saucepan or Dutch oven, heat the olive oil and garlic together over high heat and sauté the garlic just until it starts to brown. Add the onion and sauté until translucent, about

3 minutes. Add the bell pepper, zucchini, eggplant, and basil, and sauté for 3 minutes. Add the tomato concassée and bring to a boil, then remove from the heat. Season with salt and pepper. Cut a circle of parchment paper that fits just inside the pan and a 1-inch hole in the center. Place the paper on the ratatouille to cover, and cook in the oven for 20 minutes, or until all the vegetables are soft. Set aside.

TO MAKE THE HUMMUS, combine the beans, tahini, lemon juice, garlic, and ⅓ cup water in a food processor and process until smooth, adding more hot water if the hummus is too thick (it should be spoonable). Season with salt. Cover and refrigerate.

TO MAKE THE TABBOULEH, soak the bulgur in warm water for about 20 minutes, or until softened. Drain in a sieve and squeeze out the excess water by hand. Mix together the bulgur and all the remaining tabbouleh ingredients in a medium bowl. Cover and refrigerate.

TO MAKE THE RAITA, mix together all the ingredients in a small bowl. Cover and refrigerate.

TO MAKE THE CURRY OIL, combine all the ingredients in a very small sauté pan over low heat. Heat the mixture until warm, then let cool. Skim off the clear oil, discarding the spices left behind. Reserve the oil in a small bowl.

TO COOK THE RACK OF LAMB, preheat the oven to 450°. Heat the olive oil in a large oven-proof sauté pan or skillet over high heat until hot. Season the lamb with salt and pepper, then place in the pan, meat side down, and cook until golden brown, 2 to 3 minutes. Turn the racks over, put the pan in the oven, and roast for 6 to 8 minutes for medium rare, basting every 2 minutes. Remove the pan from the oven, cover loosely with aluminum foil, and let rest for 3 to 4 minutes.

Meanwhile, reheat the ratatouille.

TO SERVE, divide the hot ratatouille among 4 plates. Place a scoop of hummus above the ratatouille in the 12 o'clock position, then spoon the tabbouleh in the 4 o'clock position, and the raita in the 8 o'clock position. Cut both of the lamb racks into 6 chops. Place 3 chops on each plate between the condiments with the bone in the center of the plate. Drizzle the curry oil around the lamb. Place a popadam straight down in the hummus, with the edges being supported by the lamb chops. Place 2 cilantro sprigs in the middle of each plate.

 Letting Meat Rest

"RESTING" MEAT MEANS ALLOWING IT TO SIT FOR A FEW MINUTES IN A WARM (NOT HOT) PLACE AFTER IT HAS BEEN COOKED. WHEN MEAT COOKS, ITS JUICES FLOW TOWARD THE CENTER. IF YOU CUT A ROAST, FOR EXAMPLE, AS SOON AS IT COMES OUT OF THE OVEN, THE INTERIOR WILL BE MOIST, THE EXTERIOR WILL BE DRY, AND THE JUICES WILL RUN OUT EXCESSIVELY. RESTING THE COOKED MEAT ALLOWS IT TO REABSORB ITS JUICES EVENLY. REST STEAKS AND CHOPS FOR 5–10 MINUTES; REST ROASTS FOR 10–15 MINUTES, DEPENDING ON THEIR SIZE. WE'VE BUILT THIS TECHNIQUE INTO OUR RECIPES BY THE WAY WE ORGANIZED THE ORDER OF THE STEPS.

Pork Belly "Kakuni"
on Steamed Tatsoi with Wasabi

Serves 4 as main course, 8 as an appetizer

"Kakuni" means "square stew," a reference to the cube-shaped pieces of meat. If pork belly sounds a little intimidating, just remember, that's what bacon is. Like bacon, pork belly has a lot of fat, not all of which cooks away. But that's what gives this dish its incredible flavor—and why the portions are small. Pork belly can be hard to find; if your butcher doesn't carry it, try a Chinese market. Serve this dish with steamed rice.

1 (2½ pounds) piece of pork belly,
 about 5 by 6 inches and 1¼ inches thick
1 tablespoon peanut oil

Braising Liquid
4 cups water
⅓ cup sugar
⅔ cup soy sauce
2 cloves garlic, smashed
1 tablespoon sliced fresh ginger
1 star anise pod
1 teaspoon black peppercorns

1½ ounces shiitake mushrooms,
 cleaned and thinly sliced
½ cup julienned leek (white part only)
4 large tatsoi or small bok choy,
 about 5 inches long, halved lengthwise
2 teaspoons grated fresh wasabi, wasabi powder
 mixed with water, or prepared wasabi in a tube
1 teaspoon sesame seeds, toasted (page 68)

CUT THE PIECE OF PORK BELLY lengthwise into 2 pieces, each 5 inches by 3 inches and 1¼ inches thick. Heat the oil in a medium sauté pan or skillet over high heat until hot. Add the pork belly, skin side down, and cook, 3 to 4 minutes per side until golden brown.

Meanwhile, in an ovenproof saucepan or Dutch oven just large enough to hold both pieces of pork belly in a single layer, combine all the braising liquid ingredients and bring to a boil. Add the browned pork belly, making sure both pieces are covered with the braising liquid, and return to a boil. Skim off any foam that develops, decrease the heat to a simmer, cover, and cook for about 2 hours, or until tender. Gently transfer the pork belly to a baking dish. Strain the liquid, discarding the solids, and pour it over the pork belly. Let cool completely, then refrigerate for at least 3 hours or overnight.

WHEN READY TO SERVE, cut the pork belly into ½-inch squares, then combine them with 2 cups of the braising liquid, the shiitake mushrooms, and leek in a large saucepan. Bring to a boil, decrease the heat to a simmer, and cook until the pork belly is heated through, about 3 minutes.

Meanwhile, blanch the tatsoi (page 198).

TO SERVE, place 2 halves of the tatsoi in the center of each of 4 warmed shallow bowls. Divide the pork belly squares among the bowls, arranging them on top of the tatsoi. Spoon the sauce over the tatsoi and pork belly, then top each serving with a ½-teaspoon ball of wasabi. Sprinkle with sesame seeds.

Grilled Quail on Eggplant
and Goat Cheese "Lasagna" with Herbed Game Jus

Serves 4

Partially boned quail are easier to use and much easier to eat (in markets they are called "boneless" quail). We use the word "lasagna" to describe the layering of the ingredients in this dish, even though this version is made with eggplant, not pasta. You can also make it in a casserole to serve at a large party or buffet. It makes a nice main course for lunch and an ideal side dish with lamb or roast chicken.

1 tablespoon olive oil

¼ teaspoon minced garlic

¼ teaspoon chopped fresh rosemary

8 partially boned quail
(leg and wing bones left in)

Eggplant and Goat Cheese "Lasagna"

3 tablespoons salt

1 gallon water

2 large globe eggplants, peeled, stemmed,
and cut crosswise into ½-inch-thick disks

3 tablespoons extra virgin olive oil

Salt and freshly ground black pepper to taste

1 cup (8 ounces) fresh goat cheese without a rind

5 tablespoons plus 1 teaspoon dry bread crumbs

1 cup tomato sauce (page 20)

1 tablespoon fresh basil chiffonade

4 tablespoons freshly ground Parmesan cheese

Herbed Game Jus

1 cup game stock (page 209) or
brown chicken stock (page 209)

1 tablespoon chopped fresh flat-leaf parsley

2 tablespoons tomato concassée (page 199)

⅛ teaspoon chopped fresh thyme

½ teaspoon chopped fresh basil

2 tablespoons cold unsalted butter

Salt and freshly ground black pepper to taste

2 tablespoons unsalted butter

2 tablespoons chopped shallots

½ cup haricots verts, blanched for
1 minute (page 198)

½ cup yellow wax beans, blanched for
1½ minutes (page 198)

Salt and freshly ground black pepper to taste

4 fresh thyme sprigs, for garnish

To MARINATE THE QUAIL, combine the olive oil, garlic, and rosemary in a large mixing bowl. Add the quail and turn to coat well. Cover and refrigerate for at least 1 hour.

TO MAKE THE "LASAGNA," preheat the oven to 350°. In a large bowl, stir the salt into the 1 gallon of water. Soak the eggplant in the salted water for 15 to 20 minutes to remove the bitterness. Drain and pat dry with paper towels. Brush with the extra virgin olive oil and season lightly with salt and pepper. Place the eggplant on a baking sheet pan lined with parchment paper and bake for 10 to 12 minutes, or until soft and slightly browned. Set aside.

continued page 144

Grilled Quail on Eggplant, continued

Prepare a fire in a charcoal grill or preheat a gas grill.

Divide the goat cheese into 8 equal portions, roll each into a ball, and flatten into a disc about 3½ inches in diameter. Using four 4-inch-diameter by 2-inch-high soufflé (10-ounce) dishes, choose 4 of the largest eggplant discs and place one in the bottom of each dish. If the discs are not big enough to cover the bottom of the dish, cut a piece of eggplant to fit the space. Sprinkle each with 2 teaspoons bread crumbs and top with a goat cheese disc, 2 tablespoons tomato sauce, a pinch of basil, and 1½ teaspoons Parmesan cheese. Top with a disc of eggplant and repeat the layering process again, ending with eggplant on top. You should have 3 layers of eggplant and 2 layers of filling. Gently press evenly on the top of the eggplant to settle the layers and help them stick together.

Place the soufflé dishes on a baking sheet pan and bake for 20 to 25 minutes, or until hot. To test, insert a small knife into the center of one soufflé dish for 10 seconds, remove it, and carefully put it close to but not touching your lip; you should feel heat radiating from the knife. Set aside and keep warm.

MEANWHILE, TO GRILL THE QUAIL, season them with salt and pepper. Grill, breast side down, for 2 minutes, then turn at a 90-degree angle on the same side to make cross marks and cook 1 minute longer or until golden brown. Turn the quail over and grill for 2 minutes, or until golden brown. Transfer to a plate to rest and keep warm.

TO MAKE THE JUS, combine the stock, parsley, concassée, thyme, and basil in a medium saucepan and bring to a boil. Cook until reduced to ⅔ cup. Decrease the heat to low, add the butter, and incorporate it into the sauce by gently shaking the pan. Season with salt and pepper. Set aside and keep warm.

TO COOK THE BEANS, heat the butter and shallots in a small sauté pan over medium heat, and cook until the shallot is tender, about 1 minute. Add the beans and cook for about 2 minutes. Season with salt and pepper.

TO SERVE, carefully unmold the lasagnas by turning them upside down in the center of each of 4 warmed plates. Place 2 quail on top of each lasagna with the legs up. Top with the beans. Spoon the jus evenly over all and garnish with a thyme sprig.

Slow-Cooked Veal Cheeks
on Roasted Yukon Gold Potatoes with Salsa Verde

Serves 4

Fork-tender braised dishes like this one are what we think of as soul food, and not only is this one deeply satisfying, it's also very easy to make. Veal cheeks are among the most richly flavored meats, and cooked in this way, they taste like a world-class pot roast. Order them from a specialty butcher; veal cheeks are not as big as you may think, so figure about two to three pieces per person. Cook them the day before you serve them so the flavors can meld and develop overnight. This dish is also wonderful with mashed potatoes.

Marinade

2 cups dry red wine

4 cloves garlic, smashed

4 fresh thyme sprigs

1 cup coarsely chopped onion

½ cup coarsely chopped carrot

½ cup coarsely chopped celery

1 tablespoon black peppercorns

4 pounds veal cheeks, trimmed of extra fat
   and sinew (about 2 pounds trimmed)

Salt and freshly ground black pepper

¼ cup all-purpose flour

4 tablespoons unsalted butter

2 cups dry red wine

2 tablespoons Cognac

2 cups veal stock (page 207) or
   brown chicken stock (page 209)

2 tablespoons tomato paste

⅔ cup chopped tomatoes

½ cup sliced button mushrooms

Roasted Potatoes

1½ pounds Yukon Gold potatoes
   (about 2 inches in diameter), peeled

2 tablespoons olive oil

Salt and freshly ground white pepper

Salsa Verde

1 cup fresh flat-leaf parsley leaves

1 clove garlic, smashed

2 tablespoons capers

½ cup extra virgin olive oil

3 anchovy fillets

Pinch of crushed red pepper flakes

1 tablespoon freshly squeezed lemon juice

12 oven-dried tomatoes (page 199)

To MARINATE THE VEAL CHEEKS, combine all the marinade ingredients in a medium bowl. Add the veal cheeks, cover, and refrigerate overnight.

TO BRAISE THE VEAL CHEEKS, drain the cheeks and other solids in a colander set over a bowl for 1 hour. Reserve the liquid and solids separately. Preheat the oven to 350°. Pat the cheeks dry with paper towels. Season with salt and pepper, then dust with flour. Melt the butter in a large ovenproof sauté pan or skillet over high heat, add the cheeks, and sauté until golden brown on each side. Transfer to a dish. In the same pan, add the remaining reserved solids and sauté until caramelized, 3 to 4 minutes. Add the reserved liquid and bring to a boil. Skim off any foam that develops, then add the cheeks, red wine, and Cognac, and return to a boil. Add the stock, tomato paste, tomatoes, and mushrooms, and return to a boil. Lightly season with salt and pepper, and skim off any foam again. Cut a circle of parchment paper that just fits inside the pan and with a 1-inch hole in the center. Place the paper on the veal cheeks to cover and cook in the oven for 2 to 2½ hours, or until the veal cheeks are very tender.

Take the pan out of the oven (keep the oven on to cook the potatoes) and gently remove the cheeks; set aside and keep warm. Skim off any fat on the surface of the sauce, then puree the sauce in batches in a blender (be careful, as the sauce is very hot). Strain the sauce through a fine-mesh sieve. Rinse out the pan, return the sauce to the pan, and cook over high heat until reduced to about 3 cups. Return the cheeks to the pan and keep warm.

Meanwhile, to cook the potatoes, cut them into ½-inch-thick slices and toss them with the olive oil. Season with salt and pepper and spread them in a single layer on a rimmed baking sheet pan. Roast in the oven until soft, 20 to 25 minutes. Remove from the oven and keep warm.

TO MAKE THE SALSA VERDE, combine all the ingredients except the lemon juice in a blender and puree until smooth. Just before serving, whisk in the lemon juice.

TO SERVE, mound the potatoes in the center of each of 4 warmed plates. Place 3 oven-dried tomatoes around the potatoes, then divide the cheeks among the plates on top of the potatoes. Spoon the sauce over the veal cheeks, then drizzle about 1 tablespoon of the salsa verde around them. 🍃🍃🍃

Roasted Squab with Wild Mushroom Risotto and Pinot Noir Essence

Serves 4

We love squab! It has a sweet, gamy flavor that's almost liver-y in its richness. Because squab is very lean, it should be cooked medium rare to keep the meat from becoming dry. It pairs beautifully with the earthy flavor of mushrooms, and we often serve it over a mushroom risotto like this one. If juggling the elements of this dish seems a bit too complicated for you, you may want to skip the giblets and simply garnish the plate with the rosemary sprigs.

Pinot Noir Essence

2 cups Pinot Noir

1 cup veal stock (page 207) or
   brown chicken stock (page 209)

1 tablespoon cold unsalted butter

Salt and freshly ground black pepper to taste

Pinch of sugar (optional)

Wild Mushroom Risotto

4 tablespoons unsalted butter

6 ounces wild mushrooms such as chanterelles,
   porcini, black trumpets, or morels, cleaned
   and cut into bite-size pieces

1½ teaspoons minced garlic

Salt and freshly ground black pepper to taste

4 cups chicken stock (page 208)

½ cup chopped onion

1 cup arborio rice

¼ cup dry white wine

¼ cup freshly grated Parmesan cheese

¼ cup shredded fontina cheese

1 tablespoon chopped fresh flat-leaf parsley

 What is Deglazing? ————————

DEGLAZING REFERS TO THE PROCESS OF USING A LIQUID SUCH AS WINE, WATER, OR STOCK TO DISSOLVE FOOD PARTICLES AND DRIPPINGS LEFT IN A PAN AFTER SAUTÉING OR ROASTING. THE FLAVORFUL LIQUID IS THEN USED TO MAKE GRAVY OR SAUCE.

4 (1-pound) squabs, wingtips removed
   and giblets reserved

Salt and freshly ground black pepper

4 cloves garlic, smashed

8 (6 to 8-inch-long) fresh rosemary sprigs

6 tablespoons unsalted butter

16 baby Blue Lake green beans,
   blanched (page 198), for garnish

TO START THE PINOT NOIR ESSENCE, cook the Pinot Noir in a medium, heavy saucepan over high heat until reduced to 3 tablespoons. Add the veal stock, and cook until reduced to ⅓ cup. Set aside. Just before serving, reheat the Pinot Noir mixture and whisk in the butter. Season with salt and pepper. If the essence tastes too acidic, add a pinch of sugar to balance the acid; taste and adjust the seasoning again if necessary.

TO MAKE THE RISOTTO, melt 2 tablespoons of the butter in a medium sauté pan or skillet over high heat, add the mushrooms and sauté for 1 minute. Add ½ teaspoon of the garlic and sauté for another minute. Remove from heat, season with salt and pepper, and set aside.

In a medium saucepan, bring the stock to a simmer. In a large, heavy saucepan, melt 1 tablespoon of the butter over medium heat and sauté the onion and the remaining 1 teaspoon of garlic until translucent, about 4 minutes. Add the rice and sauté for about 3 minutes, stirring with a wooden spoon until the outside of the rice becomes opaque. Add the wine, and bring to a boil. Stir constantly, scraping the entire bottom of the pan until almost all the wine is absorbed by the rice. Season lightly with salt and pepper. Add 1 cup of the simmering stock. The rice should be kept at a fast simmer and not a boil as you stir and add stock. Stir the rice constantly until almost all the stock has been absorbed. Add ½ cup of the simmering stock and repeat the process until the rice is almost tender but still firm. Add ¼ cup stock and the sautéed wild mushrooms. Cook, stirring constantly, until the rice is tender but firm. Add the remaining 1 tablespoon butter, the Parmesan cheese, fontina cheese, and parsley, and mix well. Taste and adjust the seasoning if necessary. Remove from the heat.

MEANWHILE, TO ROAST THE SQUAB, preheat the oven to 450°. Season each squab inside and out with salt and pepper, then stuff with a garlic clove and rosemary sprig. Melt 4 tablespoons of the

butter in a large ovenproof sauté pan or skillet over medium heat. Place the squab in the pan, on one side, and cook until golden brown and crisp, about 2 minutes; turn the squab on the other side and cook about 2 minutes longer. Set the squab on their breasts and cook until golden brown, about 2 minutes. Set the squab on their backs and roast in the oven for 5 to 6 minutes, basting every 2 minutes until medium rare. To test for medium rare, insert a bamboo stick into the thickest part of the breast and hold for 5 seconds. Remove the stick and barely touch it with your lips. If the stick is warm, the squab is medium rare (flesh will be pink). Remove the pan from the oven, cover loosely with aluminum foil, and let rest for 3 to 4 minutes before cutting.

Season the reserved giblets with salt and pepper. Melt the remaining 2 tablespoons butter in a medium sauté pan or skillet over high heat until hot. Add the giblets and sauté for 2 to 3 minutes. Scrape the leaves from the bottom 3 inches of the rosemary sprigs and carefully skewer the giblets on the sprigs. Keep warm.

JUST BEFORE SERVING, cut off both whole legs (leg and thigh) at the back joint of each squab. Cut the whole breasts off including the wings and cut each breast in half horizontally (the 4 pieces should have the same shape, but 2 will have skin on them).

TO SERVE, divide the risotto among 4 warmed shallow bowls. Arrange the pieces of squab on top of the risotto in a circular pattern, alternating the different cuts. Pour off the fat from the pan the squab cooked in. Add 3 tablespoons water to the pan and bring to a boil, stirring to scrape up the browned bits from the bottom of the pan. Strain through a fine-mesh sieve and add to the Pinot Noir mixture. Finish the Pinot Noir essence. Drizzle the essence around the risotto, arrange the blanched green beans over the squab, and put the skewered giblets in the middle. *♪♪♪*

Grilled Natural-Fed Veal Chops
with Stir-Fried Japanese Eggplant in Miso Sauce

Serves 4

We like to use natural-fed veal because it's hormone-free and has more flavor than ordinary white veal. Don't be concerned if it has a little more color than what you may be used to, it's still wonderfully tender. The miso used in the stir-fry sauce is Hatcho miso, which comes from the Kyoto region of Japan and is very dark—almost black—and less salty than most other kinds. The technique of first deep-frying the vegetables before stir-frying them (sometimes referred to as "oil blanching") helps preserve their color and integrity during stir-frying. This step is a bit time-consuming, so if you want to omit it, increase the oil slightly when you stir-fry the vegetables and give them a little extra cooking time.

1 tablespoon peanut oil

2 teaspoons soy sauce

1 tablespoon mirin

4 (12-ounce) veal chops, each about 1 inch thick

Miso Sauce

1/4 teaspoon grated peeled fresh ginger

1/8 teaspoon grated garlic

1/4 cup Hatcho miso or dark miso

1 tablespoon soy sauce

2 tablespoons mirin

2 tablespoons firmly packed brown sugar

1 1/2 cups chicken stock (page 208)

2 teaspoons cornstarch mixed with 2 teaspoons water

1/2 teaspoon Asian (toasted) sesame oil

1 cup Japanese rice or short-grain rice

1 1/2 cups water

1 teaspoon sake (optional)

Vegetable oil for deep-frying

4 Japanese eggplants, stemmed and
　quartered lengthwise

1/2 onion, cut into 6 wedges

1/2 large red bell pepper, seeded and
　cut into 1/2-inch-wide strips

1/2 large yellow bell pepper, seeded and
　cut into 1/2-inch-wide strips

Salt and freshly ground black pepper

2 teaspoons peanut oil

2 uncored small bok choy, quartered lengthwise,
　blanched for 1 minute (page 198), and dried

Garnish

2 teaspoons 1/2-inch-long diagonally cut fresh chives

1/2 teaspoon sesame seeds, toasted (page 68)

1/8 teaspoon shichimi togarashi (Japanese red pepper
　mixture) or crushed red pepper flakes

4 fresh cilantro sprigs

TO MARINATE THE VEAL CHOPS, whisk together the peanut oil, soy sauce, and mirin in a small bowl. Put the chops in a glass baking dish and coat on both sides with the oil mixture. Cover and refrigerate for at least 3 hours or up to overnight, turning at least 3 times.

Preheat the oven to 350°. Prepare a fire in a charcoal grill or preheat a gas grill.

TO MAKE THE MISO SAUCE, combine the ginger, garlic, miso, soy sauce, mirin, and brown sugar in a small saucepan, then gradually whisk in the chicken stock and bring to a boil. Decrease the heat to a simmer and gradually whisk in the cornstarch mixture. Return to a boil, remove from the heat, whisk in the sesame oil, and set aside.

TO MAKE THE RICE, put the rice in a bowl and cover generously with room-temperature water. Stir the water and rice with your fingers, then drain. Repeat this process until the water runs clear, about 3 times. After the last rinse, drain the rice in a fine-mesh sieve and let drain for about 30 minutes. Transfer the rice to a small ovenproof saucepan. Add the 1½ cups water and sake, cover with a tight lid, and set over high heat until steam comes out from under the lid. Transfer the pan to the oven and bake for 12 minutes. Remove from the oven and let sit for 3 minutes. Remove the lid and gently fluff the rice with a damp wooden spatula. Put the lid back on and set aside. Keep warm. Decrease the oven temperature to 250°.

Meanwhile, to start the stir-fry, heat 3 inches of oil in a deep, heavy pot to 320°. Add the eggplant and deep-fry for 1 minute. Using a wire-mesh skimmer or slotted metal spoon, transfer to paper towels to drain. Repeat with the onions, then the bell peppers. Set aside.

TO COOK THE VEAL CHOPS, season them with salt and pepper. Grill for 5 to 7 minutes per side for medium rare. Or, heat a large skillet or grill pan over medium heat until very hot, and cook the chops for 5 to 7 minutes per side. Transfer the chops to the oven to keep warm.

To finish the stir-fry, heat a wok or heavy skillet over high heat until hot, then add the peanut oil and swirl the oil around in the wok to evenly distribute it. Add the fried vegetables and bok choy and stir-fry for 1 minute, then add one half of the miso sauce and bring to a boil. At the same time, heat the remaining miso sauce in the saucepan over medium-high heat until hot.

TO SERVE, mound the rice in the center on 4 warmed plates. Lay a veal chop on the rice with the bone sticking upwards. Place the vegetables on top of the veal chop (they can fall around the chop a little). Spoon the extra sauce around the rice. Sprinkle with the chives, sesame seeds, and shichimi togarashi, then top with a cilantro sprig. ♨♨♨

Testing for Doneness

THE EASIEST AND MOST RELIABLE WAY TO TEST MEAT AND POULTRY FOR DONENESS IS TO INSERT AN INSTANT-READ THERMOMETER, INTO THE THICKEST PART OF THE MEAT. WAIT 30 SECONDS BEFORE CHECKING THE TEMPERATURE. THE FOLLOWING CHART GIVES UNIVERSAL DONENESS TEMPERATURES FOR COOKING MEAT, AS WELL AS THE TEMPERATURE THE MEAT WILL REACH AFTER RESTING AND CURRENT USDA-RECOMMENDED COOKING TEMPERATURES, WHICH ARE HIGHER DUE TO CONCERNS ABOUT FOOD SAFETY. USE YOUR OWN JUDGMENT ABOUT WHICH IS RIGHT FOR YOU. YOU CAN ALSO GET A GENERAL IDEA ABOUT THE TEMPERATURE OF MEAT USING A METAL SKEWER, INSERTING IT FOR 30 SECONDS INTO THE THICKEST PART OF THE MEAT. REMOVE THE SKEWER AND CAREFULLY TOUCH IT TO YOUR BOTTOM LIP. IF IT IS SLIGHTLY WARM, THE MEAT IS RARE; IF IT'S WARM, THE MEAT IS MEDIUM; AND IF IT'S HOT, IT'S WELL DONE.

IN THIS CHART, "STEAK" AND "CHOP" REFER TO CUTS THAT ARE NO MORE THAN 1¼-INCH THICK. IF THE ONES YOU'RE COOKING ARE THICKER THAN THAT, USE THE TEMPERATURE FOR ROASTS.

Temp.	Cut	Remove	After resting	USDA
BLUE				
	STEAK	115–120	115–120	N/A
	CHOP	110–115	115–120	N/A
RARE				
	STEAK/CHOP	120–130	125–130	140
	ROAST	115–120	125–130	140
MEDIUM RARE				
	STEAK/CHOP	130–135	130–140	150
	ROAST	125–130	130–140	150
MEDIUM				
	STEAK/CHOP	135–150	140–150	160
	ROAST	130–140	140–150	160
MEDIUM WELL				
	STEAK/CHOP	150–165	155–165	170
	ROAST	145–155	150–165	170
WELL				
	ROAST	165	170–185	170

"WELL" IS ONLY RECOMMENDED FOR COOKING FATTY CUTS OF MEAT LIKE SPARERIBS, BOSTON BUTT, OR BRAISED DISHES. ANY STEAK OR CHOP COOKED PAST MEDIUM WELL WILL BE DRY AND TOUGH WITH MOST OF ITS JUICES COOKED OUT. MEDIUM WELL WILL SATISFY MOST PEOPLE WHO DO NOT WANT ANY RED IN THEIR MEAT.

Medallions of Lamb with Anchovy–Black Olive Sauce and Artichoke Fritters

Serves 4

"Anchovy with lamb?" That's the response we hear whenever we put this dish on the menu. So we're used to explaining that the anchovy here is not a dominant presence, but is used, in the manner of French and Italian cooking, to intensify and add depth to the sauce. With its bold flavors of kalamata olives, white wine, tomato, caper, lemon zest, and, yes, anchovy, this is a lusty sauce that's a great match for a big cabernet. You can find chickpea flour in health food stores and Indian markets. It makes a light, flavorful batter that gives fried foods a beautiful golden finish. If you don't want to deep-fry the artichokes, you can simply sauté them, or substitute another vegetable. It's fine to use store-bought tapenade in the sauce.

4 (8-ounce) lamb loins, trimmed of silver skin
1 tablespoon olive oil
Pinch of chopped fresh rosemary
Pinch of chopped fresh thyme

Chickpea Batter
1 cup chickpea flour
3 tablespoons cornstarch
1½ teaspoons baking powder
¼ teaspoon garlic powder
¼ teaspoon salt
Pinch of cayenne pepper
Pinch of freshly ground pepper
⅔ to 1 cup hot water

Anchovy–Black Olive Sauce
1 tablespoon unsalted butter
1 teaspoon minced garlic
⅓ cup dry white wine
1 cup veal stock (page 207) or
    brown chicken stock (page 209)
2 tablespoons tomato puree
Pinch of chopped fresh rosemary
2 teaspoons minced kalamata olives
⅛ teaspoon minced anchovy fillet
¼ teaspoon minced capers
Pinch of minced lemon zest
Salt and freshly ground black pepper to taste

Vegetable oil for deep-frying
4 large artichokes, cooked and quartered (page 196)
1 cup sliced onion

1 tablespoon unsalted butter
16 sugar snap peas, stemmed and blanched (page 198)
Salt and freshly ground white pepper to taste
2 cups hot mashed potatoes (page 206)
4 fresh rosemary sprigs, for garnish

To marinate the lamb loins, coat them with the olive oil and sprinkle on all sides with the herbs. Cover and refrigerate for at least 1 hour or up to overnight.

To make the batter, combine all the dry ingredients in a medium bowl. Whisk in ⅔ cup hot water until smooth, adding the remaining ⅓ cup water if necessary (the batter will be very thick). Set aside.

To start the sauce, in a medium saucepan heat the butter and garlic together over high heat and sauté the garlic until lightly browned. Add the wine and cook until reduced to 2 tablespoons. Add the stock, tomato puree, and rosemary, and cook until reduced to ⅔ cup. Set aside. Just before serving, heat the sauce and then whisk in the olives, anchovy, capers, and lemon zest. Season with salt and pepper (it won't need much salt, since the olives and anchovy are salty).

To cook the lamb loins, heat a large grill pan or sauté pan over high heat until very hot. Season the lamb with salt and pepper and grill for

2 minutes, then turn at a 45-degree angle on the same side to make cross marks and cook for 1 minute. Turn the loins over and cook 2 to 3 minutes longer for medium rare. Let rest in a warm place.

MEANWHILE, TO DEEP-FRY THE FRITTERS, preheat the oven to 250°. Heat 2 inches of oil in a deep, heavy pot to 350°. Add the artichokes and onion to the batter. Using a large spoon, scoop some of the batter, making sure you get some artichokes and onion in each scoop. Fry for about 3 minutes, or until crisp and golden brown. Using a slotted metal spoon, transfer to paper towels to drain, then transfer to a baking sheet pan and keep warm in the oven. Repeat with the remaining batter.

Melt the butter in a medium sauté pan or skillet over high heat, add the snap peas, and sauté for about 1 minute, or until heated through. Season with salt and pepper.

TO SERVE, finish the sauce. Put ½ cup of mashed potatoes in the center of each of 4 warmed plates. Put one fourth of the fritters on the upper side of the mashed potatoes. Spoon the sauce on the lower side of the mashed potatoes and arrange the snap peas between the fritters and the sauce. Cut each lamb loin into 5 medallions and place them on the sauce in a semicircle. Garnish with the fresh rosemary sprigs. 🎵🎵

DESSERTS

Almond Pithiviers
with Meyer Lemon Ice Cream and Huckleberry Sauce

This recipe makes six individual pastries, but plan on serving only four, because there's no better breakfast than warm leftover almond pithiviers with coffee. At the restaurant, if there are any left over in the morning, whoever shows up first gets a special treat.

Almond Pithiviers
24 ounces puff pastry, made with unsalted butter
1¼ cups almond cream (page 213)
1 egg yolk
½ teaspoon water
3 teaspoons sugar

Huckleberry Sauce
2 cups fresh or frozen huckleberries
   or blueberries, stemmed
¼ cup sugar
Finely minced zest of ½ lemon
2 tablespoons freshly squeezed lemon juice
1 teaspoon cornstarch mixed with 1 tablespoon water

1½ pints Meyer lemon ice cream (page 215)

To MAKE THE PITHIVIERS, roll out the puff pastry on a floured board to a ³⁄₁₆-inch thickness. Cut out twelve 4½-inch rounds. Mound 3 tablespoons of the almond cream in the center of each of 6 rounds, leaving a ¾-inch border. Brush the border of the puff pastry right up to the almond cream with the egg yolk. Be careful not to let any of the egg yolk run down the sides of the pastry, or it will not rise in that spot.

Gently lay the other 6 rounds on top of those with the almond cream, lining them up perfectly with the one below to keep it round. Using the dull side of a 3-inch-diameter pastry cutter or a drinking glass, center it over the top of each round and gently push down to seal the almond cream in. (Don't push so hard that the dough gets cut through, but hard enough to make a seal.) Along the outside edges that you have just created, run your finger over the dough to carefully seal the puff pastry out to the side.

Using a sharp paring knife, decorate the top by making shallow cuts in the top of each pithiviers, being very careful not to cut all the way through, to create crescent shapes. Next, cut the edges of the dough into a scallop pattern to make the pithiviers look like a flower (don't cut closer to the almond cream seal than ¼ inch). Add the water to the remaining egg yolk to make an egg wash and brush the tops of the pithiviers completely with the egg wash. Be careful not to let any egg wash run down the sides, or it will act like glue and the pithiviers won't rise in that spot. Transfer the pastries to a baking sheet pan lined with parchment paper and

refrigerate until the dough is set, at least 45 minutes. Preheat the oven to 375°. Remove the pithiviers from the refrigerator and sprinkle each with ½ teaspoon sugar. Bake for 10 minutes, then rotate the pan, decrease the oven temperature to 325°, and bake for 15 to 20 minutes longer, or until golden brown. Let cool slightly on the pan if serving immediately; cool completely if serving later.

MEANWHILE, TO MAKE THE SAUCE, combine the huckleberries, sugar, lemon zest, and lemon juice in a nonreactive saucepan over low heat. Cook until the sugar dissolves and the huckleberries release some of their juice, about 5 minutes. Since each batch of berries will have a different sweetness, you may need to adjust the sugar or lemon juice to your taste. Whisk in one half of the cornstarch mixture, return to a simmer, and cook until thickened, about 1 minute. Check the consistency of the sauce; if necessary, add more of the cornstarch mixture and return to a simmer. Set aside and keep warm.

TO SERVE, if necessary, warm the pithiviers in a preheated 350° oven for 5 minutes. On each of 6 plates, pool some huckleberry sauce at the top of the plate. Place a pithiviers on the other side, then place a small scoop of ice cream in the center of the huckleberry sauce.

Apple Tart
with Vanilla Ice Cream and Caramel Sauce

Throughout the year, we top this rustic-elegant puff pastry tart with almost any fruit that's in season. The almond cream seems to go with everything—peaches, apricots, pears, and even figs. The only fruit we wouldn't recommend are berries. The tart can also be made in a single, larger circle, rectangle, or square.

4 Granny Smith apples, peeled and cored

1 tablespoon freshly squeezed lemon juice

3 tablespoons unsalted butter

⅓ cup plus 1 teaspoon sugar

12 ounces puff pastry, made with unsalted butter

¾ cup almond cream (page 213)

1 egg yolk

1 teaspoon water

1 cup caramel sauce (page 213)

1 pint vanilla bean ice cream (page 214)

CUT EACH APPLE INTO 8 WEDGES and toss them in the lemon juice so they won't brown. In a large sauté pan or skillet over high heat, melt the butter, then add the ⅓ cup sugar and let cook until it starts to caramelize. Add the apples and cook, tossing frequently so that the caramel doesn't burn, for about 5 minutes, or until the apples are an even caramel color but have not cooked through. (The apples are going to cook again, so they need to retain some body.) Transfer the apples to a rimmed baking sheet pan and let cool. Transfer to a bowl and refrigerate for at least 2 hours.

Meanwhile, on a lightly floured board, roll the puff pastry out into a 10-inch square that is ⅛-inch thick. Let rest in the refrigerator for 2 hours. To assemble the tarts, cut out four 5-inch-diameter rounds from the puff pastry sheet and place them on a baking sheet pan lined with parchment paper. Mound about 3 tablespoons almond cream into the center of each round. Overlap 8 apple wedges in a circle on the almond cream, leaving a ½-inch border. (The apples will be closer together toward the center and farther apart

on the edges.) Be careful not to let any of the juice from the apples drip down the sides, or the pastry will not rise in that spot. Refrigerate the tarts for about 15 minutes to set the pastry again.

Preheat the oven to 400°. In a small bowl, combine the egg yolk with the water to make an egg wash. Brush the ½-inch border of each tart with the egg wash, taking care not to let the egg wash run down the sides, or the pastry will not rise in that spot. Sprinkle the edges of each tart with ¼ teaspoon sugar. Place the tarts in the upper third of the oven, decrease the oven temperature to 350°, and bake for 25 to 30 minutes, or until the tarts are browned on the bottom. Let cool slightly on a wire rack if serving immediately; let cool completely to serve later.

TO SERVE, if necessary, warm the apple tarts in a preheated 350° oven for about 5 minutes. Place 1 tart in the center of each of 4 warmed plates and spoon the caramel sauce around the outside of the tart. Put a scoop of vanilla bean ice cream on top of each apple tart. ♪♪

Fig Fritters
with Ginger Ice Cream

The light fritter batter we use here is a lot like tempura batter, and must be very cold when fried so that it takes on a lacy texture. Use very ripe figs, which will develop an intense, jam-like quality when they're cooked. The batter also works well with other soft fruits, such as bananas, peach wedges or apricots filled with almond cream (page 213).

Vegetable oil for deep-frying
8 large ripe brown turkey figs or
   16 black mission figs at room temperature

Fritter Batter
1 cup pastry flour
⅓ cup rice flour
⅓ cup sugar
Pinch of salt
1 egg
1 cup ice water

1 pint ginger ice cream (page 214)
¼ cup julienned crystallized ginger

HEAT 3 INCHES OF OIL IN A DEEP, heavy pot to 350°. Wipe the figs with a damp cloth to remove any dust.

TO MAKE THE BATTER, combine all the ingredients in a large bowl, and whisk until just blended; don't worry if there are a few lumps. Dip 2 figs into the batter and immediately deep-fry until golden brown, about 2 minutes. Using a wire-mesh skimmer or slotted metal spoon, transfer to paper towels to drain. Repeat with the remaining figs.

TO SERVE, put a small scoop of ginger ice cream in the center of each bowl. Cut the turkey figs in half and place 4 halves around the ice cream. If using black mission figs, keep them whole and put 4 around each serving of ice cream. Sprinkle the crystallized ginger on the ice cream.

Chocolate Truffle Cake
with Espresso Ice Cream

Makes 6 cakes

The fad of melting chocolate cake is all around us. We like the idea, but we were determined to create a version that didn't rely on half-cooked batter for the melting effect. The trick we came up with is inserting a truffle into the batter just before baking. These cakes can be baked ahead of time and reheated, and the truffles can be made in advance and frozen. The truffle recipe actually makes 8 truffles, so the cook gets a nice little bonus. To serve the truffles on their own, you can double or triple the recipe, using any alcohol you prefer in place of the Cognac; dust the finished truffles with cocoa powder.

Chocolate Truffles

3½ ounces bittersweet chocolate, chopped

1 teaspoon egg yolk

3 tablespoons heavy cream

4 teaspoons Cognac

Chocolate Tuiles

4 tablespoons unsalted butter

2 tablespoons honey

6 tablespoons pastry flour

½ cup confectioners' sugar

2 tablespoons cocoa

1 egg white

Cake

6 ounces bittersweet chocolate,
   coarsely chopped

6 tablespoons unsalted butter

3 eggs

¾ cup sugar

5 tablespoons plus 1½ teaspoons cornstarch,
   sifted

1 pint espresso ice cream (page 214)

2 tablespoons unsweetened cocoa powder
   for dusting

To MAKE THE TRUFFLES, melt the chocolate in a double boiler over barely simmering water (don't let the water touch the bottom of the bowl or the chocolate will get too hot). Remove from the heat and add the egg yolk. Whisk until just blended, being careful not to overmix, or the chocolate will become stiff and hard to work with. In a small saucepan, bring the cream and the Cognac just to a boil (if your saucepan is shallow, the Cognac may ignite; just blow it out carefully). Whisk the cream mixture into the chocolate mixture until smooth and shiny. Transfer the mixture to a smaller, deeper bowl. Refrigerate for at least 4 hours or overnight.

Using a large melon baller, form ¾-inch balls from the truffle mixture. Flatten the shaped truffles slightly into fat discs and refrigerate until ready to use. (The truffle mixture will keep, refrigerated, for up to 2 weeks.)

TO MAKE THE TUILES, in a heavy-duty mixer fitted with the paddle attachment, cream the butter and honey until light and fluffy. Meanwhile, sift together the flour, sugar, and cocoa, then add it to the butter mixture while mixing on a very slow speed. Once incorporated, add the egg white and mix to form a batter. Transfer to a smaller container and refrigerate until cold.

Preheat the oven to 350°. Make a template to spread the batter over. To do this, find a large

continued page 162

disposable plastic container approximately ¹/₃₂ inch thick. Cut a large square piece from the side of the container, then cut out a triangle shape from the square that measures about 5 inches long on two sides and 3 inches long on the third side. If the plastic starts to roll up too much, plunge it into a pot of boiling water for a minute to soften, then press between 2 pans with some weight. Use a silpat-lined baking sheet pan, or butter and flour a baking sheet pan. Lay the template down at one end and with a small spatula spread the batter to evenly fill the form. Make one final pass with the spatula in a single gesture to smooth. Carefully remove the template and repeat as many times as will fit on the baking pan. Make a couple extra in case some break (they are very fragile). Bake for 15 to 20 minutes, or until they are very dark brown and a little toasted at the edges. While they are baking, lay out a few large cans (about 6 inches in diameter) and brace them with a utensil so they don't roll. Remove the tuiles from the oven and immediately drape them over the cans so that they make a delicate arch. They form quickly. Remove from the cans and repeat until all the tuiles are formed. Let cool completely. Store in an airtight container.

TO PREPARE THE CAKES, preheat the oven to 325°. Melt the chocolate and butter together in a double boiler over barely simmering water (don't let the water touch the bottom of the bowl, or the chocolate will get too hot). Meanwhile, whisk together the eggs and sugar in a large bowl until the sugar dissolves. Whisk the chocolate mixture into the egg mixture, then gently whisk in the cornstarch just until blended. (Don't overwhisk, as too much air in the batter can cause the cakes to rise and fall too sharply.)

Line a baking sheet pan with parchment paper. Place six 4-inch-diameter by 1-inch-high rings or 8-ounce soufflé dishes on the paper. Divide two thirds of the batter among the 6 rings or dishes. Drop a truffle into the center of each ring or dish and cover with the remaining batter until the mold is three fourths full. Bake for 10 to 15 minutes, or until the tops have formed crusts but the cakes are still soft to the touch. If serving the cakes immediately, let them cool slightly so that the rings can be easily removed by pushing the cakes up through the rings (this will keep the edges of the cakes from being broken off). If using soufflé dishes, leave the cakes in the dishes. Let cool completely if serving later.

TO SERVE, if necessary, reheat the cakes in a preheated 350° oven for 3 minutes. Carefully remove the rings and transfer the cakes to one side of each serving plate using a solid metal spatula. (If using soufflé dishes, serve the cakes in the dishes.) Place a tuile, short side on the plate, against the cake (the arched point should be over the cake). Place a small scoop of espresso ice cream on the other side of the tuile. ♫

Stone-Fruit Crostata

A crostata is a rustic Italian tart that's loosely formed and thin-crusted—a style of pastry that lends itself particularly well to stone fruit, which has a lot of flavor and doesn't need to cook for a long time. We like to use the somewhat vague term "stone fruit" on our menu, because it gives us the freedom to use the best peaches, nectarines, apricots, or plums we can get our hands on that day. For a while, we called this dessert the "tart of tonight," but we got tired of all the jokes about who that might be.

Crostata Dough

2 cups pastry flour

¼ cup sugar

½ teaspoon ground cinnamon

¼ teaspoon ground nutmeg

1 cup (2 sticks) cold unsalted butter,
   cut into ½-inch cubes

¼ cup ice water

4 cups peaches, nectarines, apricots, or plums,
   peeled if desired, pitted, and cut into ½-inch slices

¼ to ⅓ cup sugar

1 tablespoon freshly squeezed lemon juice

1 egg yolk

1 teaspoon water

1 cup heavy cream

¼ cup vanilla sugar (page 216),
   or ¼ cup confectioners' sugar and ½ teaspoon
   vanilla extract

½ cup crème fraîche or sour cream

To make the dough, combine the flour, sugar, cinnamon, and nutmeg in a food processor and pulse for 1 minute. Add the butter and pulse until a pea-size crumb is formed. With the machine running, add the ice water all at once. Process just until the dough comes together. Remove from the bowl and form into a 1-inch-thick disc on a lightly floured board. Wrap the dough in plastic wrap and refrigerate for at least 1 hour or up to 3 days.

When the dough is ready to roll, combine the fruit with sugar to taste in a large bowl. Add the lemon juice.

To prepare the crostatas, roll the dough out on a lightly floured board to a ⅜-inch thickness. Cut out four 7-inch-diameter rounds. Place the rounds on a baking sheet pan lined with parchment paper. Refrigerate for 10 to 15 minutes, or until the dough is pliable but not so soft that it tears easily. Quickly divide the fruit mixture into mounds among the 4 rounds, leaving a 1½-inch border on each round. Carefully fold the border over the fruit, pleating as you go; the center of the tarts will be open. In a small bowl, combine the egg yolk and water to make an egg wash. Lightly brush the folded-over dough edge with the egg wash. Return the crostatas to the refrigerator for about 15 minutes. Meanwhile, preheat the oven to 350°. Bake the crostatas for 55 to 65 minutes, or until the dough is golden brown on top and on the bottom.

To serve, in a deep bowl beat the cream with the vanilla sugar. Fold in the crème fraîche. Place each warm crostata on a plate and spoon a large dollop of the cream mixture against the crostata, just overlapping it slightly. ♪♪♪

Lemon Crème Brûlée

Serves 6

Crème brûlée can sometimes be cloyingly sweet and rich. We think adding the lemon is the perfect way to keep things in balance. If Meyer lemons are in season, by all means use them; they add a lovely delicate flavor and perfume. Because these individual custards are made in shallow gratin dishes, it's impossible to caramelize them under a broiler, because the cream would break before the sugar caramelizes. Instead, use a small, hand-held blowtorch, available in most hardware stores and generally not very expensive. Once you get over any initial jitters about working with a flame, you'll discover how much easier this method is.

3¾ cups heavy cream

Grated zest of 2 lemons

1 vanilla bean, split lengthwise

¾ cup plus 3 tablespoons sugar

9 egg yolks

1 egg

¾ cup freshly squeezed lemon juice

PREHEAT THE OVEN to 275°. In a large saucepan, combine the cream and lemon zest. Scrape the seeds from the vanilla bean and add them to the pan, along with the bean. Bring just to a boil, then remove from the heat.

IN A LARGE BOWL, whisk together ½ cup plus 1 tablespoon sugar, the egg yolks, egg, and lemon juice. Whisk in the cream mixture quickly so that the egg does not cook. Strain through a fine-mesh sieve. Rinse and air-dry the vanilla bean, which can be used to make vanilla sugar (page 216). Divide the mixture among six 10-ounce gratin dishes. Place the gratin dishes in a roasting pan. Slide the middle rack partially out of the oven and place the pan on the rack. Pour boiling water into the pan to a depth of about ¼ inch, making sure none of the water comes over the sides and into the dishes. Very carefully slide the rack back into the oven. Bake for 15 to 17 minutes, or until the custard jiggles slightly when you tap a dish but is set. Carefully remove the gratin dishes from the water and let cool. Refrigerate for at least 3 hours.

TO SERVE, sprinkle 1 tablespoon sugar evenly over 1 custard. Use a hand-held blowtorch to evenly caramelize the sugar, keeping the blowtorch moving and about 3 inches above the dish (do only one dish at a time, or the sugar will liquefy while waiting on the custard). Repeat with the remaining custards.

Carrying a Torch

A TORCH IS A WONDERFULLY USEFUL KITCHEN TOOL. WE PARTICULARLY LIKE IT FOR CARAMELIZING THE TOP OF CRÈME BRÛLÉE (A BROILER WILL OFTEN HEAT AND BREAK THE CUSTARD BEFORE THE SUGAR CARAMELIZES). ADJUST THE FLAME TO LOW AND POINT IT TOWARD THE CENTER OF THE CUSTARD, HOLDING IT ABOUT 3 INCHES AWAY. KEEP THE FLAME MOVING TO AVOID BURNING ONE SPOT. IF THE CARAMELIZING STARTS HAPPENING TOO FAST, JUST PULL THE FLAME AWAY AND IT WILL STOP INSTANTLY. A TORCH IS ALSO HANDY FOR UNMOLDING ANYTHING MADE WITH BUTTER OR OIL, SUCH AS CAKES, TARTES, AND TERRINES. JUST RUN THE TORCH QUICKLY AROUND THE OUTSIDE OF THE MOLD. AFTER A FEW PASSES THE MOLD SHOULD SLIP OFF EASILY.

Macadamia Nut Tart
with Banana-Rum Ice Cream

Serves 4

Rather than make classic desserts that people have all kinds preconceived opinions about, we prefer to create surprising variations of our own. This macadamia nut tart, for example, is our take on pecan pie. At Spago, we used to call the filling "Buddy Pie" after those little pecan pies you can buy in convenience stores, and at Terra, we still call the filling "Buddy Mix." You can make this tart with any nut you like. You can also make a single 8-inch tart but you'll need to double the filling. We generally make a few extra of these. Hiro always steals one, saying it's his "energy bar."

pâte sucrée (page 216)

Filling

⅓ cup firmly packed brown sugar

⅓ cup sugar

¾ cup light corn syrup

1 egg

2 egg yolks

2 tablespoons Myers's Rum

2 tablespoons unsalted butter

¼ vanilla bean, split lengthwise,
   or 1 teaspoon vanilla extract

1½ cups whole macadamia nuts, lightly toasted
   (page 68)

1 pint banana-rum ice cream (page 214)

4 tablespoons unsweetened shredded coconut,
   toasted (page 68 (optional)

REMOVE THE DOUGH FROM THE REFRIGERATOR and let set for 5 minutes, or until the dough gives to a light pressure. On a lightly floured board, roll the pâte sucrée out to a ³/₁₆-inch thickness and cut out 4 rounds about 5½ inches in diameter. Place four 4-inch metal rings on a small baking sheet pan lined with parchment paper. Line the rings with the pastry rounds. Trim off the excess dough around the top. Refrigerate the lined rings for at least 30 minutes or up to 1 day if covered.

TO MAKE THE FILLING, in a medium bowl combine all the ingredients except the butter and vanilla and whisk until smooth. In a small sauté pan or skillet over medium heat, melt the butter with the vanilla bean, if using, until foamy, then allow the butter to continue cooking until it becomes a dark brown; the butter should not burn but have a toasted-nut aroma. Strain the browned butter through a fine-mesh sieve into the sugar mixture and whisk together. Add the vanilla extract, if using.

TO PREPARE THE TARTS, preheat the oven to 350°. Fill each tart with toasted macadamia nuts, packing them tightly but keeping them in one layer. Spoon the filling over the macadamia nuts to just the top of the nuts. Put the tarts in the oven and bake for 25 to 30 minutes, or until the filling rises and is golden brown. (If the tarts are over-cooked they will be hard, and if undercooked they will be mushy. The perfect tart is chewy inside and a little crisp outside.) Let the tarts cool for 10 minutes on the pan before removing the rings. To remove the rings, run a small knife around the inside of each ring, then gently lift the ring off. Serve now, or let cool completely to serve later.

TO SERVE, if necessary, reheat the tarts in a preheated 350° oven for 5 minutes. Place each tart on a dinner plate and top with a scoop of banana-rum ice cream. Sprinkle each plate and tart with the toasted coconut. ♪♪

Tart of Fromage Blanc
with Caramelized Pears

Serves 6

This is essentially a sophisticated cheesecake with a surprising depth of flavor and much less sweetness than the traditional kind. We use the term fromage blanc loosely to refer to a young white cheese—in this case, fresh goat cheese, the kind without a rind, usually sold in cylinders. We love Laura Chenel's Chef's Chevre, which is packed in 5-pound containers; the same cheese is also sold in 4- and 8-ounce logs. (Laura Chenel products are available in gourmet markets or through mail order.) You can also use this recipe to make a single 8-inch tart in a tart ring. For a tart of this size, you'll need to double the cooking time.

Pâte sucrée (page 216)

Caramelized Pears
2 Bosc pears, peeled, halved, and cored
1½ teaspoons unsalted butter
1 tablespoon sugar

Filling
½ cup plus 1 tablespoon (4½ ounces) natural
  (without gelatin) cream cheese at room temperature
½ cup plus 1 tablespoon (4½ ounces) fresh mild
  goat cheese without a rind, at room temperature
1 cup sour cream
½ cup sugar
2 eggs
Juice of ½ lemon

6 tablespoons sugar

Garnish
1 cup crème anglaise (page 214)
6 strawberries, quartered
24 fresh mint leaves

PREHEAT THE OVEN to 350°. Remove the dough from the refrigerator and let sit for 5 minutes, or until the dough gives to a light pressure. On a lightly floured board, roll the dough out to a ¼-inch thickness. Cut into six 4-inch rounds. Transfer the rounds to a baking sheet lined with parchment paper and, using a fork, pierce the dough all over so it will not rise when baked. Refrigerate for 15 minutes. Bake for about 10 minutes, or until light brown.

TO MAKE THE PEARS, cut them lengthwise into ¼-inch-thick slices. In a large sauté pan or skillet, melt the butter over high heat. Add the sugar and cook until it starts to caramelize, then add the pear slices and sauté until the pears are golden brown. Transfer the pears to a rimmed baking sheet pan and refrigerate.

TO MAKE THE FILLING, combine all the ingredients in a medium bowl and beat with an electric mixer just until smooth. (Don't beat longer, because you don't want to add air to the filling.)

TO PREPARE THE TARTS, preheat the oven to 250°. Line a baking sheet pan with parchment paper. Tear 6 pieces of aluminum foil into 5-inch squares. Put six 4-inch-diameter by 1-inch-tall pastry rings on the foil and press the foil up around the outside of the ring to keep the cheesecake mixture inside the ring. Arrange the rings on the sheet. Put a baked pastry round in each ring.

Arrange one sixth of the caramelized pears in a single layer on each round; don't overlap them. Pour the cheese mixture over the pears to the top of the ring. Bake until barely set, 30 to 40 minutes (the filling should jiggle slightly but not be browned or cracking). Let cool to room temperature, then refrigerate for at least 2 hours or up to 1 day.

Remove the pastry rings and foil by running a small knife around the inside of each ring, then gently lift the ring off. Evenly sprinkle each tart with 1 tablespoon of sugar just before caramelizing. Using a hand-held blowtorch, evenly caramelize the sugar, keeping the blowtorch moving and about 3 inches above the tart (do only one tart at a time, or the sugar will liquefy while waiting on the custard). Repeat with the remaining tarts. Or, sprinkle the sugar on 1 tart and place it on a baking sheet pan small enough to rotate under the broiler. Place the sheet under a preheated broiler 2 inches from the heat source and broil, rotating as necessary, until the sugar melts and evenly caramelizes. Repeat with the remaining tarts.

TO SERVE, place 1 tart in the center of each of 6 plates. Surround each tart with a ring of crème anglaise. Arrange 4 strawberry pieces around each tart and a mint leaf between each strawberry. ♪♪♪

Chocolate Bread Pudding
with Sun-Dried Cherries and Crème Fraîche

Makes 6 individual puddings or 1 large pudding

This dish shows up on our menu almost every winter, and we think it's the perfect way to end a meal on a cold night. When the first order of the evening is brought to the table, the aroma of warm chocolate fills the dining room, and everyone starts looking around to see where it's coming from. Within a few minutes, we usually sell several more orders. We serve the pudding in individual soufflé dishes, but you can also make it in a large dish and serve it family-style, passing the crème fraiche in a bowl on the side.

½ cup sun-dried cherries

⅓ cup Cognac

8 ounces bittersweet chocolate, chopped

3 eggs

1 cup heavy cream

½ cup sour cream

½ cup sugar

⅛ teaspoon ground cinnamon

1 teaspoon vanilla extract

3 cups ½-inch-cubed sourdough bâtard without crusts, dried overnight

Garnish

1 cup crème fraîche or sour cream

1 tablespoon confectioners' sugar, sifted

6 fresh mint sprigs

COMBINE THE CHERRIES AND COGNAC and soak for at least 2 hours, or preferably overnight.

Melt the chocolate in a double boiler over barely simmering water (don't let the water touch the bottom of the bowl or the chocolate will get too hot). Remove from the heat and let the chocolate stand over the warm water until ready to use.

In a large bowl, whisk together the eggs, cream, sour cream, sugar, cinnamon, and vanilla extract. Quickly whisk in the melted chocolate. If the chocolate does not completely melt, place the bowl back over the hot water and whisk gently until the chocolate is completely incorporated. Fold in the bread cubes, cherries, and Cognac. Let sit in a warm place until the bread absorbs the custard, 1 to 2 hours. To test, break a bread cube in half; there should be no white showing. Spoon the mixture into six 10-ounce soufflé dishes or one 8-cup dish. Clean the edges well with a damp towel to remove any chocolate drips.

Preheat the oven to 350°. Put the dish(es) in a roasting pan. Slide the middle rack partially out of the oven, and place the pan on the rack. Pour boiling water into the pan to a depth of about 1 inch, making sure none of the water comes over the sides and into the dishes. Very carefully slide the rack back into the oven. Bake for 35 to 40 minutes, or until the puddings are puffed and set to the touch. Remove the dishes from the water and let cool slightly if serving immediately; let cool completely to serve later.

TO SERVE, if necessary, cover each cooled pudding with a square of aluminum foil and reheat in a preheated 350° oven for 6 to 8 minutes. To test, stick a small knife into the center of a pudding for 30 seconds, then remove it and feel the blade; if it's not warm, keep the puddings in the oven a little longer. Whisk the confectioners' sugar into the crème fraîche or sour cream. Put a large dollop on top of each of the puddings and garnish with a sprig of mint.

To Melt Chocolate

CUT OR BREAK THE CHOCOLATE INTO SMALL PIECES. SET A HEATPROOF BOWL OVER A POT OF BARELY SIMMERING WATER, AND PLACE CHOCOLATE IN THE BOWL. DON'T LET THE WATER TOUCH THE BOTTOM OF THE BOWL, OR THE CHOCOLATE WILL GET TOO HOT, AND DON'T LET THE WATER BOIL, BECAUSE STEAM OR WATER MIGHT GET INTO IT, GIVING IT A GRITTY TEXTURE. IF THIS HAPPENS, THERE IS NO WAY TO FIX THE CHOCOLATE; FOR SOME BAKED DISHES, YOU CAN STILL USE IT, BUT FOR ICE CREAM OR TRUFFLES, YOU'LL NEED TO START AGAIN WITH FRESH CHOCOLATE.

Mixed Berry Shortcake
with Caramel Sauce

These are old-fashioned, biscuit-style shortcakes with a rich, creamy flavor and lovely crumbly texture. Strawberries are, of course, the traditional filling choice, but any combination of ripe, flavorful berries is wonderful served this way, as are peaches, apricots, or nectarines. For a refreshing change of pace, try using vanilla bean ice cream (page 214) instead of whipped cream.

Shortcake

1 cup pastry flour

3 tablespoons sugar

1½ teaspoons baking powder

Pinch of salt

4½ tablespoons cold unsalted butter, cut into small cubes

6 to 8 tablespoons heavy cream, plus 2 teaspoons for brushing

½ teaspoon vanilla extract

Fruit Compote

4 cups mixed fresh berries, hulled strawberries, raspberries, or blackberries

¼ cup sugar

1 teaspoon freshly squeezed lemon juice

1 cup heavy cream

¼ cup vanilla sugar (page 216)

½ cup crème frâiche or sour cream

1 tablespoon powdered sugar

½ cup warm caramel sauce (page 213)

To make the shortcakes, combine the pastry flour, sugar, baking powder, and salt in a heavy-duty mixer fitted with the paddle attachment and blend together on low speed. Add the butter and mix until crumbly. Combine 6 tablespoons of the cream with the vanilla, add it to the flour mixture, and mix until the dough just comes together; if necessary, add up to 2 more tablespoons cream and mix just for a second. (Depending on the temperature of the kitchen and the ingredients, the flour will absorb more or less of the cream.)

Or, to mix by hand, combine the dry ingredients on a work surface. Add the butter and toss to coat with the flour mixture. Using your fingers, a pastry blender, or 2 knives, cut the butter and flour mixture until crumbly. (Work quickly if using your fingers, so the heat of your hands doesn't melt the butter.) Make a well in the center of the mixture and add the liquid ingredients. Carefully begin drawing in the flour mixture from the sides, taking care not to let the cream run out, and stir gently until the liquid is absorbed. Do not knead the dough; it should be slightly crumbly.

On a lightly floured board, pat the dough into a disc about 1 inch thick. With a 2½-inch biscuit cutter, cut out 4 shortcakes. Re-form the scraps, pat them out, and cut an extra one (a treat for the cook). Put the shortcakes 3 inches apart on a small baking sheet pan lined with parchment paper and refrigerate until solid, about 30 minutes.

Preheat the oven to 350°. Brush each shortcake

with a little cream and bake for 45 to 50 minutes, or until golden brown on the top and bottom. (If the shortcakes flatten out too much, there was too much cream in the dough; next time add a little bit less.) Let cool slightly if serving immediately; let cool completely to serve later.

TO START THE FRUIT COMPOTE, puree 1 cup of the fruit in a blender with the sugar and lemon juice. Strain through a fine-mesh sieve and set aside.

TO SERVE, in a deep bowl, beat the cream with the vanilla sugar until stiff peaks form. Add the crème fraîche, and mix until blended. If necessary, warm the shortcakes in a preheated 325° oven for 3 to 4 minutes. Cut each one in half crosswise and place the bottoms in the center of 4 dinner plates. Dust the top halves with the powdered sugar and set aside. In a large bowl, combine the fruit puree and the remaining fruit and stir to coat. Spoon the fruit over the shortcake bottoms, then put a large dollop of the cream mixture on top of the berries. Drizzle the warm caramel sauce all around and over the fruit and cream, then put the top halves of the shortcakes on top of the cream. 🍃🍃🍃

Orange Risotto in Brandy Snaps
with Passion Fruit Sauce

Serves 6

When they see this dessert on our menu, people often ask us, "Risotto for dessert?" We just smile, and say, "Trust us." If you're a fan of rice pudding, imagine how wonderful arborio rice can be when it's sweetened, chilled, and lightened with whipped cream. We pipe this heavenly filling into crispy, lacy brandy snap cylinders, cannoli-style, and add a little tangy passion fruit sauce—the perfect balance to the sweetness of the risotto. The brandy snaps take a little practice and patience. If you're frustrated by forming them into cylinders, simply drape the warm rounds over a small bowl or cup, letting them cool in a bowl shape. Then spoon the risotto into the brandy snap bowl—not quite as dramatic, but much easier. If fresh passion fruit are unavailable, you can find passion fruit purée in some markets. If you use it, don't add the water, and taste it to determine if you need to add the sugar.

Brandy Snaps

½ cup (1 stick) unsalted butter

½ cup light corn syrup

½ cup firmly packed brown sugar

1 teaspoon vanilla extract

½ cup plus 2 tablespoons pastry flour

1 teaspoon ground ginger

Orange Risotto

1½ cups half-and-half

Finely minced zest of 1 orange

½ vanilla bean, split lengthwise

¼ cup sugar

¼ cup arborio rice

1 egg yolk

2 tablespoons unsalted butter

1 teaspoon plain gelatin

2 tablespoons Cointreau or other orange liqueur
  or orange juice

Passion Fruit Sauce

6 passion fruit

1 tablespoon granulated sugar

2 tablespoons water

1½ cups whipped heavy cream

24 orange segments

12 grapefruit segments

12 fresh mint sprigs

To make the brandy snaps, combine the butter, corn syrup, brown sugar, and vanilla in a medium saucepan over medium heat, and cook until the brown sugar is completely dissolved and the mixture is smooth. Remove the pan from the heat, add the flour and ginger, and whisk to incorporate. Strain through a medium-mesh sieve into a metal bowl and let cool. Cover and refrigerate for at least 6 hours or up to 1 week.

Preheat the oven to 325°. Heat a baking sheet pan in the oven until hot. Have a broom handle ready or a ½-inch-diameter piece of PVC pipe to wrap the brandy snaps around.

Roll 2 small pieces of dough into 2 balls the size of a quarter, and place them far apart on the hot pan. Put the pan in the oven and bake for about 12 minutes, or until the snaps have a honeycomb texture and are slightly dark; if you take them out too early, they won't hold their shape when cool. Remove the pan from the oven and wait 1 minute to allow the snaps to set (take care not to touch the snaps, as they are extremely hot). Using a spatula and working very quickly, lift up the edge of a snap; if it comes up, then quickly wrap the snap around the broom handle or pipe with the textured side facing out, to form a cylinder. Quickly repeat with the other snaps. While they

continued page 176

are cooling, put 2 more balls of dough in the oven and repeat the process. Carefully take the cooked snaps off the mold before the next ones come out of the oven and place on a flat tray to cool completely. Store in an airtight container. It is a good idea to make extra; they are so fragile you will probably break some either in forming or filling. (The broken pieces taste great with ice cream.)

TO MAKE THE ORANGE RISOTTO, preheat the oven to 350°. In a small ovenproof saucepan, bring the half-and-half, orange zest, vanilla bean, and sugar to a boil. Add the arborio rice, stir, and return to a boil. Cover the pan and put it in the oven. Cook for 30 to 40 minutes, or until the half-and-half is absorbed and the rice is tender. (If it starts to get a little color, that's all right.) Remove the rice from the oven and quickly stir in the egg yolk, then the butter. Dissolve the gelatin in the liqueur; this should take about 10 minutes, or until the gelatin blooms and becomes soft. Stir the gelatin into the rice mixture, then put the rice into a heat-resistant container and let cool completely. Place a piece of plastic wrap directly on the rice and refrigerate until chilled or for up to 2 days.

TO PREPARE THE SAUCE, cut each passion fruit in half and scoop all the pulp and seeds into a small bowl. Add the sugar and water, and mix well. Strain through a fine-mesh sieve into a bowl, pressing against the pulp and seeds with the back of a large spoon to extract all the juice. Save some seeds for garnish. Refrigerate.

Transfer the rice to a large bowl and, with a wooden spoon, fold in ½ cup of the whipped cream. The mixture will be stiff, so mix it thoroughly so there are no small lumps. Fold in ½ to 1 cup more of the whipped cream, depending on how thick the rice is, so it is light but not runny. Half-fill a pastry bag (without a tip) with the risotto. Insert it in one end of a brandy snap and fill

halfway, then finish filling from the other side. Or, if you don't have a pastry bag, use a heavy-duty self-sealing plastic bag and cut off one corner. Be gentle, as the brandy snaps break easily.

TO SERVE, make a ring of passion fruit sauce on each of the 6 plates, and sprinkle the reserved seeds on the sauce, leaving the center open. In a pattern that resembles a butterfly, alternate 3 orange and 2 grapefruit segments on either side of the plates. Place a brandy snap in the center of the plate, vertical to the fruit. Garnish with a mint sprig on either side of the brandy snap. 🎵🎵

Cooking with Vanilla Beans

TO GET THE MOST FLAVOR OUT OF A VANILLA BEAN, CUT OFF ONE END, THEN, STARTING JUST BELOW THE OTHER END, USE THE TIP OF A SHARP PARING KNIFE TO CUT ALL THE WAY THROUGH THE BEAN LENGTHWISE. SCRAPE OUT THE SEEDS AND ADD THEM TO WHATEVER YOU'RE MAKING, ALONG WITH THE BEAN. IF YOU'RE USING ONLY HALF A BEAN, FIRST CUT INTO TWO PIECES, THEN SPLIT ONE PIECE AND PROCEED AS DIRECTED ABOVE. ONCE YOU'VE USED THE BEAN, RINSE IT OFF, LET IT DRY, AND SAVE IT TO MAKE VANILLA SUGAR (PAGE 216).

Pavlova
with Frozen Yogurt and Tropical Fruit Salad

Makes 6

Although Australia has long claimed this meringue-and-fruit confection as its national dessert, recent evidence indicates that it may have been invented in New Zealand. Whatever the case, everyone agrees that it was created in honor of the famous Russian ballerina, Anna Pavlova. Lissa's grandmother used to make an enormous pavlova filled with vanilla ice cream and strawberries for every special occasion. Our low-fat version is made with homemade frozen yogurt, which is wonderfully creamy and nothing like the store-bought version.

Frozen Yogurt

2 cups low-fat plain yogurt

¼ cup sugar

½ teaspoon vanilla extract

Pavlova

3 tablespoons cornstarch

2 tablespoons plus ¾ cup sugar

1 teaspoon distilled white vinegar

½ teaspoon vanilla extract

3 ounces egg whites (about 2½ egg whites),
    at room temperature

1/8 teaspoon cream of tartar

1 mango, peeled, pitted, and cut into 1/4-inch dice

½ small pineapple, peeled, cored, and cut
    into ¼-inch dice

1 kiwi, peeled and cut into ¼-inch dice

¾ cup Passion Fruit Sauce (page 174)

To PREPARE THE FROZEN YOGURT, whisk together all the ingredients in a medium bowl. Freeze in an ice cream maker according to the manufacturer's instructions. Transfer to an airtight container and freeze for 2 hours or until completely frozen.

TO MAKE THE PAVLOVA, preheat the oven to 250°. Line a baking sheet pan with parchment paper and dust it with ½ tablespoon of the cornstarch. Mix 1 tablespoon of the sugar with the remaining 2½ tablespoons cornstarch and set aside. Mix together the vinegar and vanilla; set aside. In a heavy-duty mixer fitted with the whip attachment, beat the egg whites and cream of tartar on a low speed until foamy, then increase speed to medium and beat until soft peaks form. Turn the speed up to high and slowly beat in the remaining 1 tablespoon plus ¾ cup sugar, no more than 2 tablespoons at a time, waiting a minute between additions, until stiff, glossy peaks form, about 7 minutes. (Take your time with this step, as it is what makes a great pavlova.) Quickly add the cornstarch and sugar mixture and beat on low speed. Beat in the vinegar and vanilla. Dip a 4-ounce ice cream scoop in room-temperature water, then scoop mounds of egg white onto the parchment paper about 3 inches apart. Make a small indentation in the top of each meringue with the back of the scoop. (This will help to hold the frozen yogurt.) Place the pan in the oven and immediately decrease the oven temperature to 225°. Bake for 1¼ hours, or until the meringues are dry and hollow-sounding when you tap them on the bottom. They will color very slightly but should be close to white; if they start to brown, decrease the oven temperature to 200°.

TO SERVE, combine all the fruit in a medium bowl and gently mix. Place a pavlova in the middle of each of 6 plates and place a small scoop of the frozen yogurt on the top of each pavlova. Divide the fruit salad evenly around each pavlova, then drizzle about 2 tablespoons passion fruit sauce around and a little over the top. 🌙🌙

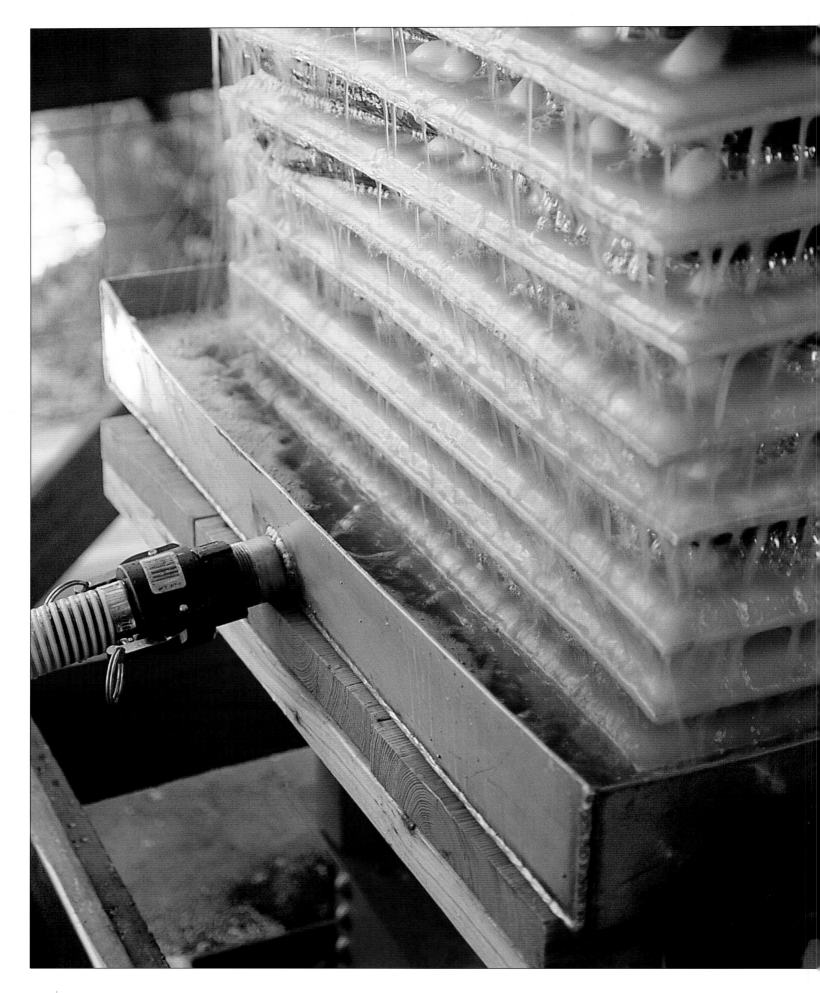

Upper left: Tim crushing apples at the Apple Farm   Upper right: Karen bottling boiled cider

Baked Apple Crème Brûleé
with Maple Cookies

This sensational dessert takes "comfort food" to a whole new level—especially because it was inspired by our friend Jerry Comfort, the executive chef of Beringer Winery. We saw a picture of his baked apples filled with crème brûlée and loved the idea, so we created our own version. (This is not uncommon for chefs. Speaking for ourselves, rather than get bogged down in reading recipes, we prefer to just look at a picture and then make up what we think the dish should be. This can be interesting when the picture is not altogether clear, and we wind up creating an appetizer from what was originally a dessert!) Wrapping the apples in cheesecloth helps them hold their shape as they bake. "Boiled cider" is made by boiling down apple cider to a sweet, thick syrup. It's available, along with many other wonderful apple products, from The Apple Farm in Philo, California (707-895-2333).

Maple Cookies (makes 24)

1 cup (2 sticks) unsalted butter

½ cup sugar

1 egg yolk

2 tablespoons pure maple syrup

½ teaspoon vanilla extract

1¾ cups pastry flour

1¼ cups finely chopped pecans

Baked Apples

6 Granny Smith, Fuji, Jonagold, or Macintosh apples

6 tablespoons firmly packed brown sugar

3 teaspoons unsalted butter

3 cups hot water

3 tablespoons granulated sugar

Crème Brûleé Custard

4 egg yolks

2 tablespoons maple sugar or brown sugar, sifted

1¼ cups heavy cream

½ vanilla bean, split lengthwise

1 tablespoon unsalted butter

3 tablespoons sugar

2 tablespoons boiled cider or maple syrup (optional)

To make the cookies, combine the butter and sugar in a heavy-duty mixer fitted with the paddle attachment and cream until light and fluffy. Add the egg yolk and beat until fully incorporated, then beat in the maple syrup and vanilla extract. Gradually stir in the flour and pecans with a wooden spoon. Divide the dough onto 2 large pieces of plastic wrap, fold the wrap over the dough, and flatten into a ½-inch-thick disk. Refrigerate for at least 3 hours or up to 2 days.

Preheat the oven to 325°. Remove one of the dough packets from the refrigerator and let it sit for about 5 minutes, until it gives a little when you push on it. Don't let the dough get too warm, or it will be difficult to roll out and will absorb more flour and make a tougher cookie. On a lightly floured board, roll the dough out with a floured rolling pin, turning the dough a little with each roll and lightly dusting the board and the dough with flour as needed. Roll to a ⅛-inch thickness. Using a maple leaf cutter, cut out as many cookies as possible from the dough, dipping the cutter in flour periodically. Transfer the cookies to a baking sheet pan lined with parchment paper. Gather the scraps, refrigerate them for a few minutes, reroll, and cut out. Place the cookies in the refrigerator for 15 minutes to let the dough set up again. Repeat with the second packet of cookie dough.

continued page 182

Bake the cookies for 15 minutes, or until lightly browned. Let cool on the pans. Store in an airtight container.

TO PREPARE THE APPLES, preheat the oven to 325°. Cut down at an angle from the shoulder of the apple to the stem and remove the top to make a 2-inch opening. With a melon baller, remove the core and some of the inside of the apple (be sure to get the hard part around the seeds), but don't cut through the bottom. Put 1 tablespoon brown sugar in each apple and top with ½ teaspoon butter. Wrap each apple in a piece of cheesecloth, then tie at the top with string. Place the apples in a deep baking dish just big enough to hold the apples closely packed. Mix the water and granulated sugar and pour it into the baking dish. Cover the pan with aluminum foil and bake for 25 to 35 minutes, or until the apples are tender but before the skin begins to loosen. Remove the pan from the oven. Let cool, then remove the apples from the liquid and remove the cheesecloth.

TO MAKE THE CUSTARD, combine the egg yolks and maple sugar in a double boiler over barely simmering water (don't let the water touch the bottom of the bowl, or the custard will burn), and whisk vigorously until the mixture becomes a pale yellow and is very thick. This will take about 8 minutes; be careful that the egg doesn't cook around the edges of the pan. Meanwhile, pour the cream into a medium saucepan. Scrape the seeds from the vanilla bean and add them to the pan, along with the bean. Bring just to a boil, then remove from the heat. Whisk the cream mixture into the yolk mixture and continue to cook over the barely simmering water, whisking periodically and checking the water level occasionally, until the custard is thick enough to coat the back of a spoon and won't drip off, 25 to 30 minutes. Remove from the heat and whisk in the butter, then strain through a fine-mesh sieve. Rinse and air-dry the vanilla bean, which can be used to make vanilla sugar (page 213). Let cool, then refrigerate until cold, about 2 hours.

TO SERVE, preheat the broiler for 15 minutes. Carefully fill each apple with the custard, then add more to slightly round the top of the custard. Sprinkle each custard with 1½ teaspoons sugar just before caramelizing. Use a hand-held blowtorch to evenly caramelize the sugar, keeping the blowtorch moving and about 3 inches above the apple (do only one apple at a time, or the sugar will liquefy while waiting on the custard). Repeat with the remaining apples. Or, sprinkle the sugar over 1 apple and place it under the broiler, 2 inches from the heat source, and broil until the sugar caramelizes, moving as needed to brown evenly. Repeat with the remaining apples. Place each apple in a shallow bowl, drizzle the boiled cider around each apple, and place 2 maple cookies on the side. 🎵

To Prevent Food from Oxidizing

SOME FOODS (SUCH AS BANANAS, APPLES, POTATOES, AND ARTICHOKES) CHANGE COLOR RAPIDLY WHEN CUT AND EXPOSED TO AIR. AN ENZYME IN THE FOOD REACTS WITH OXYGEN TO PRODUCE A CHEMICAL COMPOUND THAT GIVES THE EXPOSED SURFACES A GRAY, BLACK, OR BROWN COLOR. THIS REACTION HAPPENS FASTEST AT 100°. TO SLOW THE PROCESS DOWN, KEEP CUT FOODS IN THE REFRIGERATOR OR IN COLD WATER, OR RUB THE CUT SURFACES WITH LEMON JUICE.

Sunshine Cake
with Cashew Brittle and Peach Compote

Makes 12 individual cakes or 1 large cake

Sunshine cake is an old-fashioned dessert that is similar to angel food cake but is made with egg yolks, which give it its sunny color. Our version is based on one that became a San Francisco tradition at Blum's. We make individual cakes, but it's easier to make a single large one in an angel food cake pan. The brittle keeps for a couple of days in an airtight container, and makes a nice little treat on its own. Try making slightly larger pieces and dipping them halfway in melted dark chocolate. Let the chocolate set and serve the brittle with coffee.

Sunshine Cake

1¼ cups pastry flour

1¼ cups sugar

6 egg yolks

¼ cup water

1 tablespoon freshly squeezed lemon juice

1 teaspoon vanilla extract

8 egg whites

1 teaspoon cream of tartar

½ teaspoon salt

Cashew Brittle

1 cup sugar

¼ cup strongly brewed coffee or espresso

3 tablespoons corn syrup

2 teaspoon baking soda

1 cup toasted cashews

6 peaches, peeled and pitted

⅓ cup sugar

1 teaspoon freshly squeezed lemon juice

2 cups heavy cream, beaten to soft peaks
  and sweetened to taste

1 (½-pint) basket fresh raspberries

To PREPARE THE CAKES, preheat the oven to 325°. Sift the pastry flour into a large bowl. Add ¾ cup of the sugar, the egg yolks, water, lemon juice, and vanilla extract. Whisk until smooth.

In a large bowl, beat the egg whites, cream of tartar, and salt until soft peaks form. Gradually beat in the remaining ½ cup sugar until stiff, glossy peaks form. Fold one half of the egg whites into the yolk mixture, then fold in the other half. Fill twelve individual (3-inch) angel food pans or one 10-inch angel food cake pan three fourths full with the batter. Bake for 40 minutes, or until the cake is browned and springy to the touch. Let cool slightly. To unmold, run a knife around the inside of the cake pan and invert it. Let cool completely.

TO PREPARE THE BRITTLE, combine the sugar, coffee, and corn syrup in a medium, heavy saucepan. Bring to a boil and cook until the syrup registers 310° on a candy thermometer. Remove from the heat and carefully stir in the baking soda and cashews with a wooden spoon; the baking soda will cause the candy to foam up. Don't overmix, but once fully incorporated quickly pour the brittle out onto a baking sheet pan, and spread it into a flat layer. Set aside to cool completely. Put the brittle in a heavy plastic bag and break it up into small pieces with a rolling pin or mallet.

Cut the peaches into eighths and toss with the sugar and lemon juice. Let sit for 2 hours.

TO SERVE, place an individual cake or a generous slice on a plate. Place the equivalent of half a peach and some of the juice from the peaches along one side, then spoon the whipped cream partially over the cake. Top the whipped cream with the cashew brittle and scatter raspberries around the peaches. ♪♪♪

Sautéed Strawberries in Cabernet Sauvignon and Black Pepper Sauce with Vanilla Bean Ice Cream

Serves 4

We love this dessert. It's like an adult ice cream sundae. Berries marry beautifully with the flavor of Cabernet Sauvignon, and the pepper adds an intriguing edge. You'll find lots of other uses for the light, slightly sweet, crunchy sacristan cookies. We serve this dessert in oversized martini glasses, with a single cookie perched across the rim. It makes a stunning presentation. This is an easy dessert for a big group, as the recipe can be increased many times.

Sacristan Cookies

10 ounces puff pastry, made with unsalted butter

½ cup clear crystallized sugar or sanding sugar

½ cup finely chopped slivered almonds

1 egg yolk

1 tablespoon water

Cabernet Sauvignon and Black Pepper Sauce

1¼ cups good-quality Cabernet Sauvignon

6 tablespoons sugar

1/4 vanilla bean, halved lengthwise

1½ teaspoons cornstarch

Small pinch of freshly ground black pepper
   (about one turn of a peppermill)

Confectioners' sugar for dusting

1 tablespoon unsalted butter

4 cups fresh strawberries, hulled and cut lengthwise
   into quarters or halves, depending on size

1 pint vanilla bean ice cream (page 214)

6 fresh mint sprigs

To make the cookies, preheat the oven to 350°. On a lightly floured board, roll the puff pastry out into a 12 by 5-inch rectangle that is ⅛ inch thick. Refrigerate until solid, about 30 minutes. Line a small baking sheet pan with parchment paper and set aside. In a small bowl, mix together the crystallized sugar and almonds. In another small bowl, combine the egg yolk and water to make an egg wash. Brush the egg wash over the puff pastry. Sprinkle half of the sugar mixture evenly over the pastry, then turn the pastry over and brush the second side with the egg wash. Sprinkle with the remaining sugar mixture. Trim the edges of the dough so that it is squared, then cut it lengthwise into ½-inch strips to make 8 or 9 cookies. Take each strip and gently twist from both ends about 4 times. If the dough has gotten too soft to twist, refrigerate for 20 minutes and try again. Place the sticks on the parchment paper as straight as possible and 1½ inches apart. Refrigerate until the dough sets, about 30 minutes. Bake for 20 minutes, or until puffed and golden brown. Transfer to a rack to cool.

To make the sauce, combine 1 cup of the Cabernet Sauvignon, the sugar, and vanilla bean in a medium saucepan. Bring to a boil. Meanwhile, in a small bowl, whisk the remaining ¼ cup Cabernet Sauvignon with the cornstarch. Remove the sauce from the heat and whisk in the cornstarch mixture. Return the pan to high heat and bring back just to a boil, then set aside. (The pepper should be added at the last minute.)

To serve, dust the sacristans with confectioners' sugar. Melt the butter in a medium sauté pan or skillet over medium heat, add the strawberries, and sauté for 1 minute. Add the sauce and the pepper. Bring just to a boil, then remove from the heat. Divide the strawberries and sauce among 4 serving bowls. Place a small scoop of ice cream in the center of each bowl. Lay 1 cookie across each bowl. Put a sprig of mint next to the ice cream. ♪♪

Chocolate Mousseline on Pecan Sablé
with Coffee Granité

Serves 6

This is an intensely chocolaty dessert—a sexy bittersweet chocolate mousse on a pecan shortbread crust alongside an icy coffee granité, which cuts through the richness of the chocolate. We make these in individual baking rings, but you can also make the mousseline in an 8-inch tart ring and then cut portions at the table using a very hot knife. The granité makes a nice warm-weather dessert on its own, served with a scoop of vanilla ice cream or a dollop of whipped cream. The sablés are great as cookies on their own; just roll them out and cut into smaller circles, then bake.

Coffee Granité

1½ cups strong brewed coffee
  or espresso
1/4 cup sugar

Pecan Sablés

½ cup (1 stick) cold unsalted butter
¼ cup firmly packed brown sugar
2¼ teaspoons bourbon
¼ teaspoon vanilla extract
1 cup sifted pastry flour
½ cup pecan pieces, toasted and
  finely chopped (page 68)

Chocolate Mousselines

6 ounces bittersweet chocolate, chopped
5 tablespoons unsalted butter
½ cup heavy cream
4 eggs, separated
3 tablespoons sugar

¼ cup unsweetened cocoa powder
  for dusting

To MAKE THE GRANITÉ, mix together the coffee and sugar in a shallow glass baking dish and freeze for 1 hour. Stir with a fork, then freeze for another hour. Stir again, then let freeze completely. Just before serving, take the dish out of the freezer and scrape the granité with a fork to make small crystals of coffee. If it starts to melt, return the dish to the freezer for 30 minutes, then continue the process. Coffee granité has the texture of shaved ice or snow cone ice. Once it is prepared, return it to the freezer until serving.

TO MAKE THE SABLÉS, combine the butter and brown sugar in a large bowl. Using an electric mixer, beat until light and fluffy, then beat in the bourbon and vanilla extract. Gradually stir in the flour and the pecans with a wooden spoon just until blended. Transfer the dough to a large sheet of plastic wrap. Form the dough into a 1-inch thick disc, wrap in the plastic wrap, and refrigerate for at least 1 hour or up to 2 days.

Preheat the oven to 325°. Remove the dough from the refrigerator and gently roll it out on a lightly floured board to a ¼-inch thickness. Cut it into six 4-inch rounds. Using a fork, pierce the dough all over so that it does not rise or bubble when baked. Place the rounds on a baking sheet pan lined with parchment paper and refrigerate until firm, about 15 minutes. Bake the sablés until golden brown, 12 to 15 minutes. Remove from the oven and let cool completely.

TO MAKE THE MOUSSELINES, melt the chocolate and butter together in a double boiler over barely simmering water (don't let the water touch the bottom of the bowl, or the chocolate will get too hot). Remove from the heat and let stand over the warm water until ready to use.

IN A DEEP BOWL, beat the heavy cream until soft peaks form. Refrigerate until needed.

Combine the egg yolks and 1½ tablespoons of the sugar in a bowl. Using an electric mixer, beat until a slowly dissolving ribbon forms on the surface when the beaters are lifted. Quickly whisk the egg mixture into the chocolate mixture (you need to be quick so that the egg doesn't cook before it incorporates into the chocolate mixture). Whisk the chocolate mixture over barely simmering water until the mixture becomes very shiny and slides down the sides of the bowl, about 2 minutes (don't let the water touch the bottom of the bowl, or the chocolate mixture will get too hot). Remove from the heat and let sit for a couple of minutes to cool slightly. Gently fold the whipped cream into the chocolate mixture and set aside.

Meanwhile, clean the mixing bowl and beaters for the electric mixer and dry well. Put the egg whites in the bowl and beat until soft peaks form. Gradually beat in the remaining 1½ tablespoons of sugar until stiff, glossy peaks form. Fold the whites into the chocolate mixture until blended.

TO ASSEMBLE, take six 4-inch-diameter by 1-inch-high baking rings and place one around each sablé on the baking sheet. Fill each ring with chocolate mousseline. Scrape across the top of the rings with a long metal spatula or the back of a knife to level the mousseline. Refrigerate until set, at least 1 hour, or as long as 24 hours.

TO SERVE, remove the rings by running a knife that has been warmed in hot water around the inside of each ring, then gently lift the ring off. Put the cocoa powder in a small sieve and dust each chocolate mousseline evenly. Place 1 mousseline to one side of each of 6 dinner plates. Fill a very small bowl or an espresso cup with about ¼ cup coffee granité and place on each plate. ♪♪

Tiramisù

Serves 4

We've had Tiramisù on our menu almost since the day we opened. Every so often, we contemplate taking it off, but then we think about all those "regulars" who love it and order it every time they come in. And so it stays, like a faithful old friend. Our version is made with the traditional ingredients—espresso-soaked ladyfingers layered with a sweet mascarpone cheese filling—but the presentation is unique. We make round ladyfingers and pipe on the filling, layering everything in individual Japanese bowls. An easier approach is to double this recipe and make it in an 8-inch square cake pan, then simply spoon out portions at the table. We prefer regular espresso to decaf; it's your choice. Espresso extract can be purchased at cookware shops. Make the ladyfingers a day or two ahead of time, so they dry out a bit.

Ladyfingers (makes 25)
2½ eggs, separated
5 tablespoons sugar
¼ teaspoon vanilla extract
½ cup pastry flour
Confectioners' sugar for dusting

Mascarpone Cream Filling
1 egg yolk
1 cup (8 ounces) mascarpone cheese
3 tablespoons sugar
½ cup heavy cream

Soaking Liquid
1 cup brewed espresso
¼ cup espresso extract, or 2 tablespoons instant espresso
¼ cup Myer's rum

1 tablespoon cocoa powder for dusting

To PREPARE THE LADYFINGERS, preheat the oven to 325°. Line 2 baking sheet pans with parchment paper and set aside.

In a very clean mixer, beat the egg yolks with 2 tablespoons of the sugar on high speed until a slowly dissolving ribbon forms on the surface when the beaters are lifted. Transfer to a large bowl. Rinse and dry the beaters.

In another large bowl, beat the egg whites until soft peaks form. Gradually beat in the remaining 3 tablespoons sugar slowly until stiff, glossy peaks form. Fold one half of the egg whites into the yolk mixture. Add the vanilla extract and the remaining egg whites and fold in. Sift the flour over the egg batter and fold it in just until blended; don't overfold, or the batter will lose too much volume.

Fill a pastry bag fitted with a No. 4 (large-size round) tip half full with the batter and carefully pipe the batter onto the prepared pans into rounds about 1½ inches in diameter and spaced about 1 inch apart. Dust the ladyfingers with confectioners' sugar. Put this pan in the oven and repeat with the second pan. After each pan cooks for 5 minutes, turn it front to back so the ladyfingers will cook evenly. Bake each panful for a total of about 15 minutes, or until light brown. Remove from the oven and let cool completely on the pan before removing from the parchment paper.

TO MAKE THE FILLING, in a deep bowl beat together the egg yolk, mascarpone, and sugar, then gradually beat in the cream until very thick; don't overbeat, or the filling will break and look curdled. Cover and refrigerate.

TO MAKE THE SOAKING LIQUID, mix together all the ingredients in a large bowl.

TO ASSEMBLE THE TIRAMISÙ, choose 4 beautiful 2-cup bowls, each about 4 inches in diameter and 4 inches high. Fill a pastry bag fitted with a No. 3 (medium-size round) tip with half of the mascarpone filling. Working in batches, soak the ladyfingers in the espresso mixture, working quickly so that they don't get too wet (they should be soaked through with liquid but not soggy; squeeze one to see if it is soaked through). Place them on a plate as you finish soaking them. (How dry the ladyfingers are will determine how much soaking liquid you need; this recipe should make enough, but you may have some left over.)

Place about 1 tablespoon mascarpone filling on the bottom of a bowl, then place 2 ladyfingers on top of the mascarpone; slightly offset the lady-fingers so that only about ¼ inch overlaps. Pipe a 1½-tablespoon circle on top of the ladyfingers, being careful not to exceed their boundaries. Place 2 more ladyfingers on top of the filling with the same overlap, but at the opposite angle to the first 2, to make a cross. Pipe on another circle of filling just as in the last layer, then top with 1 ladyfinger right in the center. Pipe a circle of filling on top of the last ladyfinger, and carefully cover the bowl with plastic wrap. (If the bowl is the right size and the ingredients are in the correct amount, the last step should bring the mascarpone right to the top of the bowl or a little higher, so the plastic wrap will sit on the mascarpone.) Repeat with the remaining components. Refrigerate the tiramisù for at least 2 hours or as long as 24 hours before serving.

TO SERVE, dust with cocoa powder. 🥄🥄🥄

Apricot Tarte Tatin
with Noyau Ice Cream

Serves 4

Tarte tatin is a classic French "upside-down tart," in which the apples caramelize in their own juices on the bottom of the pan while the pastry cooks on top. The tart is then inverted to serve. This version is made with apricots, but you can use the traditional apples (which you'll need to precook a bit if you're making small tarts), as well as many other kinds of fruit. Try peaches, nectarines, pears, or small ladyfinger bananas. The light bitter-almond flavor of the noyau ice cream, which is made with apricot kernels, makes a nice complement to this tart. The tart pans we use are available through Bridge Kitchenware in New York (212-688-4220) and are called Puck tartlette pans.

8 ounces puff pastry, made with unsalted butter

½ cup brown sugar

1 tablespoon water

1 tablespoon Myers's rum

8 small ripe apricots, halved or quartered,
   depending on size (save the pits for the ice cream)

Noyau ice cream (page 215)

To MAKE THE TARTS, preheat the oven to 350°. On a lightly floured board, roll the puff pastry out to an 8-inch square that is ⅛ inch thick. Cut out four 4-inch-diameter rounds, place them on a baking sheet pan lined with parchment paper, and refrigerate.

IN A SMALL, HEAVY SAUTÉ PAN OR SKILLET over medium-high heat, melt the sugar with the water and cook until golden, swirling the pan occasionally to cook evenly. Remove from the heat and carefully stir in the rum (it will splatter). Spoon the caramel into four 4-inch-diameter by ½-inch-high nonstick tart pans, and let cool. Overlap the apricots in a circular pattern in each pan. Cover each tart pan with a puff pastry round and push the edges of the pastry down onto the pan edge to seal the contents. Make 3 small slits in the dough. Put the tarts on a baking sheet pan and bake for 1 hour to 1 hour and 15 minutes, or until the pastry is golden brown and when you lift an edge it looks cooked through. Let cool slightly to serve immediately; let cool completely to serve later.

TO SERVE, if necessary, reheat the tarts in a preheated 350° oven for about 5 minutes, or until the caramel on the bottom of the tart pan is liquid. Invert each tart onto a dessert plate and place a scoop of Noyau ice cream alongside. ♪♪♪

Feuilletée of Caramelized Bananas
with Chocolate Fudge Sauce

Serves 4

If you have access to good-quality puff pastry dough, feuilletées are quite simple to make. They're really nothing more than rectangles of baked puff pastry, which you slice open and fill—in this instance with rum-infused caramelized bananas and ice cream. Once you're comfortable making them, have fun experimenting with different fillings. Fresh strawberries or raspberries and whipped cream is a beautiful choice. You might also want to make extra chocolate fudge sauce. It's a wonderful all-purpose topping to have on hand.

12 ounces puff pastry, made with unsalted butter

1 egg yolk

½ teaspoon water

Chocolate Fudge Sauce

4 ounces bittersweet chocolate, chopped

¼ cup light corn syrup

¼ cup coffee or water

2 tablespoons sugar

6 tablespoons unsweetened cocoa powder, sifted

1 teaspoon instant espresso powder

Caramelized Bananas

4 tablespoons unsalted butter

1 cup sugar

2 tablespoons Myers's rum

¼ cup heavy cream

4 ripe bananas without large brown spots

2 tablespoons confectioners' sugar

1 pint Myers's rum–currant ice cream (page 214)

To MAKE THE FEUILLETÉES, preheat the oven to 400°. Line a baking sheet pan with parchment paper. On a lightly floured board, roll the puff pastry out into an 11 by 7-inch rectangle that is ¼ inch thick. Using a very sharp knife, trim the edges and cut the pastry into 4 pieces, each 5 inches by 3 inches, and lay the pieces on the parchment paper, evenly spaced. In a small bowl, combine the egg yolk with the water to make an egg wash. Carefully brush the top of the puff pastry with the egg wash, being careful not to let it run down the sides, because the pastry will not rise in that spot. Refrigerate until the puff pastry is very cold again, about 30 minutes. Place the pan in the upper third of the oven and bake for 7 minutes, then rotate the pan and decrease the oven temperature to 350°. Continue baking until richly brown, 30 to 35 minutes. Transfer the pastries to a wire rack to cool.

TO MAKE THE SAUCE, melt the chocolate in a double boiler over barely simmering water (don't let the water touch the bottom of the bowl, or the chocolate will get too hot). In a small nonreactive sauté pan or skillet over high heat, heat the corn syrup, coffee, and sugar to a boil. Add the cocoa powder and instant espresso, and whisk constantly until the liquid is dark and slightly thickened and you can no longer taste the graininess of the cocoa. Remove from the heat and whisk in the melted chocolate. Return the pan to medium heat and cook the mixture for a few minutes until reduced slightly and the mixture is thick and sticky and has a glossy shine. The sauce can be made in advance and reheated gently in a double boiler over hot water. It also keeps indefinitely in the refrigerator.

TO CARAMELIZE THE BANANAS, melt the butter in a large sauté pan or skillet over medium heat, add the sugar, and cook until the sugar turns a dark golden brown, about 4 minutes, stirring as necessary to keep the sugar from burning. Remove the pan from the stove and add the rum (make sure the pan is not near an open flame, or the mixture could ignite). Return the pan to medium heat and gradually add the cream, swirling the pan to help incorporate the cream (again, be careful, as the mixture will splatter). Decrease the heat to low. Peel and cut the bananas in half lengthwise, then in half crosswise. Add to the caramel and let cook without stirring for about 2 minutes, or until still firm but heated through. (To make ahead, make the caramel but don't cook the bananas until just before serving.)

TO SERVE, preheat the oven to 325°. Place the feuilletées on a baking sheet pan and heat for 2 or 3 minutes. Cut each one in half horizontally and place the bottom layer of each in the center of each of 4 dinner plates. Dust the top of each feuilletée with the confectioners' sugar and set aside. Spoon 4 banana pieces onto each feuilletée, letting the ends of the bananas stick out, 2 from each side in a chevron, or "V" shape, pattern. Spoon the caramel sauce over and around the bananas. Top the bananas with 2 small scoops of ice cream and quickly put the other piece of feuilletée on top of each serving (this will help to hold the ice cream in place). Drizzle the warm chocolate sauce around the bananas and a little over the caramel sauce.

BASIC TECHNIQUES AND RECIPES

Preparing Artichoke Hearts and Baby Artichokes

PUT 4 ARTICHOKES IN A LARGE, NONREACTIVE POT and add 8 cups water, the juice of 1 lemon, ½ cup rice vinegar, and 2 tablespoons salt. Put a small plate on top of the artichokes to hold them under the water. Bring to a boil, decrease the heat to a simmer, and cook for 15 to 20 minutes, or until easily pierced with a bamboo skewer or a meat fork. Remove from the heat and let the artichokes cool to room temperature in the cooking liquid. (This can be done up to 1 day in advance.) Remove all the leaves and dig out the choke with a teaspoon. Peel and trim the stem.

Baby artichokes (1½ to 2 inches in diameter) have almost no choke, so it doesn't need to be removed. To cook 10 to 15 baby artichokes, peel off the outer leaves leaving only the pale green to yellow leaves (these are very tender). Using a large knife, trim ½ to 1 inch off the top of the leaves to remove all spines. With a paring knife, peel the stem

down from the bottom and around the diameter of the heart to remove any tough outer fiber, then trim off the end of the stem. As you finish each artichoke, drop it into a bowl of 4 cups of water mixed with the juice of 1 lemon. Set aside.

In a large, nonreactive pot, combine 4 cups water, 2 tablespoons rice vinegar, and 1 tablespoon plus 1 teaspoon salt. Bring to a boil, then drain the artichokes and add to the cooking liquid. Put a small plate on top of the artichokes to hold them under water and simmer for 10 to 15 minutes, or until easily pierced with a bamboo skewer or a meat fork. Remove the pot from the heat, and let the artichokes cool in the cooking liquid to room temperature. Before using, check for any artichokes that have a couple of small purple leaves in the center. If there are any, gently pull them out, as they will be tough. ♪♪♪

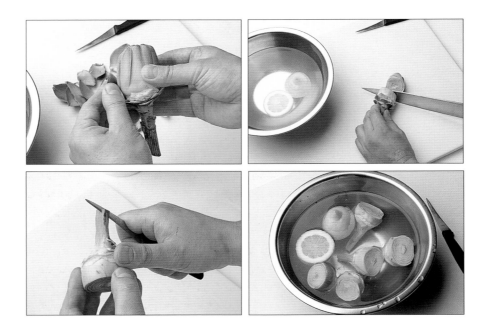

Deveining Foie Gras

To DEVEIN FOIE GRAS you first need to understand there are 2 lobes or pieces to a foie gras, a larger, more rounded posterior lobe and a smaller, flatter anterior lobe. These are connected by membranes, nerves, and veins that need to be removed. When cleaning foie gras for a terrine it is important to keep the individual lobes as intact as possible. The foie gras should be at room temperature so that it won't break as easily when you work on it; it usually comes in a vacuum pack, which can be left out of the refrigerator for 2½ to 3 hours.

Once the foie gras is at room temperature, start by separating the 2 lobes. Because of the temperature of the fat, the foie gras should have the consistency of soft clay. You should be able to clean each lobe without having it break apart into pieces. You will need to use your fingers and a small paring knife as you clean the foie gras. Place the larger lobe of foie gras smooth side down, and locate the area where the connecting membranes and veins are severed. Grasp the principal connecting membrane with your right hand and gently tug it to reveal the location of the central vein. As you pull, use your other hand to gently peel back the flesh of the liver, tracing the location of the vein. The central vein extends roughly two thirds down the middle of the large lobe before it forks into two separate directions, forming an upside down Y. Continue tracing the path of the vein by gently tugging it, pushing aside the flesh to reveal the vein, and removing any evidence of coagulated blood, vein, or membrane you encounter. The point of a small paring knife may help lift out these imperfections. Be sure to cut away any green discoloration (evidence of bile) that will give the liver a bitter taste, and use moist paper towels to clean your hands and knife as you work. Use the same procedure for the smaller lobe. When you are finished you should be left with 2 flattened, somewhat misshaped lobes of liver that are largely intact, a few smaller pieces that have broken off, and membranes and veins. Discard the membranes and veins. ♪♪♪

Preparing Beets

We cook beets in one of two ways, steaming or roasting. Either way will work fine for our recipes. Roasting the beets intensifies the flavor and lessens the moisture content. Steaming allows the beets to keep their natural moisture and will be more like store-bought canned beets. Adjust the cooking time based on beet size and age: if fresh, the beets will take a shorter time to cook. We use beets the size of ping-pong balls.

To cook the beets, cut off the green top but leave some of the stem and wash in cold water. Be sure not to break the skin, or juice will escape while cooking. If roasting, preheat the oven to 400°. Place the beets on a baking sheet pan and bake for 15 to 25 minutes, until the beets can be pierced easily with a skewer or toothpick. Let cool, then peel and cut as required. If steaming, arrange the beets in a single layer in a steamer over boiling water and steam for 15 to 25 minutes, until the beets can be pierced easily with a skewer or toothpick (check the water level periodically and add boiling water as necessary). Remove and let cool, then peel and cut as required. ♪♪♪

Roasting and Peeling Bell Peppers

If you're roasting peppers, make a big batch and pack some in olive oil. They'll keep in the refrigerator for up to a week. This roasting and peeling technique also works with fresh chili peppers.

Cook the peppers on an open flame or 2 inches from a broiler, turning them until the entire skin turns black. Put them in a bowl, cover with plastic wrap, and set aside for 5 minutes. To peel, use your fingers or a small knife to remove all the charred skin. Cut off the top and remove the seeds. ♪♪♪

Blanching and Shocking Vegetables

This technique is used to retain a vegetable's color and crispness. After blanching and shocking, the vegetable can be either eaten or recooked later.

To blanch vegetables, bring a large pot of salted water to a boil and add the vegetables all at once. It's important to use a lot of salt, which helps keep their bright color. Don't overcrowd the pot; cook in batches as necessary, since you want the water to return to a boil as quickly as possible. When the vegetables are crisp tender (this can take a few seconds or a few minutes depending on the density of the vegetable), use a wire-mesh skimmer or slotted metal spoon to remove them from the water. To shock, plunge them into ice water to stop the cooking process. As soon as they're cooled, remove the vegetables from the water to prevent them from losing flavor. ♪♪♪

Peeling and Seeding Tomatoes

THERE ARE A COUPLE OF DIFFERENT TECHNIQUES chefs use to peel a tomato. The easiest and most widely used is to core a tomato and make a small X in the bottom with a paring knife, then immerse it in a large pot of boiling water for one minute, or until the skin right next to the X starts to curl up. Only do a couple of tomatoes at a time, so the temperature of the water does not fall too much and the tomatoes overcook. Remove with a slotted spoon and plunge into ice water. Once cool, peel the skin off. The other technique is more difficult, and you will need a very sharp knife or peeler. Core the tomato, then using a sawing motion remove only the skin.

TO SEED A TOMATO, cut it in half horizontally so that you can easily remove the seeds with a spoon or your finger.

TO MAKE TOMATO CONCASSÉE from a whole peeled tomato, cut a small piece of the top and bottom from the tomato, about ¼ inch, then cut the tomato lengthwise into quarters. Lay the wedges facing up, and with a sharp knife cut away and discard the seeds and interior flesh from the outside of the tomato. The 4 pieces of tomato should be flat, cut into strips lengthwise ¼ inch wide, then cut across the strips to make a ¼-inch dice.

Oven-Dried Tomatoes

Makes 24

This technique intensifies the flavor of any tomato—even one that's not remarkably flavorful to begin with. You end up with something halfway between a fresh and a sun-dried tomato that retains its shape and juiciness and won't dissolve in a dish. These are excellent in sauces, tossed into salads, or drizzled with a little olive oil and served as part of an antipasto platter.

6 ripe Roma (plum) tomatoes
   (about 4 ounces each), cored
Salt and freshly ground black pepper to taste

PREHEAT THE OVEN TO 225°. Cut the tomatoes lengthwise into quarters. Put a wire rack in a rimmed baking sheet pan and lay the tomatoes on the rack, skin side down. Season very lightly with salt and pepper. Put them in the oven and dry for 3 to 4 hours, or until they shrink to three fourths their size but are still soft inside. (If you use a convection oven, it takes only 1 hour.) Remove from the oven and let cool. Store in a single layer in a covered container in the refrigerator for up to 4 days.

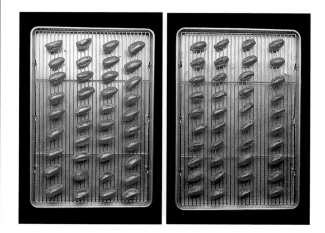

Tomato Sauce

Makes about 3 cups

If tomatoes aren't in season, use canned Italian plum tomatoes and remove the seeds if possible. To scale this recipe up, don't increase the pepper flakes and garlic quite as much as the other ingredients.

2 tablespoons olive oil
Pinch of crushed red pepper flakes
2 teaspoons minced garlic
2/3 cup finely chopped onion
2 cups diced peeled tomatoes (page 199)
1 cup tomato puree
Salt and freshly ground white pepper to taste

HEAT THE OIL, pepper flakes, and garlic in a saucepan over medium heat until the garlic is lightly browned. Add the onion and sauté until very soft, about 5 minutes. Add the tomatoes and tomato puree, bring to a boil, lower the heat, and simmer for 3 minutes. Season with salt and pepper.

Clarified Butter

Makes about 1 1/2 cups

Removing the milk solids from melted butter increases its smoking point, so you can cook with it at higher temperatures with less risk of burning.

IN A SMALL SAUCEPAN, melt 1 pound (4 sticks) of unsalted butter over very low heat. The butter should melt but not boil. Once completely melted, it will separate into three layers. On top is white foam, then a clear golden layer that is clarified butter, and under that is a milky liquid that is milk solids. Skim off the foam and discard. Ladle the clarified butter into a container; cover and refrigerate indefinitely. Discard the milk solids.

Garlic-Parsley Compound Butter

Makes about 1 1/4 cups

This flavored butter is great on grilled steak or fish. It will keep for up to a week in the refrigerator or up to a month in the freezer. To create your own variations, just replace the parsley with one or more fresh herbs, such as chervil, tarragon, or dill.

About 1½ ounces (12 cloves) garlic
About ¾ ounces (2½ cups) flat-leaf parsley leaves
1 cup (2 sticks) unsalted butter, at room temperature
1½ teaspoons salt
¾ teaspoon freshly ground black pepper
3½ teaspoons dry white wine
1 tablespoon freshly squeezed lemon juice

IN A FOOD PROCESSOR, combine the garlic and parsley, and process until finely chopped. Add the butter, salt, and pepper, and process for 10 seconds. Scrape down the sides with a spatula, then process for another 10 seconds. With the machine running, slowly add the white wine and lemon juice through the feed tube and process until well blended. Transfer to an airtight con-tainer and refrigerate for up to 1 week or freeze for up to 1 month.

 Degerming Garlic

PEOPLE SOMETIMES COMPLAIN ABOUT HAVING DIFFICULTY DIGESTING GARLIC. WHAT THEY'RE HAVING TROUBLE DIGESTING IS ACTUALLY THE GERM—THE GREEN SPROUT THAT RUNS THROUGH THE CENTER OF THE GARLIC CLOVE. REMOVING IT MAKES GARLIC MUCH EASIER FOR YOUR BODY TO PROCESS. CUT DOWN THE CENTER OF THE CLOVE AND PULL OUT ANY GREEN YOU SEE; IT SHOULD COME OUT IN A SINGLE STRIP, THE LENGTH OF THE CLOVE.

Mayonnaise

Makes about 1 cup

There are two tricks to making your own mayonnaise. First, add the oil very slowly in a thin stream. And second, don't expect the finished product to look like the store-bought kind. A food processor is a great tool for making mayonnaise.

1 egg yolk
4 teaspoons rice vinegar
1 tablespoon Dijon mustard
⅛ teaspoon salt
Pinch of freshly ground white pepper
1 tablespoon freshly squeezed lemon juice
⅔ cup corn oil

IN A FOOD PROCESSOR, combine the egg yolk, vinegar, mustard, salt, white pepper, and lemon juice. Process until blended. With the machine running, slowly add the oil in a thin stream and process until emulsified. ♪♪♪

Aïoli

You'll find this garlic mayonnaise as a condiment and flavor accent in several recipes in this book. It's also great in sandwiches and as a dip for fresh vegetables.

IN A BOWL, combine 1 cup mayonnaise with ¼ teaspoon grated garlic and ¼ teaspoon saffron threads. Stir to blend. Let sit for 1 hour, then stir again. ♪♪♪

Lemon-Mustard Vinaigrette

Makes about 3/4 cup

We suggest making this dressing fresh each time you use it, but if there's any left over, it will keep in the refrigerator for up to a week. This is a versatile vinaigrette that has lots of uses: add some fresh herbs and use it as a marinade for chicken, or add a little tomato concassée and you've got a light, fresh sauce for fish.

¼ cup freshly squeezed lemon juice
1 tablespoon Dijon mustard
½ cup extra virgin olive oil
½ teaspoon salt
¼ teaspoon freshly ground white pepper

IN A BOWL, whisk together all the ingredients. ♪♪♪

Terra House Vinaigrette

Makes 1/2 cup

This classic vinaigrette will keep for up to a week in the refrigerator.

1 tablespoon sherry vinegar
1 tablespoon balsamic vinegar
1 tablespoon Dijon mustard
2 tablespoons corn oil
¼ cup extra virgin olive oil
1 teaspoon minced shallot
Salt and freshly ground black pepper to taste

IN A SMALL BOWL, whisk together the sherry vinegar, balsamic vinegar, and mustard. Gradually whisk in the corn oil and extra virgin olive oil in a thin stream. Add the shallot. Season with salt and pepper. ♪♪♪

Ponzu

Makes about 1 1/3 cups

This lemon-soy dressing is the "oil and vinegar" of Japan. It is eaten on meat, fish, and vegetables. Made without oil, it's a great choice for people concerned about fat. You can keep ponzu in the refrigerator for up to 2 weeks.

4 tablespoons freshly squeezed lemon juice
½ cup rice vinegar
6 tablespoons soy sauce
2 tablespoons mirin
Zest of 1 lemon

IN A SMALL NONREACTIVE SAUCEPAN, combine all the ingredients and bring to a boil. Let cool and refrigerate. Remove the lemon zest before using.

Sake Marinade

Makes about 3/4 cup

This is Hiro's version of **the** Japanese mother sauce. A variation of it is used in almost every Japanese marinade and soup base, and you can use it to marinate almost anything. Once you start using it, it will become a staple in your kitchen, as it is in ours. Increase the recipe if you need more.

¼ cup soy sauce
3 tablespoons sugar
2 tablespoons mirin
2 tablespoons sake
¼ teaspoon grated peeled fresh ginger
¼ teaspoon grated garlic

IN A BOWL, whisk together all the ingredients.

Momiji Oroshi

Makes about 2/3 cup

This traditional Japanese condiment of seasoned, grated daikon is used for a variety of dishes. If you want to halve the recipe, you can save the remaining daikon and use it to make more momiji oroshi within the next day or two—the daikon should be grated fresh each time.

1 small daikon (about 1 pound), peeled
   and coarsely chopped
About ½ cup water
2 pinches of cayenne pepper
¼ teaspoon paprika

COMBINE THE DAIKON AND WATER in a blender and puree until smooth. Transfer to a fine-mesh sieve and let drain without pressing for 10 to 15 minutes. Transfer to a bowl; whisk in the cayenne and paprika. Cover and refrigerate for up to 6 hours.

Why Grate Garlic or Ginger?

WE RECOMMEND USING A GINGER GRATER (AVAILABLE IN STORES THAT CARRY ASIAN PRODUCTS) FOR BOTH GINGER AND GARLIC. GRATING GINGER ALLOWS YOU TO EXTRACT THE JUICE AND THE MEATY PULP, LEAVING BEHIND THE TOUGH, STRINGY FIBERS. IF A RECIPE CALLS FOR GINGER JUICE, PUT THE GRATED PULP IN A PIECE OF CHEESECLOTH AND TWIST THE CLOTH TO RELEASE THE JUICE. GRATING GARLIC RELEASES ITS FLAVORFUL OILS AND GIVES YOU A SMOOTH PUREE THAT'S EASY TO INCORPORATE INTO SAUCES. THIS IS PARTICULARLY USEFUL WHEN THE GARLIC IS EITHER UNCOOKED OR BARELY COOKED, SUCH AS IN MARINADES AND VINAIGRETTES. GRATED GARLIC ALSO BLENDS BEAUTIFULLY WITH OTHER INGREDIENTS. THE KIND OF GINGER GRATER WE LIKE BEST IS A SHALLOW CERAMIC BOWL WITH THE GRATING SURFACE IN THE CENTER AND A SILICON RING ON THE BOTTOM TO PREVENT SLIPPING.

Preserved Lemons

Makes 4 cups

Use these straight from the jar to add a lovely lemon flavor to all kinds of dishes. The rind of the lemon "cooks" in the salt and loses its bitterness, becoming soft and delicate. Preserved lemons can be stored in the refrigerator for up to 6 months.

10 lemons, quartered and seeds removed
2½ cups freshly squeezed lemon juice,
   or more as needed
½ cup salt

PACK THE LEMONS as tightly as possible into a 1-quart mason jar. Whisk the 2½ cups lemon juice and the salt together in a bowl, then pour over the lemons in the jar. There should be enough juice to cover the lemons; if there isn't, add more. Keep at room temperature for 1 week, each day shaking the jar to distribute the salt and juice, and opening the top for a minute or so to release any built-up gas. Refrigerate for 1 month, or until the skins become soft, as in marmalade. They are now ready to use. ♪♪♪

Pesto

Makes about 1/4 cup

In addition to the recipes in which we call for pesto in this book, we use it for all kinds of things— tossing with pasta, drizzling over boiled potatoes or any other vegetable. It's also good with grilled fish. Pesto freezes beautifully. You can store it in an airtight container or plastic freezer bag for up to a month.

1 small clove garlic, smashed
2 tablespoons coarsely chopped fresh basil
1 teaspoon coarsely chopped fresh flat leaf parsley
2 teaspoons pine nuts, toasted (page 68)
¼ cup extra virgin olive oil
2 teaspoons freshly grated Parmesan cheese
Pinch of salt
Pinch of freshly ground white pepper

IN A SMALL MORTAR AND USING A PESTLE, grind the garlic with the salt to a paste. Add the basil and parsley, and pound until they break down. Add the pine nuts and pound to amalgamate them with the other ingredients and make a chunky paste. Gradually work in the olive oil, then the Parmesan cheese and pepper. If you don't have a mortar and pestle, you can use a small food processor. ♪♪♪

Brunoise
⅛ x ⅛ x ⅛

Concassée
(SMALL DICE)
¼ x ¼ x ¼

Oblique

Julienne
1/16 x 1/16 x 1½ to 2

Mince

Chop

Medium dice

$\frac{1}{3}$ x $\frac{1}{3}$ x $\frac{1}{3}$

Large dice

$\frac{3}{4}$ x $\frac{3}{4}$ x $\frac{3}{4}$

Alumette

(MATCHSTICK)

$\frac{1}{8}$ x $\frac{1}{8}$ x 1$\frac{1}{2}$ to 2

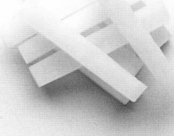

Bâton

$\frac{1}{4}$ x $\frac{1}{4}$ x 1$\frac{1}{2}$ to 2

Coarse chop

Rough chop

Fontina Cheese Polenta

Makes about 7 cups

We serve this creamy polenta soft, but if you have any left over, or just want to try a different approach, spread it into a baking pan, cover with plastic wrap, and chill, then cut it into slices (or whatever shape you like). These can be either baked in a 400° oven (sprinkled with a little extra Parmesan cheese) or sautéed in a nonstick pan until golden brown, then served as a side dish or even as a first course with a mushroom ragoût or tomato sauce.

7 cups water
Pinch of salt
1 cup polenta flour (not instant)
1 tablespoon unsalted butter
3 tablespoons freshly grated Parmesan cheese
⅓ cup shredded fontina cheese
Freshly ground black pepper to taste

IN A LARGE, HEAVY SAUCEPAN, bring the water to a boil and add the salt. Very slowly, add the polenta in a thin stream while stirring constantly with a wooden spoon. Keep the water at least at a simmer until all the polenta is added. Bring the polenta to a full boil, then decrease the heat to a simmer. (Be very careful at this stage, as the polenta is thick and hot and can burn you easily.) Simmer for 30 to 40 minutes, stirring every 2 minutes. The polenta is done when each grain is soft.

Remove from the heat. Add the butter, Parmesan cheese, and fontina cheese. Mix well and season with salt and pepper. If you need to hold the polenta for serving, put it into a heat-resistant container and cover it with plastic wrap. Put the container in a pot and fill with enough hot water to come more than halfway up the container. Keep over very low heat. ♪♪♪

Mashed Potatoes, Garlic Mashed Potatoes

Makes 4 cups

Once made, mashed potatoes can be kept warm before serving by putting them in a container that can sit in a pot of barely simmering water. If you have leftover mashed potatoes and you want to reheat them, we recommend using a microwave oven. You can also spread them thinly in an oven-proof sauté pan or baking dish, sprinkle a little cream on top, and place them in a hot oven for a few minutes, being careful not to let them brown.

2 pounds large russet potatoes, peeled
  and halved lengthwise
Salt and freshly ground white pepper to taste
⅔ cup heavy cream
3 tablespoons unsalted butter

CUT THE POTATOES CROSSWISE into 1-inch-thick pieces. (Don't cut them too small, or they will absorb too much water.) Put them in a pot, add cold water to cover, and add a pinch of salt. Bring to a boil, decrease the heat to a simmer, and cook until soft, about 10 minutes; drain. Return the potatoes to the pot and shake over medium heat for a few seconds to help the excess water evaporate. Add the cream and bring to a boil, then remove from the heat, add the butter, and stir. Transfer to an electric mixer fitted with the paddle attachment and mix until smooth. Season with salt and pepper. Or, press the potatoes through a food mill or a potato ricer, or mash them in the pot with a potato masher.

FOR GARLIC MASHED POTATOES, peel and remove the hard stem from the bottom of 10 large garlic cloves and add to the water with the potatoes. Drain with the potatoes and follow the above recipe. ♪♪♪

Veal Stock

Our veal stock is not as heavy as some. We make it milder and less concentrated so that the flavors of the other ingredients with which it's used can come through; a sauce made with stock should enhance a dish, not overwhelm it. Because it has a less assertive flavor, we're also able to use this stock with fish dishes when we want to give them a richer flavor.

5 pounds veal bones, cut into 2-inch-long pieces
2 cups dry red wine
2 tablespoons vegetable oil
1 onion, coarsely chopped
½ carrot, coarsely chopped
1 stalk celery, coarsely chopped
½ bulb garlic, halved crosswise
1 cup water
3 bay leaves
2 teaspoons black peppercorns
3 fresh thyme sprigs
2 teaspoons salt
½ cup tomato paste
3 ripe tomatoes, halved

PREHEAT THE OVEN TO 400°.

Put the veal bones in a large roasting pan and roast until golden brown, about 30 minutes. Transfer the bones to a large stockpot. Add the wine to the roasting pan set over medium heat, and deglaze by stirring to scrape up the browned bits from the bottom of the pan, then add the liquid to the stockpot.

Heat the oil in a large sauté pan or skillet over high heat, add the onion, carrot, celery, and garlic, and sauté until golden brown, about 4 minutes. Add the vegetables to the pot, deglaze the pan with the water, and add the liquid to the pot. Fill the pot with enough cold water to just cover the veal bones. Bring to a boil and skim off any foam that develops.

Add all the remaining ingredients, bring back to a boil, then decrease the heat to a simmer. Cook for at least 12 hours (at Terra, we cook the stock for 2 days, to develop the flavor even more). Keep adding hot water to maintain the water level, which you will need to do 5 to 6 times.

Strain through a fine-mesh sieve into a smaller pot and cook over high heat until reduced to about 7 cups, about 1 hour. Transfer the stock to a smaller pan. Sit the pan in a bowl of ice water to cool. Cover and refrigerate overnight. Remove the layer of congealed fat on top. Store in the refrigerator for up to 3 days or freeze for up to 1 month.

Chicken Stock

At a restaurant like Terra, there are various stocks simmering on the stove every day, and more than half the dishes we prepare are based on one or another of them. We encourage you to make your own stocks. Their flavor—especially in sauces that involve reduction—makes a real difference. This recipe can be doubled and freezes well. Use the cooked chicken for another purpose—preferably a dish with assertive flavors, such as Chinese chicken salad, since much of the flavor of the chicken will have cooked out.

5 pounds chicken bones
½ chicken (about 1½ pounds)
1 onion, coarsely chopped
½ carrot, coarsely chopped
1 stalk celery, coarsely chopped
½ bulb garlic, halved crosswise
3 bay leaves
1½ teaspoons black peppercorns
2 fresh thyme sprigs
1 teaspoon salt

Wash the bones and chicken in cold running water, taking care to rinse out the body cavity well, and put them in a large stockpot. Fill the stockpot with enough cold water to just cover the chicken bones. Bring to a boil and skim off any foam that develops. Add the remaining ingredients, bring back to a boil, then decrease the heat to a simmer. Simmer for 3 to 4 hours, skimming as necessary at the beginning. The stock is ready when the bones are easy to break; this means all the essence of the chicken has come out into the water.

Strain through a fine-mesh sieve into a smaller pot and cook over medium heat until reduced to 2 quarts. Transfer the stock to a smaller pan. Sit the pan in a bowl of ice water to cool. Cover and refrigerate overnight. Remove and discard the congealed layer of fat on top. Store in the refrigerator for up to 3 days, or freeze for up to 1 month.

Making a Second Stock

AT TERRA, WE MAKE WHAT IS REFERRED TO AS A SECOND STOCK (THE FRENCH CALL IT REMOUILLAGE) FROM THE USED CHICKEN BONES. TO DO THIS, RETURN THE CHICKEN BONES AND CHICKEN TO THE POT AND ADD HOT WATER TO JUST BARELY COVER. BRING TO A BOIL, THEN REDUCE TO A SIMMER AND COOK FOR 5 MINUTES. THEN STRAIN AS BEFORE. THE STOCK WILL BE CLOUDY AND HAVE MORE OF A GELATINOUS CHARACTERISTIC THAN THE FIRST STOCK. IT CAN BE USED IN STEWS OR IN MOST RECIPES THAT DO NOT NEED THE CLARITY OF A FIRST STOCK. MOSTLY, THOUGH, WE USE IT INSTEAD OF WATER TO MAKE OTHER STOCKS LIKE LAMB, VEAL, LOBSTER, OR SHRIMP, AS IT HELPS MAKE A RICHER STOCK RATHER THAN STARTING WITH WATER.

Brown Chicken Stock

5 pounds chicken bones
½ chicken (about 1½ pounds)
1 cup dry red wine
2 tablespoons vegetable oil
1 onion, coarsely chopped
½ carrot, coarsely chopped
1 stalk celery, coarsely chopped
½ bulb garlic, halved crosswise
1 cup water
3 bay leaves
1½ teaspoons black peppercorns
3 fresh thyme sprigs
1 teaspoon salt
¼ cup tomato paste

Preheat the oven to 400°.

WASH THE BONES AND CHICKEN in cold running water, taking care to rinse out the body cavity well, and put them in a large roasting pan. Roast until a deep golden brown, 25 to 30 minutes.

Meanwhile, heat the vegetable oil in a large sauté pan or skillet over high heat until hot, add the vegetables and garlic, and sauté until golden brown. Transfer to a large stockpot. Add the 1 cup water to the sauté pan and stir to remove any brown bits from the pan, then add the liquid to the stockpot. Transfer the roasted bones and chicken to the stockpot. Add the wine to the roasting pan set over medium heat and stir to deglaze the pan. Add the liquid to the stockpot.

Fill the stockpot with enough cold water to just cover the top of the chicken bones. Bring to a boil and skim off any foam that develops. Add the remaining ingredients, bring back to a boil, then decrease the heat to a simmer. Simmer for 3 to 4 hours, skimming as necessary at the beginning. The stock is ready when the bones are easy to break; this means all the essence of the chicken has come out into the water.

Strain through a fine-mesh sieve into a smaller pot and cook over medium heat until reduced to 7 cups. Transfer the stock to a smaller pan or a container with a lid. Sit the pan in a bowl of ice water to cool, then cover and refrigerate overnight. Remove and discard the congealed fat on the surface. Keep in the refrigerator for up to 3 days, or freeze for up to 1 month.

Duck stock: Replace the ½ chicken and chicken bones in the master recipe with duck bones.

Game stock: Replace the ½ chicken and chicken bones in the master recipe with game-bird bones, such as quail, squib, or pheasant. *♪♪*

Lobster Stock

This stock has a wonderfully rich flavor that makes sauces and soups really special. You can make it from the leftover shells of lobsters you've already eaten, or, if you need it for the lobster dish you're preparing, you can par-cook the lobsters, remove the meat from the shells and refrigerate it until you need it, then use the shells to make the stock. To crush lobster shells without making a mess, first drain any liquid from them, then wrap them in a kitchen towel and place the towel in a plastic bag. Squeeze all the air out of the bag, seal the opening, grab a hammer or mallet, and have at it.

¼ cup olive oil

3 cloves garlic, smashed

½ onion, sliced

½ carrot, sliced

Heads, legs, and shells (gills removed) of
   2 (1- to 1¼-pound) lobsters, crushed

½ teaspoon fennel seed

2 tablespoons Cognac

½ cup dry white wine

6 cups chicken stock (page 208)

Lobster juice from 2 lobsters (page 211)

1 cup tomato puree

1 tablespoon tomato paste

Tomalley from 2 lobsters (page 211)

IN A LARGE SAUCEPAN, heat the olive oil and garlic over medium heat and sauté the garlic until lightly browned. Add the onion and carrot, and sauté until tender, 3 to 5 minutes. Drain off any liquid that has accumulated at the bottom of the bowl from the lobster heads, legs, and shells, and add it to the lobster juice. Increase the heat to high and add the lobster heads, legs, shells, and fennel seed. Sauté, stirring, until fragrant, about 3 minutes. Add the Cognac and carefully light it with a long-handled match. When the flames subside, add the wine and bring it to a boil. Add the chicken stock, lobster juice, tomato puree, and tomato paste. Bring to a boil and skim once to remove any foam that develops, trying not to remove any of the oil on the surface (it holds a lot of the flavor). Simmer for 45 minutes, then add the lobster tomalley. Bring back to a boil, remove from the heat, and strain through a fine-mesh sieve. Rinse the pot and return the stock to the pot. Cook over medium-high heat until reduced to 4 cups, about 1 hour. Let cool and refrigerate for up to 3 days or freeze for up to 1 month.

Shrimp stock: Replace the lobster shells in the above recipe with about 1 pound of shrimp heads and shells. Delete the tomalley and lobster juice. ♫♫

Fish Stock

Makes 4 cups

2 pounds fish bones from white flesh fish,
    such as halibut, snapper, sole, or cod,
    cut into large pieces so they fit in the pot
½ cup thinly sliced onion
¼ cup thinly sliced carrot
¼ cup thinly sliced celery
1 cup dry white wine
3 large garlic cloves, smashed
2 teaspoons white peppercorns
1 fresh thyme sprig
1 fresh parsley sprig
4 bay leaves
2 teaspoons dried fennel seeds
1 teaspoon salt

Soak the fish in cold water in a large bowl for 1 hour to remove the blood. Drain. Transfer the fish to a large stockpot and add enough cold water to cover the bones, about 8 cups. Bring to a boil, then decrease the heat to a simmer and skim off any foam that develops. Add the remaining ingredients and return to a simmer. Cook for 45 minutes. Strain through a fine-mesh sieve and let cool. Refrigerate for up to 3 days or freeze for up to 1 month. ♪♪♪

Cooking and Shelling Lobster

Lobsters should be cooked as soon as they come from the market. If they will not be cooked immediately, rinse them under cold water and drain. Transfer to a large pan and cover with a moistened towel and refrigerate until cooking time. Rinse again before cooking.

In a large stockpot of salted boiling water, boil 1 to 1½ pounds lobsters for 5 minutes. Transfer to a bowl of ice water. Drain and refrigerate for 1 hour, or until the lobsters are completely cold. (If they are still warm when you crack them, they will lose too much juice and become dry.)

Working over a bowl to catch the juices, twist each lobster body in the opposite direction from the tail, saving as much juice as possible. Reserve the juices for stock. Crack the lobster tails and claws with a mallet and remove the meat. Reserve all the shells for stock. With a spoon, remove the tomalley, the green to almost black liver in the head and in the top of the tail. Reserve this for stock, separately from the shells and juices. ♪♪♪

Making Ravioli, Wontons, and Tortelloni

Makes 24 appetizers

Here's a "trade secret." Store-bought wonton wrappers aren't just for wontons. They make it easy to make a variety of filled pastas and dumplings. Use this basic method to make the ravioli, wontons, and tortelloni in this book. Before you start, be sure to have rice flour on hand.

FILL A PASTRY BAG with whatever filling you're using. (If you don't have a pastry bag, you can simply spoon the filling onto each wrapper.) Lay out 6 wonton wrappers in overlapping diamonds, with about ½ inch of each wrapper exposed under the wrapper above it; this will allow you to brush egg wash onto one edge of half of each wrapper without wetting the whole surface. Spread the wrappers out in a single layer. Pipe or spoon the filling into the center of a wrapper. Fold the wrapper in half to form a triangle; close tightly, pressing from the filling to the outer edge to release any trapped air. Place on a baking sheet pan lined with parchment paper that has been dusted with rice flour and cover with a dry kitchen towel. Repeat with the remaining wrappers and filling. Refrigerate.

TO MAKE TORTELLONI, follow the instructions above. After sealing the triangles, dot the end of one point on the folded side with the egg wash. With the wrapper flat on the table, place one finger in the middle of the long side against the filling and bring the two ends together behind your finger and press together, using the egg wash as glue. Store and repeat as above. ♪♪♪

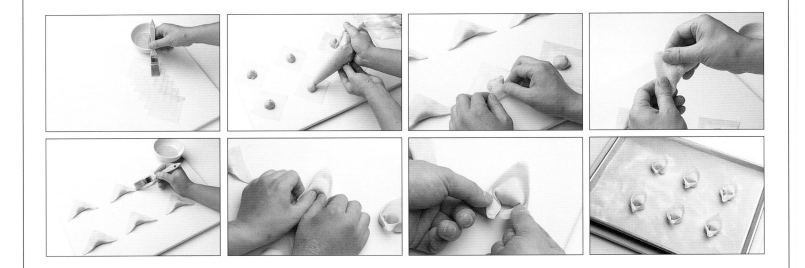

Almond Cream

Makes about 1 1/3 cups

A classic almond filling for tarts and pastries. Almond meal can be purchased at specialty food and health food stores, or you can make your own by finely chopping slivered blanched almonds, then pulsing them in a food processor to the consistency of a fine meal. Pass the meal through a medium-mesh sieve.

6 tablespoons unsalted butter, at room temperature
¾ cup confectioners' sugar
Minced zest of 1 lemon
1 egg
¼ teaspoon almond extract
¼ teaspoon vanilla extract
¾ cup almond meal
1 tablespoon pastry flour

IN A MIXER, beat together the butter and confectioners' sugar until light and fluffy. Add the lemon zest, egg, almond extract, and vanilla extract, and mix well. (The batter may look a little broken at this point, but it will come back together when you add the almond meal.) Add the almond meal and pastry flour and stir until blended. Cover and refrigerate until set, about 3 hours. Keep in the refrigerator for up to 4 days, or freeze in an airtight container for up to 1 month. 🎵

Caramel Sauce

Makes about 1 cup

This versatile sauce is great to have on hand for dressing up desserts or drizzling over ice cream. It reheats well and will keep in the refrigerator for 2 to 3 weeks. You can adjust the consistency by adding a tablespoon or so of heavy cream.

1 cup heavy cream
¾ cup sugar

IN A SMALL SAUCEPAN, bring the cream just to a boil, then set aside. Heat a medium saucepan over medium-high heat and sprinkle the sugar evenly over the bottom of the pan. As the sugar starts to melt and brown, shake and move the pan to keep the sugar from burning (this works better than stirring with a spoon). Cook the sugar to a dark golden brown, about 4 minutes. Make sure there are no sugar crystals undissolved, then very gradually add the hot cream in very small batches; take care, as the mixture will spatter and can easily burn you. Cook for 1 minute, stirring occasionally, then remove from the heat and pour into a metal bowl to cool. Keep up to 5 days. 🎵

Crème Anglaise
(Vanilla Custard Sauce and Vanilla Ice Cream Base)

Makes 1 1/2 to 2 quarts

Making your own crème anglaise takes a little extra time, but it's really worth it. From this single custard base, you can make a versatile sauce or vanilla ice cream, or an infinite number of other ice cream flavors. To make the vanilla custard sauce, simply make one-fourth of the recipe. This sauce is one of the basic elements in the "arsenal" of all clasically trained pastry chefs. It's pooled on plates, drizzled over desserts, and served hot or cold with fruit, cakes, and other confections. This sauce can be flavored, if you wish, with just about any kind of alcohol. Some suggestions: Grand Marnier, Kahlua, or rum. This ice cream base is very rich, so be careful not to run the ice cream maker for too long, which can turn the mixture into butter. If you see tiny, hard pieces of cream that have actually lost their water and become butter, you'll have to start all over again.

2 cups milk
2 cups heavy cream
1 vanilla bean, split lengthwise
8 egg yolks
½ cup sugar

IN A LARGE SAUCEPAN, combine the milk and cream. Scrape the seeds from the vanilla bean and add them to the pan, along with the bean. Bring just to a boil, then remove from the heat. Cover and steep for 20 minutes. Half fill a large bowl with ice and water, and set aside. In a medium bowl, whisk together the egg yolks and sugar. Slowly add the hot milk mixture to the yolk mixture, whisking constantly so the eggs do not curdle. Return the mixture to the saucepan and cook over medium heat, stirring constantly with a wooden spoon until the mixture coats the back of the spoon (when you wipe your finger across the spoon, the sauce should not run together immediately). Strain the custard into a bowl. Rinse and air-dry the vanilla bean, which can be used to make vanilla sugar (page 216). Set the bowl into the bowl of ice water to chill the custard as fast as possible. Stir occasionally until cool. Cover the custard and refrigerate for at least 2 hours or up to overnight.

Freeze in an ice cream maker according to the manufacturer's instructions.

Espresso Ice Cream: Using the bottom of a heavy pot, coarsely crush ½ cup coffee beans. When steeping the milk, cream, and vanilla in the master recipe, add the crushed coffee beans. Add 1½ teaspoons coffee extract (or 1 tablespoon instant espresso powder mixed with ½ teaspoon hot water) and 1 teaspoon finely ground espresso to the chilled custard, then freeze.

Ginger Ice Cream: Blanche ½ cup peeled, thinly sliced ginger in boiling water for 1 minute. (This will remove some of the acid that is in the ginger before adding it to the cream mixture, so the ginger will not cause curdling.) When steeping the milk, cream, and vanilla to the milk mixture in the master recipe, add the ginger and increase the steeping time to 30 minutes.

Banana-Rum Ice Cream: Puree 3 very ripe bananas (about 1 pound) in a food processor. Add to the cooled custard in the master recipe. Add ¼ cup Myers's rum to the chilled custard, then freeze.

Meyer's Rum–Currant Ice Cream: In a bowl, combine ⅓ cup dry currants with ½ cup Myers's rum. Soak overnight. Add to the chilled custard in the master recipe, then freeze. ♪♪

Noyau Ice Cream

Noyau is the French word for a fruit stone, and also for the flavoring made from the almond-like kernel such stones contain. You can make this ice cream with bitter almonds, but they're very hard to find in the U.S., so we use the kernels found inside apricot pits. To extract them, use a hammer or nutcracker; remove the white kernel and discard the pit. Don't use more apricot kernels than this recipe calls for, and never eat them raw, because they can upset your stomach.

7 apricot kernels
Ingredients for vanilla bean ice cream (page 214)
2 teaspoons bitter almond extract or almond extract

ADD THE APRICOT KERNELS TO THE MILK MIXTURE in the master recipe, bring to a boil, then cover and steep for 20 minutes. Strain out the apricot kernels when you strain the custard. Add the bitter almond extract to the chilled custard, then freeze. ♪♪♪

Meyer Lemon Ice Cream

Makes 1 to 1 1/2 quarts

If you can't get Meyer lemons, regular ones will work fine, but you may want to use a little less juice to suit your taste, as Meyers have a sweeter perfume and less acid.

1½ cups heavy whipping cream
1 cup half-and-half
4 teaspoons grated Meyer lemon zest
1 vanilla bean, split lengthwise
6 egg yolks
¾ cup sugar
1 cup freshly squeezed Meyer lemon juice

IN A LARGE SAUCEPAN, combine the cream, half-and-half, and lemon zest. Scrape the seeds from the vanilla bean and add them to the pan, along with the bean. Bring just to a boil, then remove from the heat. Cover and steep for 20 minutes. Half fill a large bowl with ice and water, and set aside. In a medium bowl, whisk together the egg yolks and sugar. Slowly add the hot milk mixture to the yolk mixture, whisking constantly so the eggs do not curdle. Return the mixture to the saucepan and cook over medium heat, stirring constantly with a wooden spoon, until the mixture coats the back of the spoon (when you wipe your finger across the spoon, the sauce should not run together immediately). Strain the custard into a bowl. Rinse and air-dry the vanilla bean, which can be used to make vanilla sugar (page 216). Set the bowl into the bowl of ice water to chill the custard as fast as possible. Stir until cool. Stir in the lemon juice. Cover and refrigerate for at least 2 hours or up to overnight. Freeze in an ice cream maker according to the manufacturer's instructions. ♪♪♪

Pâte Sucrée

Makes 13 ounces

Pâte sucrée, or sweet pastry dough, has a very fine texture or crumb and is good for any pastry or pie recipe, open or covered. This recipe may make a little more than you need; just tightly wrap any leftover dough in plastic wrap and freeze for up to a month.

1⅓ cups pastry flour
¼ cup sugar
½ cup (1 stick) cold unsalted butter,
    cut into small cubes
1 egg yolk
2 tablespoons heavy whipping cream
¼ teaspoon vanilla extract

COMBINE THE PASTRY FLOUR AND SUGAR in a heavy-duty electric mixer fitted with the paddle attachment, and mix on low speed. Add the butter and mix until crumbly. In a small bowl, mix together the egg yolk, cream, and vanilla extract, then add it to the flour mixture and mix until the dough just starts to come together. (Do not mix longer than this, or the dough will be tough.) Wrap in plastic and refrigerate for 1 hour or up to 3 days.

TO MAKE THE DOUGH BY HAND, whisk together the egg yolk, cream, and vanilla in a small bowl and set aside. Mix together the flour and sugar in a large bowl. Add the butter and toss to coat with the flour mixture. Using your fingers, a pastry blender, or 2 knives, cut the butter into the flour mixture until it resembles large crumbs. Work quickly so the heat of your hands doesn't melt the butter. Make a well in the center of the mixture and add the liquid ingredients. Carefully begin drawing in the flour mixture from the sides, taking care not to let the egg run out. Mix gently until the liquid ingredients are absorbed. Do not knead the dough. Shape into a ball, wrap in plastic, and refrigerate for 1 hour or up to 3 days.

Vanilla Sugar

Makes about 2 cups

This sugar is lovely for sweetening whipped cream or crème fraîche and even to use in coffee or espresso. Once made, it can be stored in a dry place indefinitely.

4 to 5 previously used, cleaned, and dried
    vanilla beans
2½ cups confectioners' sugar

PREHEAT THE OVEN to 350°. Put the vanilla beans on a baking sheet pan and sprinkle with ¼ cup of the confectioners' sugar. Roast in the oven for about 15 minutes, or until the vanilla beans are dry and brittle but not burned. Let cool. Break the beans into small pieces and put them in a food processor with the remaining 2¼ cups confectioners' sugar. Pulse the machine until the vanilla beans become a fine dust. Sift the mixture through a fine-mesh sieve; discard the bits that don't go through. Keep the sugar in an airtight container.

Acknowledgments

Leading up to and in the life of a restaurant there are many people who have inspired, guided, and cared for us along the way. Words alone will never be enough to thank them or to show the love and respect we have for their support. We hope they have always known how we feel, and we want others to know what they have done for us and meant to us.

To Carl Doumani and Joanne Doumani, for trusting us with their money and believing that we could run a restaurant. Also, for waking Lissa up after returning home from a special evening and sharing with her the night and the food they ate—those words made sweet dreams.

To Yutaka Sone and Kyomi Sone, who allowed Hiro to come to the United States for one year but didn't complain when he stayed longer. They gave Hiro an understanding and appreciation for the best that comes from the land and what it takes to grow it.

To Carol Doumani, for believing in us and giving us a nudge, then bringing our ideas to Ten Speed Press.

To Wolfgang Puck and Barbara Lazaroff, without whom none of this would be possible. Destiny is one thing, but our coming together and our relationship were a stretch of the imagination. They set the example for us to strive towards in cooking, business, and love.

To Nancy Silverton, who told Lissa's mom that Lissa wasn't burning everything when she probably was, and who had the patience and generosity to teach her art.

To Pam Hunter, who from the beginning whispered our names in all the right people's ears at just the right time.

To Lorena Jones and Kathy Hashimoto, for both making us nervous and calming us down, then directing us into making a book we could be proud of.

To Faith Echtermeyer, who photographed Terra and our suppliers. Without her eye, the soul of this restaurant and the beauty of the abundant bounty that is available to us from local producers could not have been caught on film.

To Hiroaki Ishii and Kaoru Sakuraba, who came from Japan to photograph our food with the intensity that we believe it has.

To our army of testers, who all made sure that each of the recipes worked at home: Art Finkelstein, Lisa Drinkward, Jan Dykema, Ann Leach, Stephen Dukas, Gwen Hopkins, John Gavin, Anani Lawson, Sarah Walz, Tim Mosher, Julia Tang, Laura Schweers, Gabrielle Quinonez, Tammy Matz, David Schmitt, Patrick Brawdy, Catherine Durand, Alan Steen, Greg Denton. Especially to John Giannini for organizing them and Hiro.

To all the Terra employees over the years, for all their hard work. We have always prided ourselves on the professionalism of the staff and the rapport we have with our customers. Everyone who works at Terra makes this possible. We are more than a team or family, we are what makes this work.

And, most of all, to all of our customers, who over the years have given us much joy and passion for what we do. We do it for them. Every restaurant should remember that. Without customers like ours, our restaurant would be dark.

Most of the dishes in this book are comprised of two or more subrecipes, many of which can be used in other dishes and can be incorporated into your own menus. This index gives hints on how we would use these recipes and hopefully will inspire you to come up with new ideas of your own. Feel free to experiment.

Vinaigrettes	Other Serving Possibilities
BALSAMICO AND CAPER VINAIGRETTE (PAGE 6)	Drizzle over grilled vegetables, roasted chicken, or grilled veal chop.
BLACK OLIVE–BALSAMICO VINAIGRETTE (PAGE 86)	Sauce for fish, vegetables, or good for steak.
GINGER-MUSTARD VINAIGRETTE (PAGE 2)	Goes with cold Asian noodles, also salads with roasted chicken or pork.
LEMON-CAPER VINAIGRETTE (PAGE 72)	Use as a dressing for seafood salads or artichokes.
LEMON-CORIANDER VINAIGRETTE (PAGE 24)	Makes a light sauce for delicate fish.
PARMESAN-BALSAMICO VINAIGRETTE (PAGE 13)	Like a Caesar dressing, great with romaine, sprinkled with Parmesan cheese.
SPICY LEMON-GINGER VINAIGRETTE (PAGE 20)	Cold pasta salads and grilled fish.
TOMATO–BLACK OLIVE VINAIGRETTE (PAGE 92)	Any fish, or paillard of meat.
WHOLE-GRAIN MUSTARD AND SOY VINAIGRETTE (PAGE 31)	Lightly drizzle on anything grilled.

Condiments	
ANCHOVY-GARLIC MAYONNAISE, (PAGE 18)	Use as a salad dressing or as a dip for crudités.
CHIVE-MUSTARD SAUCE (PAGE 4)	Dip or sauce for any crustacean.
LEMON-CAPER AÏOLI (PAGE 94)	Drizzle over fish or serve as a sauce for fried fish.
PISTOU (PAGE 52)	Drizzle over grilled vegetables or fish and meats.
THAI CHILI MAYONNAISE (PAGE 39)	Use as a sauce for any fish, shrimp, and lobster.

Sauces	
CABERNET SAUVIGNON SAUCE (PAGE 132)	This goes great with any meat.
CABERNET SAUVIGNON SAUCE (PAGE 104)	This works well with any meat or big-flavored fish such as monkfish or salmon.
CHARDONNAY CREAM SAUCE (PAGE 32)	This goes well with any fish or shellfish.
CURRY-SHRIMP SAUCE (PAGE 97)	Sauce for Asian noodles or any crustacean.
GORGONZOLA CREAM SAUCE (PAGE 68)	This is good with grilled steak; also toss with pasta or boiled small potatoes.
HERBED GAME JUS (PAGE 143)	Light sauce for game, chicken, or veal.
MISO SAUCE (PAGE 150)	Veal or pork or a more substantial fish.
PINOT NOIR ESSENCE (PAGE 148)	This intense sauce is good with veal or pork.
PRESERVED-LEMON BEURRE BLANC (PAGE 100)	This is a good sauce for fish and shellfish.
SALSA VERDE (PAGE 146)	Braised meat or grilled vegetables.
SPICY SWEET AND SOUR SAUCE (PAGE 34)	This sauce works like a traditional sweet and sour sauce with pork or chicken.
SUN-DRIED CHERRY SAUCE (PAGE 115)	This is perfect with any game or roast turkey.
TAHINI SAUCE (PAGE 8)	Serve as a traditional dip with pita bread; also good with fish, eggplant, and lamb.
THAI RED CURRY SAUCE (PAGE 78)	Wonderful with any lighter meat or fish.
TOMATO-GARLIC-CAPER SAUCE (PAGE 82)	Lovely with other fish.

Side Dishes

APPLE AND SWEET POTATO PUREE (PAGE 115)	This goes with pork, roasted chicken, and turkey.
ARTICHOKE FRITTERS (PAGE 152)	Serve as a passed appetizer or side dish.
AVOCADO MOUSSE (PAGE 25)	Makes a great dip for crudite or chips.
BASMATI RICE (PAGE 78)	A fragrant rice is wonderful with any dish.
BRAISED ENDIVE (PAGE 128)	This is good with pork, chicken, fish, or scallops.
BRANDADE (PAGE 104)	Serve hot in a soufflé dish with croutons as a shared appetizer; also, these can be rolled into small balls, dipped in breadcrumbs, and deep-fried, then served with a tomato sauce to dip.
CAPONATA (PAGE 107)	Add to an antipasti platter or serve as a first course.
FRENCH FRIES (PAGE 117)	Serve anytime, all the time.
HUMMUS (PAGE 140)	Serve with pita bread.
ISRAELI COUSCOUS (PAGE 130)	This is lovely served with stews or fish.
LENTILS WITH PANCETTA (PAGE 118)	This is perfect with any game bird or pork.
PICKLED RED ONIONS (PAGE 110)	Make these for a picnic or with any game.
POTATOES ALIGOTE (PAGE 132)	This is great with any meat that has lots of flavor.
POTATO LATKES (PAGE 38)	Serve with chicken or meat; traditionally, it's served with applesauce, but it's also great with caviar.
RAITA (PAGE 140)	Update this classic with poached salmon.
RATATOUILLE (PAGE 140)	Toss with pasta, or serve alongside any meat or fish.
ROASTED YUKON GOLD POTATOES (PAGE 146)	Another great potato dish.
SESAME TUILES (PAGE 20)	Good as a snack cracker.
SOURDOUGH BREAD STUFFING (PAGE 115)	Good with any game bird, also chicken and turkey.
TABBOULEH (PAGE 140)	This would make a wonderful salad to start a meal.
YAM PUREE (PAGE 110)	Serve this beautiful dish with turkey, chicken, and game.

Vegetarian Dishes (Serve as first courses or main courses. For recipes that call for stock, use vegetable stock.)

EGGPLANT AND GOAT CHEESE "LASAGNA" (PAGE 143)	A perfect main course.
GNOCCHI (PAGE 68)	This is great served with mushroom sauce, tomato sauce, or brown butter and Parmesan cheese.
MALFATTI (PAGE 123)	Serve with a tomato sauce and Parmesan cheese.
RISOTTO MILANESE (PAGE 134)	For a main course, add sides of sautéed vegetables.
STIR-FRIED EGGPLANT (PAGE 150)	Serve with Miso Sauce and rice.
WILD MUSHROOM RISOTTO (PAGE 148)	This is perfect just as it is.

Miscellaneous

CHICKPEA BATTER (PAGE 152)	Use this as a batter with other vegetables.
DA SPICE MIX (PAGE 110)	This is a wonderful rub for any pork, chicken, beef, or rich fish.
MISO MARINADE (PAGE 2)	This is great for chicken, beef, pork, white fish.
SEARED FOIE GRAS (PAGE 48)	Serve with Sun-Dried Cherry Sauce (page 115).
SOY-GINGER MARINADE (PAGE 28)	A little like teriyaki, but better, this is great for grilling pork, steak, chicken, and white fish.

A

Acqua Pazza, 90

Aïoli

    basic recipe, 201

    Lemon-Caper Aïoli, 94

Almonds

    Almond Cream, 213

    Almond Pithiviers, 156–57

    meal, 213

    Sacristan Cookies, 185

Anchovies

    Anchovy–Black Olive Sauce, 152–53

    Anchovy-Garlic Mayonnaise, 18

Apple Farm, 179, 181

Apples

    Apple and Sweet Potato Puree, 115–16

    Apple Tart, 158

    Baked Apple Crème Brûlée, 181–82

    preventing oxidation of, 182

Apricots

    Apricot Tarte Tatin, 190

    Noyau Ice Cream, 190, 215

Artichokes

    Artichoke Fritters, 152–53

    Daube of Lamb Shoulder and Artichokes, 120–21

    Goat Cheese and Artichoke Spring Rolls, 22, 43

    preparing, 196

    preventing oxidation of, 182

Arugula and Tomato Salad, 22

Asparagus, Ragout of Morel Mushrooms and, 80

Avocado Mousse, 25

B

Bacon, Smoked, and Wild Mushroom Vol-au-Vent, 11, 43, 139

Bain-marie, 40

Baked Apple Crème Brûlée, 181–82

Baked Mussels in Garlic-Parsley Butter, 15

Balsamico and Caper Vinaigrette, 6

Bananas

    Banana-Rum Ice Cream, 165, 214

    Feuilletée of Caramelized Bananas, 192–93

    preventing oxidation of, 182

Basil

    Pesto, 203

    Pistou, 52

Beans

    Foie Gras Tortelloni with Fava Beans, 67

    Fried Haricots Verts, 18–19

    Grilled Swordfish Steak with Tuscan White Beans, 107

    Hummus, 140

    Japanese Eggplant Salad, 27

    Soup au Pistou, 52–53

    Spaghettini with Tripe Stew, 70–71

    White Bean–Tomato Salad, 30

Beef

    Daube of Oxtail, 126

    Grilled Dry-Aged New York Steak, 132

    Grilled Miso-Marinated Beef Salad, 2–3

Beets

    Dungeness Crab Salad with Beets, 25

    preparing, 198

    Tomato-Beet Gazpacho, 46

Bell peppers

    Ratatouille, 140–41

    Red Bell Pepper Coulis, 58

    roasting and peeling, 198

Berry Shortcake, Mixed, 172–73

Beurre Blanc, Preserved-Lemon, 100

Black Olive–Balsamico Vinaigrette, 86

Black-Olive Oil, 94

Bocuse, Paul, xi

Bone Marrow Risotto, 62

Braised Endive, 128

Brandade, 104

Brandy Snaps, 174, 176

Bread

    Bread Crumb Crust, 118–19

    Chocolate Bread Pudding, 170–71

    Garlic Croutons, 54

    Morel Mushroom Croutons, 57

    Panzanella with Feta Cheese, 6

    Sopa de Ajo, 51

    Sourdough Bread Stuffing, 115–16

Brittle, Cashew, 183

Broiled Sake-Marinated Chilean Sea Bass, 102–3

Broths. *See also* Stocks

    Acqua Pazza Broth, 90

    Court Bouillon, 39

    Shiso Broth, 102

    Brown Chicken Stock, 209

Butter

    about, xxvi

    Clarified Butter, 200

    Garlic-Parsley Compound Butter, 200

    mounting sauces with, 101

C

Cabernet Sauvignon and Black Pepper Sauce, 185

Cabernet Sauvignon Sauce, 104, 126, 132

Cakes
　　Chocolate Truffle Cake, 160, 162
　　Sunshine Cake, 183
Capellini with Smoked Salmon, 72
Caponata, 107
Caramelized Onions, 54
Caramelized Pears, 166
Caramelizing, 164
Caramel Sauce, 213
Cashew Brittle, 183
"Cassoulet" of Quail Confit, 118–19
Catfish, Fricassee of, 82
Caviar
　　Capellini with Sevruga Caviar, 72
　　Crème Vichyssoise with Caviar, 49
Chanterelle mushrooms
　　Chanterelle Mushroom and Lentil Soup, 48
　　Sautèed Maine Scallops with Chanterelle
　　　　Mushrooms, 76
Chardonnay Cream Sauce, 32–33
Cheese
　　Eggplant and Goat Cheese "Lasagna," 143–44
　　Fontina Cheese Polenta, 206
　　Goat Cheese and Artichoke Spring Rolls, 22, 43
　　Goat Cheese Ravioli, 52–53, 64
　　Gorgonzola Cream Sauce, 68
　　Kabocha Pumpkin Ravioli, 65
　　Malfatti with Rabbit and Forest Mushrooms
　　　　Cacciatore, 123–24
　　Panzanella with Feta Cheese, 6
　　Parmesan-Balsamico Vinaigrette, 13
　　Potatoes Aligot, 132
　　Tart of Fromage Blanc, 166–67
　　Tiramisù, 188–89
Chenel, Laura, 23, 166
Cherries
　　Chocolate Bread Pudding with Sun-Dried
　　　　Cherries, 170–71
　　Sun-Dried Cherry Sauce, 115–16
Chicken
　　Brown Chicken Stock, 209
　　Chicken Stock, 208
Chickpeas (garbanzo beans)
　　Chickpea Batter, 152
　　Hummus, 140
Chinese Egg Noodles, 69
Chive-Mustard Sauce, 4–5
Chocolate
　　about, xxvi
　　Chocolate Bread Pudding, 170–71
　　Chocolate Fudge Sauce, 192–93
　　Chocolate Mousseline, 186–87

　　Chocolate Truffle Cake, 160, 162
　　Chocolate Truffles, 160
　　Chocolate Tuiles, 160, 162
　　melting, 171
Chutney, Pear, 40–41
Citrus fruit, segmenting, 25
Clams
　　Acqua Pazza, 90
　　cleaning, 85
　　Jus de Mer, 84–85
Clarified Butter, 200
Coffee
　　Coffee Granité, 186
　　Espresso Ice Cream, 160, 214
　　Tiramisù, 188–89
Comfort, Jerry, 181
Confit, Quail, 118
Cookies. *See also* Tuiles
　　Maple Cookies, 181–82
　　Pecan Sablés, 186
　　Sacristan Cookies, 185
Corn and Masa, Potage of, 58–59
Court Bouillon, 39
Couscous, Minted Israeli, 130–31
Crab
　　cleaning soft-shell, 59
　　Dungeness Crab Salad, 25
　　Dungeness Crab Wontons, 34–35
　　Peeky Toe Crab Risotto, 98–99
　　Potage of Sweet Corn and Masa with
　　　　Fried Soft-Shell Crab, 58–59
Crayfish, Sacramento Delta, 35, 39
Cream, xxvi
　　Crème Anglaise, 214
　　Crème Brûlée
　　Baked Apple Crème Brûlée, 181–82
　　Lemon Crème Brûlée, 164
　　Crème Vichyssoise with Caviar, 49
Crème Vichyssoise with Caviar, 49
Croquettes of Copper River Salmon, 80
Crostata, Stone-Fruit, 163
Croutons
　　Garlic Croutons, 54
　　Morel Mushroom Croutons, 57
Cucumbers
　　Raita, 140
　　Salmon and Tuna Tartare on Cucumber Discs, 42
　　Tomato-Cucumber Salad, 8
Currant Ice Cream, Myers's Rum–, 214
Curry Oil, 140–41
Curry Sauce, Thai Red, 78
Curry-Shrimp Sauce, 97

D

Daikon

    Momiji Oroshi, 203

Da "Mud," 110

Da Spice Mix, 110

Daube of Lamb Shoulder and Artichokes, 120–21

Daube of Oxtail, 126

Deep-frying, 81

Deglazing, 148

Dill Sour Cream, 38

Dipping Sauce, 36

Doneness, testing for, 151

Dough

    Pâte Sucrée, 216

    puff pastry, xxvii

Dressings. *See also* Mayonnaise

    Balsamico and Caper Vinaigrette, 6

    Black Olive–Balsamico Vinaigrette, 86

    Ginger-Mustard Vinaigrette, 2

    Lemon-Caper Vinaigrette, 72

    Lemon-Coriander Vinaigrette, 24

    Lemon-Mustard Vinaigrette, 201

    Parmesan-Balsamico Vinaigrette, 13

    Ponzu, 202

    Spicy Lemon-Ginger Vinaigrette, 20

    Terra House Vinaigrette, 201

    Tomato–Black Olive Vinaigrette, 92

    Whole-Grain Mustard and Soy Vinaigrette, 31

    Whole-Grain Mustard Vinaigrette, 22, 25

Duck

    Duck Stock, 209

    Grilled Duck Breast on Foie Gras, 115–16

    Merlot-Braised Duck Legs, 139

Dumplings, Shrimp, 102–3

Dungeness Crab Salad, 25

Dungeness Crab Wontons, 34–35

E

Eggplant

    Caponata, 107

    Eggplant and Goat Cheese "Lasagna," 143–44

    Japanese Eggplant Salad, 27

    Ratatouille, 140–41

    Stir-Fried Japanese Eggplant, 150–51

Endive, Braised, 128

Escabeche of Lake Smelt, 14

Espresso Ice Cream, 160, 214

F

Feuilletée of Caramelized Bananas, 192–93

Figs

    Fig Fritters, 159

    Lamb Shanks Braised in Petite Syrah with Black Mission Figs, 112–13

Fish

    Acqua Pazza, 90

    Anchovy–Black Olive Sauce, 152–53

    Anchovy-Garlic Mayonnaise, 18

    Brandade, 104

    Broiled Sake-Marinated Chilean Sea Bass, 102–3

    Capellini with Smoked Salmon, 72

    Croquettes of Copper River Salmon, 80

    Escabeche of Lake Smelt, 14

    Fish Stock, 211

    Fricassee of Catfish, 82

    Gravlax on Potato Latkes, 35, 38

    Grilled Fillet of Pacific Salmon, 78–79

    Grilled Lingcod with English Peas, 98–99

    Grilled Rare Tuna, 8–9

    Grilled Swordfish Steak, 107

    Grilled Tournedos of Tuna, 94

    House-Cured Sardines, 30

    Pan-Roasted California White Bass, 100–101

    Pan-Roasted Local Halibut, 84–85

    Pan-Roasted Medallions of Salmon, 104–5

    Poached Skate Wing, 95

    salmon, boning, 105

    Salmon and Tuna Tartare, 20–21, 42

    Sautéed Pesto-Marinated Tai Snapper, 92–93

    Tataki of Tuna, 31

Flour, xxvi–xxvii

Foie gras

    Chanterelle Mushroom and Lentil Soup with Sautéed Foie Gras, 48

    deveining, 197

    Foie Gras Terrine, 35, 40–41

    Foie Gras Tortelloni, 67

    Grilled Duck Breast on Foie Gras, 115–16

Fontina Cheese Polenta, 206

Forni Brown, xix, 5, 106

French Fries, 117

Fresh Tomato Sauce, 64

Fricassee of Catfish, 82

Fricassee of Miyagi Oysters, 32–33

Fried Haricot Verts, 18–19

Fried Rock Shrimp, 4–5

Fried Squid Tentacles, 86–87

Frozen Yogurt, 177

Fruit. *See also* individual fruits

    Fruit Compote, 172–73

    Mixed Berry Shortcake, 172–73

    segmenting citrus, 25

    Stone-Fruit Crostata, 163

    Tropical Fruit Salad, 177

G

Game. *See also* individual game
Game Stock, 209
Herbed Game Jus, 143–44
Garbanzo beans. *See* Chickpeas
Garlic
Aïoli, 201
Anchovy-Garlic Mayonnaise, 18
browning, 53
degerming, 200
Garlic Croutons, 54
Garlic Mashed Potatoes, 206
Garlic-Parsley Compound Butter, 200
grating, 202
Sopa de Ajo, 51
Spring Garlic and Potato Soup, 57
Tomato-Garlic-Caper Sauce, 82
Gazpacho, Tomato-Beet, 46
Ginger
Ginger Ice Cream, 159, 214
Ginger-Mustard Vinaigrette, 2
grating, 202
Soy-Ginger Marinade, 28
Spicy Lemon-Ginger Vinaigrette, 20
Gnocchi, Potato, 68
Goat cheese
Eggplant and Goat Cheese "Lasagna,"
143–44
Goat Cheese and Artichoke Spring Rolls,
22, 43
Goat Cheese Ravioli, 52–53, 64
Tart of Fromage Blanc, 166–67
Gorgonzola Cream Sauce, 68
Granité, Coffee, 186
Grapefruit
Dungeness Crab Salad with Ruby Grapefruit, 25
segmenting, 25
Gravlax on Potato Latkes, 35, 38
Gremolata, 134–35
Grilled Dry-Aged New York Steak, 132
Grilled Duck Breast on Foie Gras, 115–16
Grilled Fillet of Pacific Salmon, 78–79
Grilled Lamb Tenderloins, 130–31
Grilled Lingcod with English Peas, 98–99
Grilled Miso-Marinated Beef Salad, 2–3
Grilled Natural-Fed Veal Chops, 150–51
Grilled Quail on Eggplant and Goat Cheese
"Lasagna," 143–44
Grilled Rare Tuna, 8–9
Grilled Spice-Rubbed Pork Chops, 110–11
Grilled Swordfish Steak on Caponata, 107
Grilled Tournedos of Tuna, 94

H

Halibut, Pan-Roasted Local, 84–85
Haricots Verts, Fried, 18–19
Herbed Game Jus, 143–44
Herb Oil, 130
House-Cured Sardines, 30
Huckleberry Sauce, 156–57
Hummus, 140

I

Ice cream
Banana-Rum Ice Cream, 214
Espresso Ice Cream, 160, 214
Ginger Ice Cream, 159, 214
Meyer Lemon Ice Cream, 156, 215
Myers's Rum–Currant Ice Cream, 214
Noyau Ice Cream, 190, 215
Vanilla Bean Ice Cream, 158, 185, 214

J, K

Japanese Eggplant Salad, 27
Jus de Mer, 84
Kabocha Pumpkin Ravioli, 65
"Kakuni," Pork Belly, 142

L

Lacquered Quail, 28–29
Ladyfingers, 188
Lamb
Daube of Lamb Shoulder and Artichokes, 120–21
Grilled Lamb Tenderloins, 130–31
Lamb Shanks Braised in Petite Syrah, 112–13
Medallions of Lamb, 152–53
Roasted Rack of Lamb, 140–41
Langoustines, Grilled, Sautéed Pesto-Marinated
Tai Snapper with, 92–93
Latkes, Potato, 38
Lemon
Lemon-Caper Aïoli, 94
Lemon-Caper Vinaigrette, 72
Lemon-Coriander Vinaigrette, 24
Lemon Crème Brûlée, 164
Lemon-Mustard Vinaigrette, 201
Meyer Lemon Ice Cream, 156, 215
Ponzu, 202
Preserved-Lemon Beurre Blanc, 100
Preserved Lemons, 203
Spicy Lemon-Ginger Vinaigrette, 20
Lentils
Chanterelle Mushroom and Lentil Soup, 48
Lentils with Pancetta, 118–19
Lingcod, Grilled, with English Peas, 98–99

Lobster
cooking and shelling, 211
Lobster Salad in Rice Paper, 35, 36–37
Lobster Stock, 210
Lumpia wrappers, 22

M

Macadamia Nut Tart, 165
Malfatti with Rabbit and Forest Mushrooms
   Cacciatore, 123–24
Maple Cookies, 181–82
Marinades
about, 92
Miso Marinade, 2
Sake Marinade, 202
Soy-Ginger Marinade, 28
Mashed Potatoes, 206
Matsusaka, Kazuto, xi, xii
Mayonnaise
Aïoli, 201
Anchovy-Garlic Mayonnaise, 18
basic recipe, 201
Lemon-Caper Aïoli, 94
Ponzu Mayonnaise, 20
Thai Chili Mayonnaise, 39
Meat. *See also* individual meats
resting, 141
testing for doneness, 151
Medallions of Lamb, 152–53
Merlot-Braised Duck Legs, 139
Meyer Lemon Ice Cream, 156, 215
Minted Yogurt, 130–31
Mirin, xxvii
Miso
about, xxvii, 150
Miso Marinade, 2
Miso Sauce, 150
Mixed Berry Shortcake, 172–73
Miyagi Oysters in Ponzu, 10, 42
Momiji Oroshi, 203
Morel mushrooms
Morel Mushroom Croutons, 57
Ragout of Morel Mushrooms and Asparagus, 80
Mousseline, Chocolate, 186–87
Mushrooms
Chanterelle Mushroom and Lentil Soup, 48
Chinese Egg Noodles with Shiitake
   Mushrooms, 69
Malfatti with Rabbit and Forest Mushrooms
   Cacciatore, 123–24
Morel Mushroom Croutons, 57
Mushroom Sauce, 11

Petit Ragout of Sweetbreads and Mushrooms, 16–17
Ragout of Morel Mushrooms and Asparagus, 80
Sautéed Alaskan Spot Prawns with Black Trumpet
   Mushrooms, 97
Sautéed Maine Scallops with Chanterelle
   Mushrooms, 76
Wild Mushroom and Smoked Bacon Vol-au-Vent,
   11, 43, 139
Wild Mushroom Risotto, 148–49
Mussels
Baked Mussels in Garlic-Parsley Butter, 15
cleaning, 15
Jus de Mer, 84–85
Mussel Saffron Soup, 54
Mustard
Chive-Mustard Sauce, 4–5
Ginger-Mustard Vinaigrette, 2
Lemon-Mustard Vinaigrette, 201
Whole-Grain Mustard and Soy Vinaigrette, 31
Myers's Rum–Currant Ice Cream, 214

N

Napa Cabbage, Poached Skate Wing on, 95
Napa Valley Verjus Sauce, 128
Neal, Jim, xiv
Neyers, Barbara, xiii
Noodles. *See* Pasta and noodles
Noyau Ice Cream, 190, 215
Nuts, toasting, 68

O

Oils
Black-Olive Oil, 94
Curry Oil, 140–41
deep-frying with, xxvii, 81
Herb Oil, 130
olive, xxvii
Tobiko Oil, 20
vegetable, xxvii

Olives
Anchovy–Black Olive Sauce, 152–53
Black Olive–Balsamico Vinaigrette, 86
Black-Olive Oil, 94
oil, xxvii
Tomato–Black Olive Vinaigrette, 92
Onions
Caramelized Onions, 54
peeling pearl, 131
Pickled Red Onions, 110
Oranges
Orange Risotto in Brandy Snaps, 174, 176
segmenting, 25

Ossobuco with Risotto Milanese, 134–35
Oven-Dried Tomatoes, 199
Oxidizing, 182
Oxtail, Daube of, 126
Oysters
    about, 32
    Fricassee of Miyagi Oysters, 32–33
    Fried Miyagi Oysters, 94
    Miyagi Oysters in Ponzu, 10, 42

P
Paillards of Venison, 117
Pancetta, Lentils with, 118–19
Pan-Roasted California White Bass, 100–101
Pan-Roasted Local Halibut, 84–85
Pan-Roasted Medallions of Salmon, 104–5
Pan-Roasted Quail, 128–29
Panzanella with Feta Cheese, 6
Parchment paper, 135
Parmesan-Balsamico Vinaigrette, 13
Passion Fruit Sauce, 174, 176
Pasta and noodles. *See also* Ravioli; Tortelloni
    Capellini with Smoked Salmon, 72
    Chinese Egg Noodles with Gulf Shrimp, 69
    Lacquered Quail with Hong Kong Noodles,
       28–29
    Minted Israeli Couscous, 130–31
    Spaghettini with Tripe Stew, 70–71
Pastry. *See also* Puff pastry; Tarts
    Pâte Sucrée, 216
    Pavlova with Frozen Yogurt, 177
Peach Compote, 183
Pears
    Caramelized Pears, 166
    Pear Chutney, 40–41
Peas, English, Grilled Lingcod with, 98–99
Pea Tendrils, Chinese Egg Noodles with, 69
Pecans
    Maple Cookies, 181–82
    Pecan Sablés, 186
Peeky Toe Crab Risotto, 98–99
Pesto
    basic recipe, 203
    House-Cured Sardines with Pesto, 30
    Sautéed Pesto-Marinated Tai Snapper, 92–93
Petit Ragout of Sweetbreads, 16–17
Pickled Red Onions, 110
Pinot Noir Essence, 148–49
Pistou, 52
Pithiviers, Almond, 156–57
Poached Skate Wing, 95
Polenta, Fontina Cheese, 206

Ponzu
    basic recipe, 202
    Japanese Eggplant Salad, 27
    Miyagi Oysters in Ponzu, 10, 42
    Poached Skate Wing with Ponzu, 95
    Ponzu Mayonnaise, 20
Pork
    Grilled Spice-Rubbed Pork Chops, 110–11
    Pork Belly "Kakuni," 142
Potage of Sweet Corn and Masa, 58–59
Potatoes
    Brandade, 104
    Crème Vichyssoise with Caviar, 49
    French Fries, 117
    Garlic Mashed Potatoes, 206
    Mashed Potatoes, 206
    Potatoes Aligot, 132
    Potato Gnocchi, 68
    Potato Latkes, 38
    preventing oxidation of, 182
    Roasted Yukon Gold Potatoes, 146–47
    Spring Garlic and Potato Soup, 57
Prawns. *See* Shrimp
Preserved-Lemon Beurre Blanc, 100
Preserved Lemons, 203
Puck, Wolfgang, xi, xii, xiii
Pudding, Chocolate Bread, 170–71
Puff pastry
    about, xxvii
    Almond Pithiviers, 156–57
    Apple Tart, 158
    Apricot Tarte Tatin, 190
    Feuilletée of Caramelized Bananas, 192–93
    Sacristan Cookies, 185
    Wild Mushroom and Smoked Bacon Vol-au-Vent,
       11, 43, 139

Q
Quail
    "Cassoulet" of Quail Confit, 118–19
    Game Stock, 209
    Grilled Quail on Eggplant and Goat Cheese
       "Lasagna," 143–44
    Lacquered Quail, 28–29
    Pan-Roasted Quail, 128–29

R
Rabbit and Forest Mushrooms Cacciatore, 123–24
Radicchio Salad, 13
Ragout of Morel Mushrooms and Asparagus, 80
Raita, 140
Ratatouille, 140–41

Ravioli

Goat Cheese Ravioli, 52–53, 64

Kabocha Pumpkin Ravioli, 65

making, 212

Red Bell Pepper Coulis, 58

Resting, 141

Rice

Basmati Rice, 78–79

Bone Marrow Risotto, 62

Orange Risotto in Brandy Snaps, 174, 176

Peeky Toe Crab Risotto, 98–99

Risotto Milanese, 134–35

Roasted Risotto-Stuffed Monterey Squid, 86–87

Wild Mushroom Risotto, 148–49

Rice Paper, Lobster Salad in, 35, 36–37

Rice vinegar, xxvii

Risottos. *See* Rice

Roasted Rack of Lamb, 140–41

Roasted Risotto-Stuffed Monterey Squid, 86–87

Roasted Squab, 148–49

Roasted Yukon Gold Potatoes, 146–47

Robuchon, Joel, xii

Romoglia, Johnny, xii

Rum

Banana-Rum Ice Cream, 165, 214

Myers's Rum–Currant Ice Cream, 214

S

Sablés, Pecan, 186

Sacramento Delta Crayfish, 35, 39

Sacristan Cookies, 185

Sake

about, xxvii

Broiled Sake-Marinated Chilean Sea Bass, 102–3

Sake Marinade, 202

Salads

Arugula and Tomato Salad, 22

Dungeness Crab Salad, 25

Grilled Miso-Marinated Beef Salad, 2–3

Japanese Eggplant Salad, 27

Lobster Salad in Rice Paper, 35, 36–37

Panzanella with Feta Cheese, 6

Radicchio Salad, 13

Tomato-Cucumber Salad, 8

Tropical Fruit Salad, 177

Warm Scallop Salad, 24

White Bean–Tomato Salad, 30

Salmon

boning, 105

Capellini with Smoked Salmon, 72

Croquettes of Copper River Salmon, 80

Gravlax on Potato Latkes, 35, 38

Grilled Fillet of Pacific Salmon, 78–79

Pan-Roasted Medallions of Salmon, 104–5

Salmon and Tuna Tartare, 20–21, 42

Salsa Verde, 146–47

Salt, xxvii

Sambal chili, 20

Sardines, House-Cured, 30

Sauces

Anchovy–Black Olive Sauce, 152–53

Cabernet Sauvignon and Black Pepper Sauce, 185

Cabernet Sauvignon Sauce, 104, 126, 132

Caramel Sauce, 213

Chardonnay Cream Sauce, 32–33

Chive-Mustard Sauce, 4–5

Chocolate Fudge Sauce, 192–93

Crème Anglaise, 214

Curry-Shrimp Sauce, 97

Dipping Sauce, 36

Fresh Tomato Sauce, 64

Gorgonzola Cream Sauce, 68

Herbed Game Jus, 143–44

Huckleberry Sauce, 156–57

Jus de Mer, 84

Miso Sauce, 150

mounting, with butter, 101

Mushroom Sauce, 11

Napa Valley Verjus Sauce, 128

Passion Fruit Sauce, 174, 176

Pesto, 203

Pinot Noir Essence, 148–49

Pistou, 52

Preserved-Lemon Beurre Blanc, 100

Red Bell Pepper Coulis, 58

Salsa Verde, 146–47

Spicy Sweet and Sour Sauce, 34

Sun-Dried Cherry Sauce, 115–16

Tahini Sauce, 8

Thai Red Curry Sauce, 78

Tomato-Garlic-Caper Sauce, 82

Tomato Sauce, 200

Vanilla Custard Sauce, 214

Sautéed Alaskan Spot Prawns, 97

Sautéed Maine Scallops, 76

Sautéed Pesto-Marinated Tai Snapper, 92–93

Sautéed Strawberries, 185

Scallops

choosing, 24

Dungeness Crab Wontons, 34–35

Sautéed Maine Scallops, 76

Warm Scallop Salad, 24

Sea bass

Brandade, 104

Sesame Tuiles, 20
Shad Roe, Roasted, 100–101
Shiso Broth, 102
Shortcake, Mixed Berry, 172–73
Shrimp
    Chinese Egg Noodles with Gulf Shrimp, 69
    Curry-Shrimp Sauce, 97
    deveining, 69
    Dungeness Crab Wontons, 34–35
    Fried Rock Shrimp, 4–5
    Sautéed Alaskan Spot Prawns, 97
    Shrimp Dumplings, 102–3
    Shrimp Stock, 210
Silverton, Nancy, xi
Skate Wing, Poached, 95
Slow-Cooked Veal Cheeks, 146–47
Smelt, Escabeche of Lake, 14
Snow Peas, Sautéed Alaskan Spot Prawns with, 97
Sopa de Ajo, 51
Soups
    Chanterelle Mushroom and Lentil Soup, 48
    Mussel Saffron Soup, 54
    Potage of Sweet Corn and Masa, 58–59
    Sopa de Ajo, 51
    Soup au Pistou, 52–53
    Spring Garlic and Potato Soup, 57
    Tomato-Beet Gazpacho, 46
Sour Cream, Dill, 38
Sourdough Bread Stuffing, 115–16
Soy sauce
    about, xxvii
    Soy-Ginger Marinade, 28
    Whole-Grain Mustard and Soy Vinaigrette, 31
Spaghettini with Tripe Stew, 70–71
Spago, xi–xiii, xv
Spicy Lemon-Ginger Vinaigrette, 20
Spicy Sweet and Sour Sauce, 34
Spring Garlic and Potato Soup, 57
Spring Rolls, Goat Cheese and Artichoke, 22, 43
Squab
    Game Stock, 209
    Roasted Squab, 148–49
Squid, Roasted Risotto-Stuffed Monterey, 86–87
Stir-Fried Japanese Eggplant, 150–51
Stirring, 13
Stocks. *See also* Broths
    Brown Chicken Stock, 209
    Chicken Stock, 208
    Duck Stock, 209
    Fish Stock, 211
    Game Stock, 209

    Lobster Stock, 210
    second, 208
    Shrimp Stock, 210
    Veal Stock, 207
Stone-Fruit Crostata, 163
Strawberries
    Mixed Berry Shortcake, 172–73
    Sautéed Strawberries, 185
Striped bass
    Acqua Pazza, 90
Stuffing, Sourdough Bread, 115–16
Sugar, Vanilla, 216
Sumac, 8
Sun-Dried Cherry Sauce, 115–16
Sunshine Cake, 183
Sweet and Sour Sauce, Spicy, 34
Sweetbreads, Petit Ragout of, 16–17
Sweet Potato and Apple Puree, 115–16
Swordfish Steak, Grilled, 107

T
Tabbouleh, 140
Tahini
    Hummus, 140
    Tahini Sauce, 8
Tai snapper
    about, 92
    Acqua Pazza, 90
    Sautéed Pesto-Marinated Tai
        Snapper, 92–93

Tarts
    Apple Tart, 158
    Apricot Tarte Tatin, 190
    Macadamia Nut Tart, 165
    Stone-Fruit Crostata, 163
    Tart of Fromage Blanc, 166–67
Tataki of Tuna, 31
Tatsoi, Steamed, Pork Belly "Kakuni" on, 142
Terra House Vinaigrette, 201
Thai Chili Mayonnaise, 39
Thai Red Curry Sauce, 78
Tiramisù, 188–89
Tobiko Oil, 20
Tomatoes
    Acqua Pazza, 90
    Arugula and Tomato Salad, 22
    Caponata, 107
    concassée, 199
    Daube of Lamb Shoulder and Artichokes, 120–21
    Fresh Tomato Sauce, 64
    Oven-Dried Tomatoes, 199
    Panzanella with Feta Cheese, 6

Tomatoes, *continued*
peeling and seeding, 199
Ratatouille, 140–41
Spaghettini with Tripe Stew, 70–71
Tomato-Beet Gazpacho, 46
Tomato–Black Olive Vinaigrette, 92
Tomato-Cucumber Salad, 8
Tomato-Garlic-Caper Sauce, 82
Tomato Sauce, 200
White Bean–Tomato Salad, 30
Torches, 164
Tortelloni
Foie Gras Tortelloni, 67
making, 212
Tortillas
Potage of Sweet Corn and Masa, 58–59
Tripe Stew, Spaghettini with, 70–71
Troisgros, Pierre, xii
Tropical Fruit Salad, 177
Truffles (confection)
Chocolate Truffles, 160
Truffles (fungus)
Foie Gras Tortelloni with Périgord Truffle, 67
Petit Ragout of Sweetbreads and White Truffle
Oil, 16–17
Tuiles
Chocolate Tuiles, 160, 162
Sesame Tuiles, 20
Tuna
Grilled Rare Tuna, 8–9
Grilled Tournedos of Tuna, 94
Salmon and Tuna Tartare, 20–21, 42
Tataki of Tuna, 31

V
Vanilla
beans, cooking with, 176
Vanilla Bean Ice Cream, 158, 185, 214
Vanilla Custard Sauce, 214
Vanilla Sugar, 216
Veal
Bone Marrow Risotto with Braised Veal Shanks, 62
Grilled Natural-Fed Veal Chops, 150–51
Ossobuco with Risotto Milanese, 134–35
Slow-Cooked Veal Cheeks, 146–47
Veal Stock, 207
Vegetables. *See also* individual vegetables
blanching and shocking, 198
cutting, 204–5
Grilled Miso-Marinated Beef Salad, 2–3
oil, xxvii

oil blanching, 150
Soup au Pistou, 52–53
Venison, Paillards of, 117
Verjus
about, 128
Napa Valley Verjus Sauce, 128
Vichyssoise, Crème, with Caviar, 49
Vinaigrettes. *See* Dressings
Vinegar, rice, xxvii
Vol-au-Vent, Wild Mushroom and Smoked Bacon,
11, 43, 139

W
Warm Scallop Salad, 24
Water bath, 40
Whisking, 13
White Bass, Pan-Roasted California, 100–101
White Bean–Tomato Salad, 30
Whole-Grain Mustard and Soy Vinaigrette, 31
Wild mushrooms
Malfatti with Rabbit and Forest Mushrooms
Cacciatore, 123–24
Mushroom Sauce, 11
Petit Ragout of Sweetbreads and Mushrooms, 16–17
Wild Mushroom and Smoked Bacon Vol-au-Vent,
11, 43, 139
Wild Mushroom Risotto, 148–49
Wine
about, xv–xvi, xxvii
Cabernet Sauvignon and Black Pepper Sauce, 185
Cabernet Sauvignon Sauce, 104, 126, 132
Chardonnay Cream Sauce, 32–33
Lamb Shanks Braised in Petite Syrah, 112–13
Merlot-Braised Duck Legs, 139
Pinot Noir Essence, 148–49
Wontons
Dungeness Crab Wontons, 34–35
making, 212

Y
Yamaguchi, Roy, xiii
Yam Puree, 110–11
Yogurt
Frozen Yogurt, 177
Minted Yogurt, 130–31
Raita, 140

Z
Zucchini
Caponata, 107
Ratatouille, 140–41